Mercer Smith

# Building a Support Team Your Customers Will Love

A CX Guide for today and every day after

*CXOXO: Building a Support Team Your Customers Will Love*
©Mercer Smith

All rights reserved. This book or any portion thereof may not be reproduced or used in any manner whatsoever without the express written permission of the publisher except for the use of brief quotations in a book review.

ISBN: 979-8-89217-630-9 (print)
ISBN: 979-8-89217-631-6 (eBook)

# Advance Praise for CXOXO

"This is hands down the best playbook you can find for growing a CX team and building strategy. It has everything you need to build a team, create strategy for growth, and communicate effectively to your customers."

    *- Bill Bounds, CX Consultant, Former Director of Customer Support at Mailchimp*

"I've often encountered a new situation in my support career and thought, "What would Mercer do?" Mercer has years of experience leading teams but doesn't rely on her own experience alone. She is a community builder and an unfillable sponge of knowledge. She is always asking new questions and absorbing the lessons that others have learned — and then she turns around and shares it, in this case in a book called *CXOXO*. Unlike typical "thought leaders" in the CX space, Mercer truly walks the walk earning the respect of everyone. I'm a better leader and human being because of my interactions with her and because she brought this book into the world."

    *- Sarah Betts, Senior Manager of Customer Support at Alyce*

"I've always been amazed by Mercer's fresh and practical insights, which have personally guided me in improving my work in customer experience. *CXOXO* is no different. Her success over the past decade isn't just impressive; it's a source of real inspiration for me, showing how adaptable and skilled she is. Trusting in Mercer's thought leadership and this book feels like a no-brainer to me."

    *- Susana De Sousa, CX Consultant, Former Director of CX, AirBnb, Loom, and OpenPhone*

"Mercer is a treasure-trove of support wisdom and customer care. Always generous with her time and knowledge, I've learned so much from her just through our meaty conversations — and now she's given us a book! A real gem."

    - *Stephanie Lundberg, CX Writer*

"Mercer's insights will help you and your team succeed while building a culture of courage and safety. If you want your team to be excellent, you need to regularly inspect your internal expectations—and that process should come from an intention to grow together and mutual care for one another and customers. CXOXO guides you in how to do that, and more. It turns out that giving a shit is high leverage!"

    - *Tyler Sellhorn, Former Director of CX at Yac*

"Mercer is an authority on all things customer experience, but more importantly she's a pillar in the CX community. She has guided, supported and inspired myself and so many others. Her impact is everywhere—including in this book you hold in your hands!"

    - *Thomas Hils, Head of Support at Replo, former Zapier and CoinTracker*

"Mercer consistently and meaningfully champions for others by spotting potential in us that we can't see in ourselves, and this book is a proxy to that. She is less interested in climbing ladders and more interested in adding ladder rungs behind her."

    - *Kristi Ernst Thompson, Senior Technical Support Specialist at Help Scout*

"Mercer has a wealth of knowledge gained through years of building solid CX teams and crafting experiences that customers love. CXOXO is a must-read for anyone looking to level up their CX skills and become a true pro in the field."

    - *Matt Dale, CX Consultant, former VP of Customer Support at Illuminate Education*

"Mercer is a voice worth listening to in the customer experience space. She brings a decade of knowledge to the table, which is obviously valuable, but she combines it with an authentic and human-centric style of leadership that's refreshingly unique. When anyone asks me for resources in the CX space, Mercer, and now this book, are the first things I mention every single time."

> - Jeremey Duvall, Former Support Leader at Zapier, Automattic, and WordPress

"Mercer is passionate about nurturing teams to be the best they can be – and it truly comes through in *CXOXO* when she writes about the best approach to take as a CX leader. She understands that nothing in the customer experience space is black and white, and is a refreshing voice helping others work out how to make things colorful."

> - Grace Cartwright, Senior Content Specialist at Klaus

"If you're building a support function this is a must-have. The road can feel quite unknown. This book gives a very clear guided outline of not only how to succeed, but also, feels like a personal partner towards making it a reality. Honestly, I'm going to have my whole support team read it together."
- Neal Travis, Found of Growth Support

"This is the book I wish had existed when I got started in customer support."

> - Ben McCormack, Consultant, Former Director of Support for Trello, FullStory, and Saltbox

"Mercer is a fearless, authentic leader who speaks from her heart, experience, and great CX intuition. She not only looks to help others, but also learn from them in a true servant-leader fashion. This book will lead anyone to feel inspired and motivated to do great things and be their true self."

> - Andrew Rios, Director of Customer Support, Turntide Technologies

# CONTENTS

Chapter 1: CX Isn't an Afterthought .......................................... 1

Chapter 2: What You Need to Know
Before Getting Started ..................................................... 10

Chapter 3: Picking Your Channels ........................................... 20

Chapter 4: Building Your Support Operations ................. 95

Chapter 5: How to Hire (and Keep) a
High-Performing Team ..................................................... 173

Chapter 6: What to Measure ................................................. 208

Chapter 7: The Finances of CX .............................................. 219

Chapter 8: Scaling Up ............................................................. 246

Chapter 9: Creating a Customer-First
Company Culture .............................................................. 260

Chapter 10: Bringing in Help ................................................. 283

Chapter 11: The End ............................................................... 309

Index ........................................................................................ 310

# CHAPTER 1:
# CX Isn't an Afterthought

I started my career in customer experience (CX) at the tender age of 13. My high school, a private boarding school in the Northeastern United States, called Northfield Mount Hermon (Go Hoggers!), required every person to do four hours of work per week on school grounds. So, you could work in the dining halls, clean school buildings, work on the school farm, or like me, you could be a Residential Computer Consultant (RCC) and spend your time sitting in the library during study hall wearing a bright orange shirt like a literal lighthouse in a storm. I spent my time every evening Monday through Thursday helping folks figure out how to use Microsoft Word formatting or remove the virus they got on their machine after downloading a mislabeled Linkin Park song from Limewire. It certainly wasn't glamorous, but it was a job—and I quickly learned to love it. Not just love it, but see the value in it enough to build an over-20-year career in it, and strive to help others do the same.

If you're here, I don't need to convince you: you already know how important the customer experience is. Maybe you are someone who is just starting to build their career and wants to get an insider's look about what you should be thinking about. Equally possible is that you are heading up CX at a larger company, and want to get some in-depth case studies and information to gut-check your assumptions. Most likely, though, is that you're a middle-of-the-road manager who gives a hoot about your customers and is always looking to learn.

Since that job in the library, I have worked at companies like PartnerHero, Trello, Atlassian, Campaign Monitor, Wistia, Appcues, and Venafi; along with some less-well-known, now-defunct, businesses such as Panraven, Pixelitis, and Assembly. I have consulted and written for numerous other organizations as well, such as Help Scout, Nicereply, and HubSpot.

Throughout your reading, you can expect supporting anecdotes from my various experiences as well as learnings I've gleaned from peers and the communities that I'm a member of: CX Heroes, ElevateCX, and Support Driven.

We've designed this book to be used as a guide. You can read it in sequence, or flip around to the specific sections that you are interested in. We would suggest reading through, at least, this first chapter, just to get a grounding into the context for the book. But after that, the world is your oyster (unless you're allergic, in which case the world is your… playground?).

Let's get to it.

## What Is Customer Experience?

The real question is: what *is* customer experience? In order to define this business motion and set context for the rest of this book, it's important that we nail down a common definition.

For the purposes of this text, customer experience consists of the smaller touchpoints that a business uses to cultivate a relationship with their users and customers. That includes the help desk and knowledge base, any user education or onboarding, customer support, and even outreach.

While some of these traditionally fall under marketing, especially in the pre-sales context, a strong customer experience professional will consider each of these within the scope of their role as well. After all, when we can view CX holistically rather than spread piecemeal across several different business functions, we cultivate a better experience. It is better for one organization or individual to own something than it is to have shared responsibility, in most cases.

Consider, for instance, a head chef in a kitchen: there are individual teams responsible for meat, sides, sauces, and plating, but the head chef knows everything that is happening and has a handle on all of it. Without the head chef, it would certainly be *possible* for the kitchen to run, but it would take much more effort to reach the same level of efficiency. Ownership makes things possible in a much shorter, less effortful timeline.

Many of the business functions that are used interchangeably with CX, such as customer support, customer success, or UX, are usually just a *part* of the customer experience, rather than the whole thing.

**TL;DR: customer experience is the multiple touchpoints that a customer has with your brand both pre- and post-purchase.**

## Support Versus Success

Okay, so we've established that customer experience is not necessarily just customer support *or* customer success. However, how do those things differ? There are several different industry definitions of these two functions, but the ones that we will be assuming for this book are:

Customer support is reactive and addresses issues for customers after they have already had them. Typically it is broken out into technical support (technical issues such as bugs within a product or item) and product support (guidance on how to use a product or service). It includes knowledge base articles, written and video support, and in-app functionality. It also usually encompasses individuals who have not yet purchased your product and customers. Customer support is also often one-to-many, rather than dedicated. Some companies are exploring dedicated enterprise support as well, which bridges the gap between customer support and customer success.

Customer success is proactive and focuses on teaching *customers* about the best practices of using your product. It is not usually available for individuals who are not paying for your product, often referred to as *users*. It is often more consultative and personalized than customer support. Although there is one-to-many customer success, often customer success managers are responsible for a few specific "accounts," and they build deeper knowledge of those business needs and goals with the product. Customer success can encompass onboarding as well, or it may be built out as a separate section of the CX team.

Some teams are small enough or immature enough that you may hear of customer service folks doing customer success work and vice versa. Ultimately, for a truly mature Customer Experience organization, both should be separated out and allowed to focus on what they do best.

## Why You Need CX from the Start

Every single interaction that your customer has with your brand is an opportunity to get them more deeply invested in what you are offering. There are many different reasons why this investment may have value, from fiscal impact to loyalty, and it is ultimately one of the most important things you can inspire from your users and customers.

When I worked at Wistia, we worked hard to create delight every step of the way. A dedicated customer experience-focused person was one of the first ten hires, and this shows through in the relationship that the brand has built with its customers, even through today, ten years after, all of those original hires have left (myself included).

We "dog-fooded" our own product, meaning that we used our product just as our customers would. We created delightful videos for almost every need (holiday autoresponders! documentation! yearly "wrap-up" summaries!) and showed folks exactly what they could do with "video for business." But more importantly, every decision we made, from the color selection on the website through to the dropdown styling on our contact form, was made with the customer in mind and after deep cross-functional deliberation.

This is deeply important. From when customers first come to your website and try to find information about your pricing, to when they are looking for the option to cancel, you owe it to your customers to take care of them. This is *especially* true if you are a small business just trying to get started: you need all of the customers you can get.

It can be tempting to look at CX as only a cost center; after all, the fiscal impact isn't as immediately obvious as, say, a product sale. However, the long-tail return of good customer experience is much higher:

- 89% of consumers are more likely to make another purchase after a positive customer service experience. (Salesforce Research)
- 93% of customers are likely to make repeat purchases with companies who offer excellent customer service. (HubSpot Research)
- Increasing customer retention rates by just 5% can increase profits by between 25% and 95%. (Bain and Company)
- 68% of consumers say they are willing to pay more for products and services from a brand known to offer good customer service experiences. (HubSpot)
- Businesses can grow revenues between 4% and 8% above their market when prioritizing better customer service experiences. (Bain & Company)
- Only one in five consumers will forgive a bad experience at a company whose customer service they rate as "very poor." (Nearly 80% will forgive a bad experience if they rate the service team as "very good.") (Qualtrics XM Institute)
- 78% of customers have backed out of a purchase due to a poor customer experience. (Glance)

## Drive Better Product

Beyond the financial value, CX also can serve as a strong insights driver. For a small business that is still trying to identify market fit, learning what customers think and feel and acting on it could mean the difference between failure and success.

We saw this at Venafi, which pivoted to launching a new SaaS version of their long-term on-premise security services after receiving *years* of feedback that their customers wanted to move to the cloud. Without this change, they could have lost out on huge market share of a new and evolving market. Without a team dedicated to interfacing with your customers, you too could lose out on those key insights that can help you improve your strategy and business.

CX isn't just support. It is not just answering tickets. It is not just helping customers buy. Your CX encompasses everything your customer *experiences* with your product: your onboarding, your web experience, and even the process of canceling your account—all need to be considered in a strong CX strategy.

The [Kaizen Method and Philosophy](#) is a competitive strategy for business in which every employee at a business works together to create a culture of constant improvement. The thinking is, you can always make or do things better, even if they seem to work well at a particular moment. Beyond that, everything is an opportunity to improve. What that means is that every single touchpoint across everywhere in your brand is an opportunity to continue to improve and perfect your customer experience—why wouldn't you want to get started on that right away?

Especially on small teams, the opportunity to use this "kaizen" way of thinking is huge. As a smaller team, all of your team members should participate in responding to or solving customer inquiries. Yes, even (especially!) your developers and engineers. Talking with customers is the best way to understand the direct impact of the choices that each team makes. For instance, if an engineer builds a certain feature that ends up causing a lot of support inquiries, they can then see the direct impact of that choice if they are tasked with working in the inbox. Every interaction is an opportunity for them to improve the product offering.

Of course, this stops being scalable as a business grows, but is a great opportunity to start cultivating a customer-first culture at smaller companies. This seed being planted early will help teams looking to build more fully-fledged CX teams as they grow.

## Understanding and Building to Your Personas

As a small team, many companies take a less-targeted approach for their market. Rather than honing in on a specific ideal customer type, it's easier to cast a broad net and try to see who you can nab. For instance, one of the struggles that I had crafting the CX strategy for early startup Appcues was encouraging the rest of the executive team to truly get crispy on *who* we wanted to serve and why. Why say that you just want to go after female business owners specifically in the SMB SaaS space when you *could* go after female business owners in SaaS in general.

When you're just getting started, it can feel painful to limit yourself when you want *everyone* to buy your brand. However, using a wider approach rather than honing in, limits your ability to develop and understand the needs of your target audience and how they can be met by your product and CX services.

Different demographic groups approach support in different ways. For instance, millennials like to have fewer touch-points with other people when using a product. When they have problems with your product they are likely to churn if they do not have quick access to customer service, *and* if that customer service doesn't support them in the way they want to be helped. We expand upon this point in the next chapter ("What You Need to Know Before Getting Started"). The point is, when you invest in your CX strategy and team from the start, you have someone keeping their thumb on the pulse of your core audience and their needs and desires, which means that you can more deeply evolve both your CX and your product as you move forward.

As you start to grow and need to make more mature CX motions, your team will be well-prepared with key insights that they've gleaned from their experiences. Without this functionality, you find yourself trying to build a CX strategy with minimal actual experience of the people you're trying to craft for.

## Staving Off Support Debt

In software development, technical debt is the implied cost of future reworking required when you choose to build an easier but more limited solution instead of a better solution that would take more time. The same thing exists in customer experience.

Unlike financial debt, support debt cannot be repaid. But like financial debt, it can accumulate "interest" in the sense that it becomes more difficult to rectify the longer you leave it. The longer your team uses existing systems or engrains the "bad" process into their day-to-day, the harder it will be to rip out, rectify, or change. Take, for example, this story from Providence Business News in 2023:

> In response to continued high call volume and long wait times, the R.I. Department of Human Services announced Thursday its call center will be offline one day a week so that staff may catch up on backlogged applications for public benefits.
>
> Dubbed "processing Wednesdays," the pilot program will begin Feb. 8 and "is focused on increasing operational efficiency and improving customer service by refocusing call center staff on processing applications, recertifications, updating customer files, reports, and other operational tasks," said the agency in a press release. "These tasks are crucial to reducing the backlog of claims which cause a slowdown in overall processing."

Rather than taking the time to assess and address the issues with their debt, the RIDHS is choosing to shut down their CX operations for one whole day a week. Imagine how that might be different had they taken the time to nail down their workflows and create effective CX processes from the start? Some examples of where this usually comes into play for CX teams are:

- Data and analytics
- Help desk systems
- Macros and automation
- CX leadership

For example: it's true that you may not need a fully-fledged data strategy right from the start, but having a dashboard with reports and the ability to grow in complexity as needed can be a great first step in your CX strategy. It can be attractive to put together scrappy solutions that let you move fast when your business is just getting started or dismiss more complex aspects as "unneeded."

However, if you set things up appropriately from the start you create a better experience for your customer in the moment and the future. You also create a better experience for your employees by giving them the best, most efficient processes right from the start.

# CHAPTER 2:
# What You Need to Know Before Getting Started

Let's consider my experience at Appcues again. We had, up until that point, grown healthfully and regularly, expanding our customer-base through marketing and great customer care. However, as we approached trying to raise our second round of funding, we had started to experience stagnation. We were considering the available market, rather than the target market, meaning that the group of people who we were trying to convince to buy our product was too large.

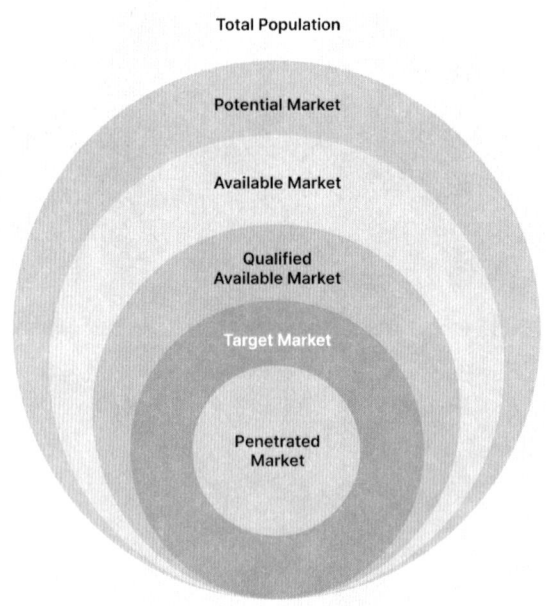

If you aren't super-familiar with marketing concepts, no worries. Consider the messages "Hey, everyone!" versus "Hey, you in the red shirt with brown hair!" The "Hey everyone!" is the total population, whereas the "Hey, you in the red shirt with brown hair!" is more specific, making it a bit closer to a target market. Effectively, this meant our marketing wasn't as incisive or effective as it used to be—we were addressing everyone when we needed to address a specific audience. Because of that, fewer people were buying than had previously.

And, it wasn't just our sales and marketing that was affected by this—our customer experience strategy was, too. We were trying to create an experience that encompassed *everyone's* needs, because that is who we had decided was our target audience, rather than trying to target the needs of a smaller, more honed audience. Beyond that, we were trying to do so with limited resources, having just done two rounds of lay-offs. Honing the audience that we were trying to reach was integral both to getting more qualified customers *and* creating CX that wasn't just a buffet of options, but was a tailored, personalized experience that considered the needs of a target customer (like someone in a red shirt with brown hair).

Maybe you're just starting a business and want to make sure that you get everything right from the start. Maybe you've let your support organization grow organically, and you're just starting to have the space to be more intentional about it. Maybe you have hit a critical mass of customers and just need *someone* to manage them.

The thing that all of those scenarios have in common is the need to plan. Rather than just letting things happen, you are now in a position to *think* about what it is that you need, and to be strategic about the creation of your CX strategy. As you get started, here are the things that you need to be thinking about and what they impact. As you go, each of these intricacies will layer on top of each other to create a more holistic picture of what the future of your strategy could look like.

## Who Are Your Users and Customers?

It may sound like a given, but there are many products and service organizations that do not have an ideal customer or user in mind when they are designing an experience. While not all of your support or CX strategy should be dictated by what your customers want and need, without having a persona in mind as you design, you end up trying to please everyone—and thus pleasing no one.

If your organization has a marketing team, this is an ideal time to make friends with them. Talk to them about who *they* perceive to be the ideal customers for your product. These are typically called "personas."

Personas are fictional profiles that represent groups of similar people in a target audience. Your marketing team uses them to figure out how to reach people on a more personal level, while delivering the right messages, offers, and products at the right time.

Once you understand the *marketing* perspective around these personas, compare them to the types of people who you see reaching out for support or engaging in your documentation or community. If not all of your personas are interacting with your support org, figure out a way to prioritize the ones that are, while still serving the ones that aren't (yet).

For instance, if your marketing team has an Enterprise Persona, but those types of customers never interact with your support organization, it's a good opportunity to figure out why, and what you can do better to provide them support. For instance, maybe they only interact with your customer success team, or perhaps you don't have any Enterprise documentation written. Both of these are solvable issues, but not ones that you would notice until understanding who your customer is.

When making decisions that will impact your customers, it's always good to have a "representative" in mind that you can test your theories against. Like, if you are considering adding chat to your support organization, think about whether any of your personas want it, would actually use it, and how. You *must* understand who your customers are. Imagine how they would use whatever service offering prior to implementing it.

## What Kinds of Interactions Are You Having?

So many times, businesses assume that they have to have every single channel available for every customer to use 24/7; but that's actually not the case. In fact, if you try to cover too much at once, your team may end up dropping the ball. It is a best practice to focus on what your customers *actually* need and serve them where they are at, rather than trying to make every possible avenue available.

We ran into this when Trello was acquired by Atlassian. The team at Atlassian wanted Trello support to take on both chat and community support because that was how the Atlassian customer service team had always handled their larger customer demographic. That said, the Trello support team had supported more than 15 million customers over just email and social media for years with no complaints.

If there are no conversations in your inbox asking for a chat channel—and it's never something that has come up in an NPS response or a CSAT survey—you probably don't need to rush to get chat support on your site. While it may be helpful and beneficial in the long run, there are likely other places where your energy should be focused.

Evaluate the conversations that exist in your current support channels to understand where most of your volume is coming from. You should be able to understand how many interactions come through each channel (if you have more than one), and what topics they are on. For example, if asked, you should be able to deliver an output like this:

- 75% of conversations come in via email through the "Contact Us" form on the site.
- 15% come through via a direct email to the hello@company.com email address.
- 10% of inquiries come through DM on Facebook.

From that breakdown, you should also be able to speak to something like this:

Of the conversations that come through the "Contact Us" form,

- 30% are about account management.
- 25% concern best practices.
- 20% are for refunds and returns.
- 15% are about bugs/escalations.
- 10% feature requests.

Having this information is important, because it allows you to understand where you need to focus your attention, and areas of opportunity that you could improve with a new CX strategy. You could, for instance—from looking at the sample insights above—determine that you need to evaluate your documentation around your top emailed topic (account management), or add a support hire to manage Facebook inquiries, if you haven't already.

Beyond that, this information is helpful to share with your product, marketing, and leadership teams. For more information on the value of this sharing, head to Chapter 9, "Building a Customer-Centric Culture."

## What Are Your Customer Expectations?

Different industries have different expectations. As much as you might like to not do phone support for flexibility and efficiency reasons, if your customers expect to be able to call you because of your industry (say, banking) or their work (say, restaurant employees), and you don't have a phone number, you're already in the trust hole.

- By understanding your personas, you are already half of the way there. Your personas should help you gain perspective on key expectation drivers, such as:
- Business size (can affect channel selection and SLAs).

- Age (for instance, Millennials like to have fewer touch-points with other people when using a product).
- Industry (see our banking or restaurant industry example above).
- Job type (do they prioritize asynchronous conversations?)
- Product need (when something goes wrong with the product, how painful is it for the customer? Is it life-or-death or a nice-to-have?)

Understanding customer expectations gives you a rubric and goals to try to meet as you design your CX strategy and experience.

## How Many Customers Do You Have?

This applies to both *right now* and how many you have forecasted over the future. This largely determines how much effort and energy you will need to put into scalability to start. If your business model is a low-cost, high-growth product, you should design your strategy with scale in mind—implementing automation, focusing on processes, and creating ways to find efficiencies.

At FogCreek, the creators of Trello, there was a policy that every user of their software, whether paid or free, deserved to be supported the same. As the CX experience for Trello came together, this was built into the model. We *knew* we needed to support a huge amount of customers while not spending a ton of money staffing up support. We supported many millions of folks with just six people by placing an emphasis on tooling from the very start.

If you do not have a lot of customers or your model has fewer customers at a more significant price point, you should prioritize a strategy that enables you to deliver more white-glove service: more phone or video calls, individualized attention, and perhaps even account assignment. Understanding your current customer count and goals for future customer growth helps you understand which areas to prioritize in your customer experience strategy.

## Where are your customers located?

Not all businesses need 24/7 support—at least not from the start. Knowing where your customers are located and when they usually reach out helps you to craft a staffing strategy for the future that encompasses all the time zones that you might need.

At Wistia, for instance, we assumed that we needed weekend support as we grew, primarily because 24/7 support is lauded as such an important tactic for "great CX." However, at that time, when we looked we saw that very few people reached out over the weekends or evenings, but the ones who did were usually in dire straits. Rather than having a whole team on point, we just needed to have someone keeping an eye for critical situations. We saved ourselves time and energy by paying attention to time zones and actual customer need, rather than going off gut.

Many help desks will offer a report that shows you when your busiest and least busy times are. Use this data in conjunction with location data to create a future-proof plan to staff accordingly.

Beyond just the technicalities of staffing, different countries also may have different legislatures or needs, depending on your industry. By knowing key customer locations early, you set yourself up for legal success, too.

## What Is Your Contact Rate?

Your contact rate is defined as what percentage of your users reach out to use your support services. If you don't already know your contact ratio, you can easily define it: you already know how many users you have. Divide that number by the number of users that have reached out for support in a given time period (usually a month or a year). You can also calculate this by using just customers to see if the metric changes after folks get access to paid resources, if you offer things like customer success, or paid advanced triaging.

If you're looking for improvement in this metric, things like great self-service support, fixing any bugs, being super-clear about what your product does, and having a clean product design should all be prioritized in your support strategy.

$$\text{Contact rate} = \frac{\text{\# of contact}}{\text{\# of users}}$$

Now, picture a graph that looks like a hockey stick—that's the growth you're aiming for with this metric. You want it to start off slow, like the handle of the stick, and then level out at the top. However, you don't want customers to stop reaching out altogether; there's a point where the work you put into deflecting tickets should even out the growth.

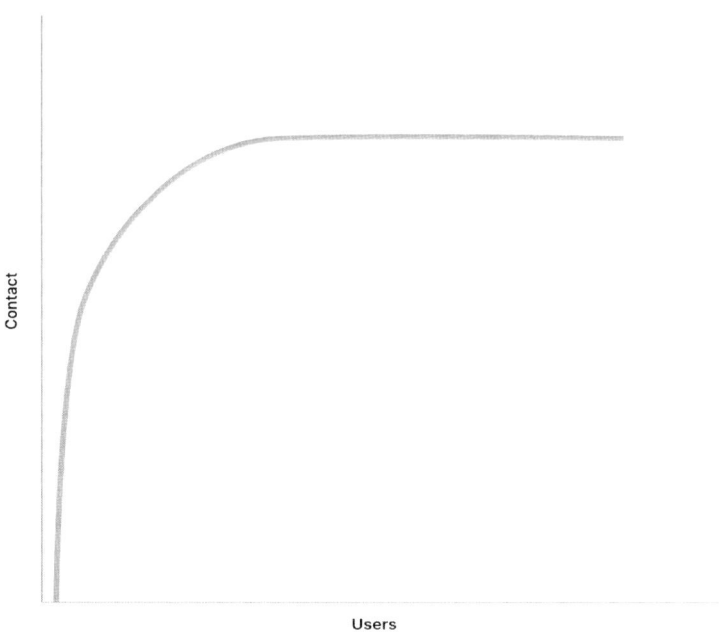

Using the data that you now have after learning more about your types of customer interactions, you can understand your contact rate across specific areas of support as well. Let's say you spot a trend where chats about account management are blowing up way more than other topics. That's your cue to chat with your product team and see if the account page needs a revamp, or maybe you just need to beef up the user instructions.

## Determining the Size and Structure of the Team

This isn't something that you need to have answered right from the start, but it's good to begin thinking about as you get started. Here are a few prompts to get the juices flowing: What are your "must haves"? For instance, do you need folks in the office?

When you move to 24/7, do you want to "follow the sun," do night shifts, or something else?

- Do you need to follow specific legal guidelines?
- Do you want to outsource?
- Do you want to lean heavily on self-service support and ticket deflection, or is having a personal human touch important?
- Do you want to offer tiered support, or do you want to enact "swarming"?
- Should support and customer success be separated?
- Does customer success include onboarding, or is that separate?

It's best to dream big and then start to scale back or minimize as needed. Having answers to these questions will help you understand the types of tools you'll need, and what kind of budget you will need to put forward for personnel.

## How Much Money Does Your Team Have?

Customer support and CX in general are often seen as "cost centers" rather than a place where budgets can be put to use. Start conversations early about what kind of budget your team has for tooling and staffing. It is much easier to have a pool of money that you are able to take from and are forecasted to be able to use, than going to your business leaders and asking for an additional budget every time a new tool or need comes up.

Having this information allows you to have clear expectations about what is within reason for your business, and what just isn't feasible. For instance, if you're working with a tight budget, integrating with a fancy AI provider that costs $10,000 every month may not be in your budget, but cross-training one of your support team members to manage bots in your helpdesk might be.

These pieces of information are all, individually, quite easy to aggregate and can have a huge impact on the future of your organization. Knowing the answers to these questions ahead of time, rather than finding them in the moment, make conversations and decisions about strategy easier to make and more streamlined.

# CHAPTER 3:
# Picking Your Channels

CX has a rich and lengthy history, stretching back to as early as 3000 BC. In those days, traders navigating long distances on boats had their own ways of treating customers well—and it certainly didn't merit a CSAT or NPS survey. Over time, as customer service evolved, so did the tools we used for it.

In this chapter, we'll delve into individual support channels like live chat, email, phone, and social media, discussing their strengths and best applications for your company's needs as you grow. If you already have your channels picked, or are looking for a primer on each, this is a *great* chapter for you. However, it doesn't read very much like a chapter and more like informational segments about each channel. That's intentional! It's meant to be a reference. However, it may bore you to tears to read through, unlike some of the other chapters, so feel free to just skim it or use it as needed.

## How to choose the right channels for your team

While both omni-channel and multi-channel approaches have their merits (and lots of businesses use them), it's wise to assess each channel independently rather than assuming they all fit your company's or customers' needs—the example in the previous chapter of Atlassian's CX leadership assuming that what worked from them would also work for Trello support is a great example of this.

Thankfully, selecting the right channel doesn't require rocket science; it boils down to understanding your customers' traits and those of your team, and if you did the work of the previous chapter, you should already be good to go there.

Here are some factors to think about when determining the optimal channel for your customers:

Customer Demographics and Communication Preferences

According to a study by MarketingDive, those aged 25 and below lean towards social media for customer service, while those above 55 opt for telephone contact. The middle (25- to 54-year-olds) prefers email, followed by mobile apps. Different demographics exhibit clear preferences for particular platforms. Understanding your user base's demographic makeup can help you make informed decisions about which support channels will work best for them.

## Type of Support You Provide

The nature of your product influences the type of inquiries you receive. Simple products may lead to quick, straightforward interactions, while more technical products might require deeper troubleshooting. Different channels excel at different troubleshooting styles. Email suits asynchronous communication for complex queries, while chat is ideal for quick retail-like interactions. Phone calls can ease customer anxiety and are valuable for building trust. Understanding your product's intricacies and the common types of inquiries can help match channels effectively.

## Long-Term Strategy

Consider where you want your product and support strategy to evolve. This foresight aids in selecting the right platforms to provide optimum customer support. For instance, if you know that in the long run you would like to be able to automate or triage lots of conversations automatically, email and chat (or social media) may be better suited to that than other channels.

## Team Bandwidth

Different channels demand varying levels of team engagement. Phone support demands focused attention, whereas chats and emails can be multitasked. If your team is limited in size but you're keen on offering phone support, consider implementing it for specific customer tiers or paying clients. For instance, at Venafi, which offered an expensive security product, we gave phone or video call support to everyone. For freemium products like Appcues and Trello, which offer basic features at no cost and charge a premium for supplemental or advanced features and thus have a large number of free users that also need support, phone support wasn't tenable to offer as a solution.

Balancing customer attraction with team capacity is crucial; an overloaded team could lead to prolonged wait times, undermining the allure of certain support channels.

In terms of scalability, email, chat, social media, phone, and video chat/in-person support are ranked from most to least scalable. Evaluate your team size and conversation volume to determine the most suitable channels.

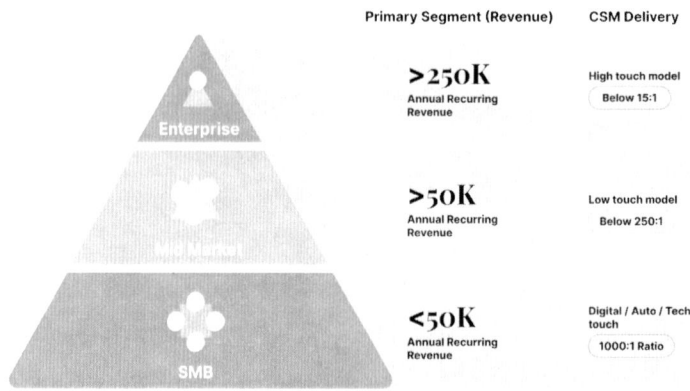

Prioritize maintaining a swift first response time and high quality as you make decisions—the more channels you add, the more thinly spread your team will become. The more they have to focus on, the more potential there is for quality to drop. It is better to do a few things well than everything poorly.

By assessing customer demographics, the nature of your interactions, future strategy, and team capacity, you can make informed choices about the most fitting support channels for your business.

## Email

Email is an OG support channel, and has remained a main staple for providing support since its introduction in the 1990s. Email is dynamic in that it can be used for solving quick one-off issues, or it can be used to delve deeper into a question or bug.

For every amazing thing about a channel, there are usually at least a few things that aren't so excellent, and email is no different:

| Pros | Cons |
| --- | --- |
| Excellent for a first channel when opening up support at a small or just starting company. | Fairly limited in terms of where you can offer it and how seamless you can make it. While you can provide an email address, you aren't able to create the email and take the work out of the process, like you are with other platforms. |
| A great form of support for asynchronous communication — this is especially important for things like debugging or troubleshooting that can't be done instantly, or close-to-instantly. | Not great if you need to give someone a step-by-step walkthrough as they are doing something. |

| | |
|---|---|
| Simple and straightforward to set up and maintain. | Less feature-full in terms of tracking information, reporting, and other "fancier" features, like screen sharing, that other support channels offer. |
| Useful for tools that allow for scaling: saved replies, autoresponders, automated SLA workflows, and more can help level up your team without needing more people. | Limited in functionality to the point where, if this is your sole point of contact and you have an outage, it may be difficult to respond to everyone who has an issue at once. |
| Doesn't require any additional installation on the customer's side, and allows your employees to work from wherever they are. | The asynchronicity makes it difficult to build deep or meaningful relationships with customers, so it might not be the best if you have a customer success or sales team that needs to do that. There's no real-time method of communication. |
| Email makes it easy to follow-up on past or outdated conversations. | Email can mean your customers wait a little bit longer than they might have normally so that they can get a proper response. |

## Features and Functions to Prioritize in Your Search

Customers expect timely, helpful responses, and the right email support tool can empower your team to deliver just that. But with a plethora of options available, how do you choose the best one?

Before diving into the sea of available tools, it's essential to take a step back and assess your business' unique needs. Factors such as the size of your support team, the volume of emails you receive, your budget, and anticipated future growth can play a crucial role in your decision-making process. Once you've gotten that nailed down (which you should have done in Chapter 2), here's a guide to help you pick the ideal customer support email tool for your business.

## Essential Features

- User-Friendly Interface: A tool may have all the features in the world, but if it's challenging to use, it's not going to be effective. Look for intuitive dashboards, easy navigation, and a minimal learning curve.

- Prioritization and Categorization: Your tool should be able to classify and prioritize emails based on preset rules. This ensures urgent matters get addressed first.

- Integration with Knowledge Base or FAQ: An integrated FAQ or knowledge base can assist in providing quick, automated yet relevant responses to frequently asked questions.

- Collaboration Features: Can multiple agents work on the same email thread? Can they leave notes for one another? Collaboration is key for complex queries that might need a team effort.

- Advanced Search: Your agents should be able to swiftly locate past interactions using keywords, email IDs, or other filters. This aids in providing context during customer interactions.

- Customizable Templates: While personalization is crucial, having customizable templates for common queries can speed up response times.

- Reporting and Analytics: Gain insights into metrics like response times, resolution rates, and customer satisfaction. This helps in continual service improvement.

## Advanced Features to Consider

- AI-Powered Suggestions: Some modern tools offer AI-driven suggestions to agents, helping them craft responses quicker.

- Sentiment Analysis: By analyzing the tone of incoming emails, the tool can prioritize based on the urgency perceived from the customer's sentiment.

- Multilingual Support: If you have a global customer base, translation tools or multilingual support can be a game-changer.

## Scalability

Your chosen tool should grow with your business. If you anticipate expanding your support team or increasing your customer base, ensure that the tool can handle that growth.

- Security and Compliance: Given that email interactions might contain sensitive data, security should be a top priority. Ensure that the tool complies with GDPR, CCPA, or any other relevant data protection regulations.

- Price: While it's essential to stay within budget, remember that the cheapest option may not always offer the best value. Consider the tool's features and the potential ROI when determining its worth.

- Team or customer base growth: Some email tools work really well for smaller teams, but not as you need to scale and add complexity. Using your evaluation from Chapter 2, find a tool that fits your dream future team as well as your team right now.

## Customer Support and Training

Ironically, while choosing a support tool, consider the kind of support and training the software company provides. A company that offers comprehensive training sessions, detailed documentation, and prompt customer support can save you from potential operational hiccups. You know they'll be there to help when you run into trouble and that their values align with your own.

Choosing the right customer support email tool is a strategic decision that can profoundly impact your customer relationships. Take the time to research, take advantage of trial periods, and read reviews. Remember, the goal is to enhance efficiency, streamline operations, and most importantly, delight your customers.

So, now that you know the pros and cons of using email support versus leaving it behind, let's talk about how you can knock every message you write out of the park.

## Best Team Practices with Email Support

These should all be implemented in your support processes if you are using email to support your customers.

### Send an Autoreply to Let Them Know You Got Their Email

Every business I have ever worked in CX for has ensured that some kind of informational autoreply is sent back to customers after they reach out. If you aren't doing this already, get started. It's table stakes.

If you can't get back to a customer immediately, it's a good practice to send a quick acknowledgement of their message. Without an automatic response, they might be unsure if their email even reached you. An autoresponder can also clue them in on your office hours or any holidays that might delay your reply. Being transparent about these details not only keeps things clear but also helps foster trust with your clientele.

### Be Honest

When a customer reaches out with a query or request, it's best to be upfront with them. For instance, if they're asking about a feature that isn't on your roadmap, it's more beneficial for both sides to be honest from the get-go. It might be challenging to decline requests, but it provides clarity and avoids setting unrealistic expectations. This approach not only ensures a smoother experience for the customer but also helps your support team manage their tasks more efficiently.

## Use Saved Replies, and Make Sure They're Up to Date

Saved replies often act as a secret weapon, especially as your team begins to expand and the volume of queries increases—we made almost excessive use of them at all of the high-volume, low-tech SaaS companies for which I worked. By establishing a set of predefined responses for common situations, you're not only speeding up the process but also ensuring consistency in your team's communication. Think about those recurring questions—maybe they're about a new feature, a significant outage, or popular feature requests. These are prime candidates for saved replies.

Additionally, consider those troubleshooting steps that the team repetitively guides customers through. A classic example is guiding a customer to clear their browser cache. Instead of typing out the steps each time, a saved reply can come in handy, leading to quicker resolutions and a more efficient use of resources.

However, it's essential to remember that the customer service landscape is always evolving. What was relevant a few months ago might not be pertinent today. So, once you've set up your saved replies, it's crucial to review and update them periodically. This is especially key if you are an early-stage start-up and expect the product or offering to be changing frequently. After all, providing outdated or incorrect information can quickly frustrate a customer, undermining the trust you've worked hard to establish.

## Pay Attention to Your Metrics

When it comes to evaluating the performance of a customer support team, many companies tend to skim the surface, relying mostly on straightforward metrics. While metrics like response time or Customer Satisfaction Score (CSAT) are undoubtedly important, they often don't tell the whole story. To truly understand the intricacies of your support operations, it's beneficial to take a more holistic approach.

Instead of solely focusing on individual metrics, consider pairing them up or delving into more nuanced indicators. For instance, one might analyze the correlation between a reduced first response time and its subsequent effect on CSAT scores. Do customers express higher satisfaction when they get quicker initial responses?

Another insightful metric is the first contact resolution ratio, which highlights the effectiveness of your support team in resolving issues during the initial interaction. A lower ratio might prompt you to investigate potential areas of improvement, training needs, or process enhancements.

At Panraven, a now-defunct company that helped customers make printed books out of their cruise ship photos, we ultimately determined that if we responded within an hour from their first message, the CSAT took a huge jump upwards into the positive. Anything beyond an hour was an almost instant detractor. The reason? People reached out when they were in the middle of making their book, which usually took one to two hours. If we didn't get to them before they were "done" or the need had passed their mind, they perceived us as having failed them.

This led us to making a triage queue and instantly assigning brand new tickets to respond to *first*—an approach that runs counterintuitive to how most businesses function, by answering the oldest tickets first. By prioritizing the newest tickets for a few of our team members, and having one person focused on taking the "old" tickets that were past an hour in wait time, we boosted our customer satisfaction rate exponentially.

When you dig deeper into these layered metrics, you're setting the stage for a richer understanding of your customer behavior, preferences, and pain points. This not only leads to better-informed decisions but also ensures a continually evolving and improving customer support experience.

## Let Your Agents Personalize Their Emails

Many companies recognize the value of having a tone and style guide to ensure consistency in their communication. These guides serve as a compass, directing the brand voice in a harmonious direction, which is undeniably beneficial. However, while uniformity has its place, there's also something to be said for individuality. One of my coworkers at Wistia, Jordan, sometimes chose to respond to emails with "Ahoy [name]," which seemed totally out of this world to me and my standard "Hey there, [name]!," but it worked for him and his customers usually loved it.

It's essential to convey to your team that, while the guidelines are there to offer direction, they shouldn't feel confined by them. Encourage your team members to infuse their unique personalities into their interactions with customers. After all, nobody truly enjoys speaking with a monotonous, scripted entity. It's those personal touches, the hint of genuine human interaction, that can transform a mundane email exchange into a memorable customer experience.

That said, it's equally important to stress the significance of adaptability. While personal flair is encouraged, team members should remain attuned to the customer's mood and adjust their tone accordingly. If they detect a hint of frustration or discouragement from the customer, it might be wise to dial back the personality a bit and approach the conversation with empathy and understanding. It's all about striking the right balance to ensure effective and positive communication, something we'll delve deeper into as we move forward.

## Make a Defined "Support Style" and Align it with Your Brand.

It's evident that brands have cultivated unique identities, and this doesn't stop at logos or advertising; it extends to customer support styles as well. Take, for instance, Buffer, which is renowned for its upbeat and optimistic approach to customer interactions. On the other hand, you have brands like Shinesty, which have adopted a more playful, even slightly flirtatious, tone.

Every company has its unique DNA, and this distinctiveness should manifest in every touchpoint with the customer. It's not just about having a brand; it's about living it, even in areas as seemingly mundane as customer support.

If your company has invested time in developing brand guidelines— which it absolutely should— it's paramount that your support style mirrors these guidelines. This ensures a consistent experience for the customer, irrespective of the medium or department they're interacting with. But while adherence to the brand's essence is crucial, it's equally important to leave some room for interpretation.

Once your marketing team rolls out brand guidelines, share them with your support teams. Allow them to internalize these guidelines and then mold their support style around them. By giving your team the autonomy to define their specific flavor of support—within the broader confines of the brand identity—you're not just ensuring brand consistency, but you're also fostering a sense of ownership and pride in the way they engage with customers. After all, it's in those small, personalized interactions where real brand loyalty is built.

## Best Agent Practices for Email Support: Share These with Your Team!

### Use Proper Formatting That Will Make Your Email Easier to Read

The range of email tools available is more advanced and user-friendly than ever before. With the latest and greatest email tools at your fingertips, you're not just limited to basic functions like bolding, italicizing, or underlining text. These modern tools empower you with a plethora of formatting options, such as crafting ordered and unordered lists, designing tables, and seamlessly integrating various types of images and other functional elements into your emails.

Harnessing these features is key to optimizing communication. Consider using bullet points or ordered lists when you're guiding a customer through a process or set of instructions. When there's a specific point or detail that demands the customer's attention, don't hesitate to use bold or italicized fonts to draw their eyes to it. By fully leveraging these formatting capabilities, you ensure that your message is not just received, but understood. This clarity in communication minimizes back-and-forth, leading to a more efficient and satisfying experience for both you and your customer.

## Greet Them and Thank Them

Email communication, especially in a business context, is more than just relaying information. It's also an opportunity to build and nurture relationships. This starts from the very moment you address your customers. A warm greeting sets the tone for the entire conversation, signaling to the recipient that they're valued and appreciated.

Always begin your email by acknowledging the customer warmly. A simple gesture like thanking them for reaching out not only demonstrates your professionalism but also establishes a friendly rapport. Phrases like, "Hey there! Thanks so much for getting in touch," or "I see what you're getting at!" or "Hello! I'm glad you brought this to our attention," can be quite effective.

And just as it's essential to start the conversation on a positive note, wrapping up your email cordially is equally crucial. Encourage open communication by inviting them to share further questions or feedback.

For instance, concluding with, "I hope this clears things up. However, should you have any more queries or need further clarity, please don't hesitate to reach back," not only keeps the communication channel open but also reassures the customer of your support.

Lastly, ensure your greetings and sign-offs resonate with your brand's voice and your personal style. Whether you opt for a traditional "Hello" or a more playful "Ahoy," the key lies in consistency and making sure it aligns with the overall tone of your message. Remember, it's these little nuances that can make email communication more personable and effective.

## Use Snippets for Quicker Responses

Efficiency and personalization often go hand-in-hand. One tool that bridges this gap is the use of "snippets." Think of snippets as concise versions of saved replies, tailored specifically to your communication style and frequent responses. Instead of using generic templates, snippets allow for a more personal touch, echoing phrases or responses you often use. For instance, tools like TextExpander can be invaluable in crafting and utilizing these snippets, ensuring that while you save time with pre-drafted content, your emails still resonate with a genuine and personal tone. Integrating snippets into your workflow can thus streamline communication while retaining that essential human touch.

## Mirror Their Behavior

Think of customer support like dancing at a party. You want to match your partner's vibe, right? If your customer emails you sounding super frustrated or upset, it's probably not the best time to be all cheerful and toss in jokes. It's like trying to breakdance when your partner's doing a slow waltz—it just doesn't fit. On the flip side, if they're chatting with loads of exclamation marks and sending fun GIFs, then absolutely dive into that fun conversation. But remember, if they're reaching out with something heavy, like their business closing down, it's probably not the moment for that hilarious GIF you've had on standby. Just read the mood and go with it!

## KPIs for Email Support

Email, being a dominant channel for customer interaction, requires a specific set of metrics to ensure optimal performance. By keeping a close eye on these Key Performance Indicators (KPIs), you can adjust strategies, streamline processes, and consistently deliver a top-tier customer experience. Here's a deep dive into the must-track KPIs for email support:

- First Response Time (FRT)
    - What it measures: The average time taken for a customer to receive their first response after submitting an email query.
    - Why it's important: A swift FRT can significantly impact customer satisfaction. The quicker a customer knows their issue is being addressed, the more valued they feel.

$$\text{Average 1st response time} = \frac{\text{Total time taken to send the first response during selected time period}}{\text{The number of tickets whose first responses were sent in the selected time period}}$$

- Average Resolution Time
    - What it measures: The average time taken to completely resolve an issue from the moment it's reported.
    - Why it's important: While quick responses are great, customers ultimately want their issues resolved promptly. This metric can highlight efficiency and effectiveness in problem-solving.
- First Contact Resolution (FCR) Rate
    - What it measures: The percentage of email inquiries resolved in the first interaction.
    - Why it's important: A high FCR rate signifies that issues are addressed effectively without the need for back-and-forth, leading to higher customer satisfaction.
- Customer Satisfaction (CSAT)
    - What it measures: Direct feedback from customers post-interaction, typically gathered through a simple survey.

- Why it's important: CSAT offers insights into the customer's perception of your service quality, allowing you to make informed improvements.
- Ticket Volume
  - What it measures: The total number of email support requests received in a specific timeframe.
  - Why it's important: Monitoring ticket volume can help in resource allocation, understanding product/service issues, and anticipating busy periods.
- Agent Utilization Rate
  - What it measures: The percentage of time an agent spends on support-related tasks versus their available working time.
  - Why it's important: This KPI ensures that agents are neither overwhelmed (leading to burnout) nor underutilized (resulting in wasted resources).
- Escalation Rate
  - What it measures: The percentage of tickets that need to be escalated to higher support tiers or specialized teams.
  - Why it's important: A high escalation rate might indicate a gap in agent training or knowledge, requiring intervention.
- Email Bounce Rate
  - What it measures: The percentage of sent support emails that are returned undelivered.
  - Why it's important: Bounced emails mean unresolved issues. Monitoring this can help in maintaining the integrity of your support database and ensuring customers receive essential information.
- Net Promoter Score (NPS)

- What it measures: Willingness of customers to recommend your service or product to others based on their support experience.
- Why it's important: NPS can act as a predictor of growth and customer loyalty, giving you a broader view of how support impacts the overall brand image.

• Knowledge Base Engagement

- What it measures: The frequency with which customers access your support articles or self-help resources.
- Why it's important: High engagement can indicate the effectiveness of your self-service resources, whereas low engagement might mean customers can't find the help they need on their own.
- KPIs act as the pulse of your email support strategy. By regularly monitoring and analyzing these metrics, businesses can not only pinpoint areas of improvement but also celebrate and build upon their strengths. Remember, the ultimate goal is to provide an unmatched support experience, turning every email interaction into an opportunity for building stronger customer relationships.

# Live Chat

Many companies start with either phone or email as their main source of support, since those are the two that most folks are familiar with. However, the landscape is changing as businesses recognize key demographics prefer live chat and social media messaging over other platforms for support. Depending on the company and what product or service they're selling, they may skip right over email and phone, and go straight to chat.

There are some strong benefits to using this lightweight tool, and also some big areas of opportunity to consider.

| Pros | Cons |
| --- | --- |
| Chat support is cheaper than phone support. Over the phone, an agent can only talk with one customer at a time, but if they are chatting online, they can handle several conversations simultaneously without affecting the level of service or customer experience. | According to the research, when customers contact companies by email, the majority of them expect a reply within 24 hours or less. (Help Scout email benchmarks report) Conversely, the optimal response time for online live chat interactions is less than a minute, and some customers may even leave your website if they have to wait for a reply for more than two minutes. |
| Many customers don't even want to take the time to make a call; they would rather have things be instantaneous. Luckily, modern technology and live chat allow customers to get support anywhere, even in a crowded subway. | Sometimes AI is not perfect. While there are definitely some chatbots that are outstanding and can answer basic questions or make it easier for your customers, that's not all of them. |

| | |
|---|---|
| If you don't have enough time or team members to provide live chat support to all your customers, you can choose to only offer it to certain types of customers or only on certain pages. For example, you could make chat available only to your VIP customers, or only place the chat button on pages where a fast response would make a difference (like cart or checkout pages, or your top exit pages). | Automatic chat invitations are annoying if misused, but can make a huge difference to your conversion rate if used correctly. |
| Live chat can be a great addition to your knowledge base or to the help section of your site. Add a chat button to those pages and let your customers contact you if they didn't find the answer to their question or if they are having trouble understanding the article. | Live chat tools need to integrate into support inboxes to have any real context for your support team members to use. If you want to provide a great customer experience over live chat, your messenger tools need to have excellent integration offerings. |
| There's no need to install anything or switch between tabs or apps to chat with your company's support team. Your customers can get support on the spot and can easily use screen sharing or co-browsing features. | Going by the statistics, you only have half a chance of having a good live chat interaction: 47% of customers haven't had a positive live chat experience in the past month. |

| | |
|---|---|
| Agents will likely get asked the same questions pretty frequently. With live chat, they can use canned responses or saved replies and reply to more chats. | According to Kayako, scripted responses are obnoxious to your customers; 29% of consumers say they find scripted responses most frustrating, and 38% of businesses agree. |

Considering these pros and cons for your business alongside the data about your customer base and team needs generated in Chapter 2, is a great way to understand if live chat will be a good fit for your team. If you've decided to move forward with using chat as a channel, here are some tips on how to best make use of its benefits and work around its weaknesses.

## Best Team Practices with Live Chat

### Customize Your Chat Window

Most chat services will offer you the option of customizing what your chat windows look like. Update the look of your chat window so it matches the design of your site, and try adding a profile picture of your agent and information such as their name and title. Customizing the design makes the chat experience less jarring, and gives your customers a human being to connect with.

We do recommend using real photos rather than cartoons or avatars, but do not recommend requiring your agents to use their actual name or pictures of themselves. Using a real picture instead of a drawn image can help differentiate between live agents and bots and create space for empathy if your customer is angry. Users are more likely to vent rage on an anthropomorphized bot than they are a human, and are scientifically proven to be able to reign in their rage more when dealing with an "actual" person, versus an anthropomorphized bot. Beyond that, they are almost more likely to vent their anger on bots that have been anthropomorphized versus "regular" bots—sorry C3PO.

## Use Targeted Proactive Chat

There are certain pages on which proactive chat can be incredibly effective rather than obnoxious to your customers. While a bubble popping up on an account page could feel annoying, high-traffic pages like pricing pages, new feature announcements, or help documentation can be great places to put a proactive chat that reaches out to customers before they need to go digging too deep.

This is a true driver for customer delight, and can be a great deflection tool for teams looking to scale more efficiently or dealing with high volumes. For instance, at Trello when we enabled proactive tooling on our customer support site, through a tool that was then called Solvvy but has since been acquired by Zoom, we got a 26% deflection rate. This was *great* for our customers because they no longer had to wait for a response, but even better for our support team. Now, they were able to take the time that would have been dedicated to answering a quarter of incoming tickets and use it on other projects to continue bettering the customer experience.

Even if you don't have it up all the time, consider dealing with seasonal spikes, or times of lower staffing efficiency, by adding these proactive chats to relevant pages. At Wistia, we only added proactive chat to our pricing page during the beginning of the year, when most companies were fresh into a new year's marketing budget, and looking to spend the business' hard-earned cash.

## Use an Optional Pre-chat Survey

One of the biggest problems with live chat is that it sometimes misses out on the contextual availability of other channels. Without integrations pulling information in from your other services (which comes up below), all that your agent has to go on is past chat history. Offering a small pre-chat survey for the customer to fill out can help gain additional context that otherwise you might miss out on. It also could save your agents from having to ask the customer for more details or re-ask basic questions once they are chatting with your customer.

If your team doesn't have the ability to integrate chat for additional context, consider offering a pre-chat survey as a way for both your customer and your support team to be set up for success.

### Implement Chat Transfer

No one should be expected to know everything. It's possible (and probable) that there will come times when your agents might not be able to answer the question being asked of them. In that case, it becomes important and valuable for them to be empowered to escalate or transfer their ticket to someone else on the team.

When evaluating chat tools, make sure that the one you pick has something like this so that one agent can easily pass a conversation to another if they have to. If your team doesn't have triage or escalation paths built into your strategy, the ability to transfer to another person may be less pressing, but the ability to transfer to another channel could still be impactful. For instance, if a technical conversation comes through, it's not going to be best solved in a chat, but would be better over video or email.

### Integrate Live Chat with Your Help Desk and CRM

Context can be one of the most important tools that an agent has at their disposal. Being able to better understand where in the customer journey someone is, or what they've already reached out to support about, can save an agent a ton of time and the customer tons of effort. Provide better context for your agents by integrating your helpdesk and CRM with your chat service. That way, instead of wondering and taking extra time to go back and dig, or even worse, asking the customer a question they've already been asked, the information is right at your team's fingertips.

This also keeps a running track record of all of the conversations that a customer has had with a company. So, if your customer success team is trying to understand customer health, or your sales team is interested in cross-selling a new product, they can go back and view all historical conversations and better understand your customer's sentiment.

Now that we've covered some of the best practices and key considerations at a team level, let's dive deeper into how agents can make the most of it with chat support.

## Best Agent Practices for Live Chat

The agents are the folks that are going to be using the product day-to-day. While you can't enforce these policies, they can be great to encourage as best practices.

### Introduce yourself and give a polite goodbye

When you start a conversation with a customer, just like you would if you were talking to them in real life, start it with a polite introduction. Saying something like "Hi there Bonnie! My name is Jane, and I'll be helping you today" can set the tone for a good conversation. Similarly, after you've resolved the customer's issue, say goodbye to them, and let them know you'll be there if they need anything else. Something like "Thanks for your time today, Bonnie. I'm glad we could resolve this, but let us know if you run into anything else." is an excellent way to let the customer know that you genuinely care about their problems. This is called an "invitation to return," and should be included in *every* customer interaction, live or otherwise.

### Use Saved Replies

Not every question is going to be unique. You will get some questions that are repeated somewhat frequently. In those cases, keep track of your most commonly asked questions and make use of saved replies—also known as canned responses—to make the most of your and the customer's time.

Keep in mind that saved replies can be a double-edged sword, though, if they provide outdated or incorrect information. Before hitting the send button, make sure you've customized or modified the saved reply to the point that it makes sense to the specific customer you're talking to. This could include updating information like their name or including additional information like relevant docs.

## Pattern Match the Person You Are Speaking with

Do you speak the same way to your parents as you would to your best friend? Probably not. Everyone has slightly different ways of communicating, depending on which circle they are currently in. This is called "accommodation," and can be done subconsciously or by choice. With customers, it is something that you most often need to do by choice. Mirror the way that the customer is engaging. For example, if they are using a lot of emoticons and emojis, you can do the same. If, instead, they are speaking tersely and without a lot of expressiveness, you can keep your communication sparse: use minimal exclamation points and no gifs or emojis. Just like in spoken conversation, this will help put your customers at ease and make them feel seen.

## Set Appropriate Expectations

In a verbal conversation, if you have to pause, you usually say "Hold on just one second, I'm going to go do something." Similarly, if you have to go and dig up an answer or ask a colleague about something for the customer when having a chat conversation, let them know. They won't mind, as long as you tell them that you'll be gone and set proper expectations. If you just disappear with no answer for several minutes while they wait for you, they're likely going to start to get frustrated. Telling them from the get-go defuses some of that potential anger and makes them feel like they are in the loop.

When evaluating tools, look for products that let you provide customers with a transcript at the end. Many people like to write down information from support interactions for use later but aren't as quick as they'd like to be and miss out on getting it down. Some tools keep the conversation history forever, so a visitor can come back anytime and review previous messages, but some customers still prefer to have chat transcripts emailed to them. Find a tool that can do at least one of these things.

### Send Links when Possible

Similar to the previous point: If you send a person who is having trouble with documentation via a link, they are able to keep that link and use it later when they run into the problem again. They could also potentially, if needed, send it to their friend or someone else trying to use your service. Links save you from typing far too much into a chat window and keeping your message from being digestible, and they give your customer resources to use later on.

Once a customer navigates to a link and is able to look at your documentation, they may also find other useful information that keeps them from having to reach out another time. Win/win!

### Use Chat Transcripts to Update Your Documentation

Chat transcripts are the best, as we've already noted, and customers love them. Beyond the benefit to customers, transcripts can be a gold mine for written content. Because your team has to do so much quick, on-the-fly assistance, it can be a great place to find useful nuggets that can be put into existing documentation or turned into new documentation as needed.

Consider having a team member go through transcripts once a week and see what is there that you can pull and put into your docs to make them even better and more useful for your customers. Alternatively, you could add a flag that team members can use for specific chats to indicate they may be useful fodder for a doc.

## KPIs for Live Chat

As with any support channel, it's imperative to measure live chat's effectiveness. Here's a breakdown of the best KPIs (Key Performance Indicators) to consider tracking for live chat support.

1. First Response Time (FRT): This is the time taken to send the first response after a customer initiates a chat. A shorter FRT is often associated with higher customer satisfaction, as it shows customers that their queries are prioritized.

2. Average Resolution Time: This KPI measures the average time it takes to resolve a customer's issue or inquiry once they've initiated a chat. Faster resolution times usually indicate efficient support processes and knowledgeable support teams.

3. Chat Duration: The average length of a chat session. While quick resolutions are good, very short chat durations might indicate unresolved issues or dissatisfied customers.

4. Customer Satisfaction Score (CSAT): Post-chat surveys can give valuable insights into how satisfied customers were with the chat experience. A simple question like, "Were you satisfied with the support you received?" can provide a wealth of data.

5. Chat Abandonment Rate: This measures the percentage of chats initiated by customers but abandoned before they were addressed by an agent. A high rate might indicate long wait times or other barriers to effective communication.

6. Total Chats Handled: This is a measure of volume. Tracking this can help with staffing decisions, identifying peak chat times, and assessing the overall demand for chat support.

7. Concurrent Chats: The number of chats an agent handles at the same time. This metric can provide insights into agent efficiency, though it's important to balance it with quality of service.

8. Escalation Rate: The percentage of chats that need to be escalated to a higher authority or different department. A high escalation rate might indicate training needs or areas where front-line agents lack sufficient resources.

9. Transfer Rate: Similar to escalation, this measures how often chats are transferred between agents. Frequent transfers can frustrate customers and may highlight gaps in team expertise or coordination.

10. Proactive Chat Success Rate: If your team uses proactive chats (initiated by the agent based on customer behavior), this KPI evaluates how many of those engagements result in positive outcomes, whether that's a resolved query or a completed sale.

Incorporating these KPIs into your analytics arsenal will provide a comprehensive picture of your live chat's performance. Regularly reviewing and acting upon these metrics ensures that your support team continues to meet and exceed the expectations of your customers, driving both satisfaction and loyalty. Remember, the aim isn't just to measure but to enhance the live chat experience continually.

## Phone Support

Phone support is like the granddaddy of all support channels. After all, the good ol' telephone was the go-to way before chatbots and emails came into play. Even though it might feel a bit vintage now, it has stuck around for some real reasons. Did you know that over 60% of customers still prefer a phone call for quick issue resolution? And there's something about hearing a human voice that makes things feel more personal. So, while it might seem retro, there's a lot going for phone support that keeps it relevant.

| Pros | Cons |
| --- | --- |
| Promotes trust with your customers. People love being able to see a phone number on a website, because it makes them feel like there is a real person there who they are able to get in touch with. Chat and email can feel very "fake" or distant to people; whereas phone, to some demographics, feels very tangible. | Hard to scale. Because phone support requires so much attention and effort from the agents providing it, it can be difficult to scale. Instead of chat or email where you can implement tools and workarounds that scale as you grow, with phone support you just have to hire more people. That can get pretty expensive. |
| Creates higher brand value. Phone support can provide a human connection in an otherwise sometimes entirely online experience. If your competitors don't provide support via phone, it can help increase the value of your brand, as it's perceived as an added product and service that you provide. Also, phone support is the fastest channel for solving customer complaints, as you can get the issue resolved within the same conversation. | Phone trees can be a bummer to navigate, and customers can get stuck lost in them or, worse yet, have to call back to re-navigate. If you don't have a simple, straightforward phone tree, it can be an even worse experience than someone giving poor service via email. It's worse still because it's not even the fault of any person on the team, and likely the individual that ends up answering the support inquiry call will get the brunt of all of that customer's frustration. |

| | |
|---|---|
| Better evolution of your brand. Because you're closer to your customers, instead of simply relying on analytics like bounce rate, click-through rate, and conversion rate, you can talk directly to customers about their thoughts and feelings. You can also solicit feedback about your products to help improve. This not only helps your company and team evolve quicker, but it also makes customers feel valued because you care about what they think and feel. | Phones are disruptive to work. Anyone who has a phone has experienced being deep in something only to be drawn out of it by the buzz or ring of a phone or text. For phone support agents, this is ten times worse, as the volume of calls they receive is so great that they seldom get the option of working on something outside of their queue, especially not with boxed-out time. |
| Phone support is perceived as faster by customers because they have an immediate response from a person. Even if, ultimately, the time it takes the support agent to answer the question is a little bit longer, the fact that they answered the phone immediately (or very quickly) makes all the difference to most customers. | Slower and more time-consuming for employees. Unlike email or chat, it is very difficult to multitask when on the phone. For example, if a customer says something over the phone, and an agent doesn't catch it, they have to ask again. Via email or chat, the agent can just reread the transcript to see if something is missing. These kinds of small things mean that any agent answering support calls needs to always be "switched on" or they might miss a detail that could potentially frustrate a customer. |

| | |
|---|---|
| The phone is great for one-on-one communication. When trying to clarify something with a customer directly, the phone can be an excellent way to gain a better understanding of what they're running into trouble with. | It is hard to keep everyone in the loop at once on the phone, though. While you can do group calls or conference calls, it's better to keep context and track of who is saying what in written format. Talking on the phone does not lend itself to multiple people being needed to solve an issue. |

Now that you have the lay of the land with what you can look forward to and what you can dread when it comes to phone support, we've put together a few tricks of the trade to make it easy as you start your new journey.

## Best Team Practices for Phone Support

### Offer a Callback Option

Scaling phone support can pose unique challenges. Although phone interactions offer a rich, personalized touch, they demand undivided attention from support teams. Imagine a customer's frustration: they dial in for urgent assistance and are met with endless hold music. Every minute on hold can dent their trust, making them question their importance to the company.

To address this, modern businesses are turning to advanced phone support systems. Features like automated callbacks not only respect the customer's time but also streamline operations for agents. Instead of enduring long hold times, customers can continue with their day and receive a call when an agent is available. This integration not only enhances the overall user experience but also offers valuable insights into call patterns, helping businesses make informed decisions.

For total transparency, I have never worked at a company that had high enough phone volume to necessitate the use of IVR, but have been on the receiving end of an automated callback and always recommend it to my consulting clients. If you are offering phone support to a large group of users, you might run into trouble when it comes to scaling if you fail to consider tooling like this.

## Keep Your Phone Navigation System Simple

I cannot tell you how many times I have called a company, followed the prompts diligently, and then zoned out and accidentally pressed the wrong button. I instantly dread needing to go back through the complex phone navigation tree that I took to get to where I was, or even worse, end up telling the person that answers that I've made a mistake. I feel anxious. I debate hanging up and just forgetting that I needed support at all. Sometimes, I even do just that. Don't make your customers feel this way.

Maintaining a simplified and intuitive phone navigation system is paramount. It's essential to design your phone tree in a manner that allows users to retrace a step without starting over. It's not just about minimizing errors but creating a system where rectification is easy and efficient. Consider segmenting your phone lines based on the specific departments—sales, success, and support. This not only prevents customers from delving deeper into numeric combinations but also offers them a more targeted assistance pathway.

But what about those ungodly hours when most of the world is asleep, and your team is off the grid? The reality is, customers operate in various time zones and on personal schedules. They might reach out anytime, even if you've explicitly listed your business hours. To maintain a customer-centric approach, consider investing in an after-hours answering service. There's a distinct warmth and reassurance in speaking to a real person, even if it's just to leave a message. If you can't do this, consider doing as my children's dentist Tiny Texans Pediatric Dentistry has done: send a text message including detailed information about what the customer could be calling about. Include your open hours, details that customers need to escalate, and other ways to get help beyond talking on the phone.

This human touch can make all the difference, proving to customers that they are genuinely valued, rather than letting them drift into the abyss of an unattended voicemail. In the end, it's all about ensuring that every touchpoint, even if it's just a phone call, enhances the customer experience.

## Best Agent Practices for Phone Support

While we know that, as a leader, you are not likely to be in the phone queues answering calls, these are some great best practices to remind your team.

### Stand Up While Calling

We often underestimate the role our posture plays in communication, especially over the phone. Think about it: when you're seated for extended periods, especially in repetitive tasks like answering calls, there's a tendency for lethargy to set in. This can inadvertently translate into your voice, making you sound disinterested or fatigued. This is far from ideal when aiming to offer stellar customer service.

Standing up while conversing with a customer over the phone can be a game-changer. Not only does it enable you to project your voice better, making you sound more vibrant and present, but it can also elevate your overall energy levels. When you incorporate light movement, like pacing around your workspace, it further aids in keeping your mind alert and active. This simple act can boost circulation, helping oxygenate your brain and fending off that mid-call fatigue.

So, if you ever find yourself drifting into monotony or feeling a bit sluggish during phone interactions, remember this little trick. Stand up, stretch those legs, and watch how it refreshes both your body and your conversation!

## Smile While You Call

Ever heard the old tip about smiling while you're on the phone? It might sound like something your grandma would advise, but there's some real science behind it. On the phone, your voice is the star of the show. And believe it or not, popping a smile can jazz up your tone in ways that genuinely make a difference.

Next time you're on a call, especially with a customer, give it a whirl. Start with a grin at the beginning, keep it up when troubleshooting, and even flash those pearly whites if you've got to share some not-so-great updates. You may be surprised at how it can change the vibe of the conversation.

So, why does it work? Smiling tweaks the sound of your voice, making you come across as friendlier and more relatable. Even if they can't see it, folks on the other end can sense that warmth. It's like giving your words a cozy blanket. Who knew such a simple trick could be a game-changer in phone chats? Give it a try and see how it spices up your interactions!

## Save True Warmth and Enthusiasm Until You Hear the Customer's Name

You know that feeling when you first meet someone and there's a rush to make a connection, but you're not quite sure how? The natural instinct is to lean into enthusiasm and charm. But just like in-person interactions, phone conversations benefit from a touch of authenticity.

Imagine you're at a social gathering. Would you immediately start gushing about how thrilled you are to meet someone you've just been introduced to? Probably not, right? It might feel forced or even disingenuous. Instead, you would likely take a moment to learn a bit about them, listening to their story or understanding their perspective. This approach helps build a genuine connection, ensuring the relationship starts on a solid footing.

Similarly, when chatting with customers over the phone, it's a good idea to resist going overboard with excitement from the get-go. Wait until they've shared a bit about themselves and their situation. Let the warmth and enthusiasm flow naturally as the conversation progresses. This not only feels more genuine but is genuine, fostering a sense of trust and understanding. It's a win-win: the customer feels heard, and you create a sincere rapport, laying the groundwork for a fruitful interaction.

## Features and Functions to Prioritize in Your Search

When you're on the hunt for an effective phone support system, here's a list of key features to consider:

- Interactive Voice Response (IVR): This automated system helps in guiding callers through menu options using voice recognition or touch-tone commands, ensuring they reach the most suitable agent or department.

- Call Routing: Automatically directs calls to the right department or the next available agent based on predefined criteria.

- Call Queuing: Ensures that calls are lined up and handled in the order they are received when agents are busy.

- Call Recording: Allows companies to record and archive conversations for training, quality assurance, or compliance purposes.

- Real-time Analytics and Reporting: Provides insights into metrics like call duration, call volume, first-call resolution, and agent performance.

- Multi-channel Support: Integration capabilities that allow agents to switch seamlessly between phone calls, live chats, emails, and other communication channels.

- Call Forwarding: Enables calls to be forwarded to different numbers or devices, which can be useful for remote or distributed teams.

- Voicemail-to-Email: Converts voicemails into email format so agents can listen to them directly from their inbox.

- Call Monitoring and Whispering: Allows supervisors to listen in on calls for training purposes, and "whisper" to agents without the caller hearing.

- Hold Music or Messages: Provides callers with music or informational messages while they wait.

- Conference Calling: Allows multiple participants on a single call, aiding in resolving complex issues that might require input from different departments.

- CRM Integration: Seamless integration with Customer Relationship Management software ensures that agents have immediate access to caller history and information.

- Callback Option: Allows customers to request a callback rather than waiting in a queue, improving customer experience.

- Customizable Caller ID: Lets businesses choose what number or name appears on the recipient's caller ID.

- Scalability: The system should be able to handle growth, whether it's an increase in call volume or adding new agents.

- Security Features: Encryption, fraud prevention, and other security features to protect both the company and its customers.

- Mobile App Integration: Allows agents to take calls and access the system features on-the-go.

- Skill-based Routing: Matches callers with agents based on specific skills, expertise, or knowledge.

- Customizable Scripts: Provides agents with suggested scripts or responses to ensure consistency and accuracy.

- Multi-language Support: Essential for businesses with a global customer base, offering support in multiple languages.

Remember, the best phone support system for your business will depend on your specific needs, customer base, and operational requirements. It's essential to do thorough research and perhaps even test a few options before settling on one.

## KPIs for Phone Support

To ensure optimal performance, businesses employ a range of KPIs. But which are the most critical? Let's dive in and decipher the vital KPIs that every phone support team should monitor.

1. First Call Resolution (FCR): Quite simply, this KPI measures how often customer issues are resolved in a single call. An impressive FCR rate often correlates with high customer satisfaction. It means your agents are both competent and efficient, addressing customer needs without transferring calls or requesting callbacks.

2. Average Handle Time (AHT): This metric calculates the average duration taken to address and resolve a customer's call, including the hold time and the follow-up tasks post-call. While it's crucial not to rush calls, a consistently high AHT might indicate a need for better training or system improvements.

3. Service Level: Often defined as the percentage of calls answered within a specific time-frame, this KPI helps gauge the accessibility and efficiency of your support team. A common benchmark might be answering 80% of calls within 20 seconds.

4. Abandon Rate: No one likes being on hold. The abandon rate measures the percentage of callers who hang up before speaking to an agent. A high rate might indicate long wait times, understaffing, or issues with your Interactive Voice Response (IVR) system.

5. Call Volume: Simply put, this is the total number of incoming calls within a specific period. Monitoring spikes or drops in call volume can offer insights into potential issues, promotional successes, or areas needing attention.

6. Customer Satisfaction (CSAT): After resolving a call, many companies send out short surveys to gauge customer satisfaction. The resulting score offers a direct insight into the quality and effectiveness of your phone support.

7. Agent Occupancy: This metric indicates how busy your agents are by assessing the time spent handling calls against available working time. It's a fine balance—you want your agents occupied but not to the point of burnout.

8. Net Promoter Score (NPS): By asking customers how likely they are to recommend your service to others, NPS offers a broader view of your service quality. While not exclusive to phone support, it's a crucial metric to understand the overall impact of your customer service.

9. Cost per Call: Every call incurs costs, in terms of manpower, technology, or infrastructure. By monitoring and optimizing the cost per call, businesses can ensure profitability without compromising on service quality.

10. Agent Turnover Rate: High turnover can be costly and disruptive. Monitoring this KPI can highlight dissatisfaction within your team and indicate areas for improvement in training, support, or working conditions.

## Social Media Support

Over the past two decades, social media has dramatically transformed the digital landscape. It's interesting to think back to the early 2000s when I was struggling to learn HTML to differentiate myself on platforms like MySpace and various blogging sites, and how far we have come. These were just the precursors to giants that followed: Meta (Facebook), X (Twitter), Snapchat, and Instagram, among others. As these platforms burgeoned, they reshaped how we communicate, forging new pathways and expectations for customer engagement.

But here's the real deal: as our customers evolve in their digital preferences, our approach to support needs to keep pace. If your customer prefers tweeting their concerns rather than sending an email, that's where your support team should be—right in the thick of it, responding to that tweet. But what determines the necessity of social media support for a brand?

Well, it's not a one-size-fits-all answer. Just because social media is the rage doesn't mean every business must jump on the bandwagon. I wouldn't want to see my bank, for instance, hamming it up on TikTok.

Some customer demographics might prefer traditional channels over sliding into your DMs. In contrast, others may see social platforms as their primary (or even sole) point of communication.

So, how do you navigate this terrain? The key is understanding your users. Take the information that you gleaned in our first chapter. Dive deep into analytics, conduct surveys, or simply ask them where they would like to connect with you. By identifying where your users are most active and what they prefer, you can tailor your support strategy, ensuring it aligns with their expectations and offers them the most seamless experience. After all, when considering CX, being where your customers are is half the battle won.

| Pros | Cons |
| --- | --- |
| Social media offers much greater customer engagement. With such a huge reach, you have the possibility of reaching immensely large audiences. For marketing, for example, if you post something that captures your audience's imagination, it can be shared by anyone it resonates with, giving you a chance for it to go viral and increase its audience exponentially. | Additional resources may be needed to manage your online presence, especially if you have a particularly small or scrappy team. While the software tools and cost of entry may be inexpensive, the cost in terms of time is significant. To successfully employ social media both in marketing and support, you need to invest substantial amounts of time over a long period to see good results and customer feedback. |
| It grants you greater access to international markets. If your support team is capable of supporting multiple languages or your product is offered in multiple countries, it can be useful for you to be able to reach all of your customers in one space. Social media allows for that! | Social media is immediate and needs daily monitoring. If you don't actively manage your social media presence, especially if you've set precedence for providing social media support, your customers might grow angry. |

| | |
|---|---|
| It offers a huge opportunity for customer feedback. Because social media is a 24/7 communications channel, you will get instant feedback on your marketing campaigns, product releases, and any other new changes from your company. That means that you'll know about bugs almost instantly, or be able to update and fine-tune your marketing posts in the moment. It can also provide you with an immediate and honest assessment of your products or services as well as the content you are putting out. For better or for worse. | Using social media causes you to run the risk of unwanted or inappropriate behavior on your social media profiles, including bullying and harassment. It can also lead to things like negative public criticism, information leaks, or hacking. |

Social media is a huge opportunity to conduct market research about your customers directly. There are many simple, free, or low-cost monitoring tools for social media that allow you to learn basic information about the market you are in. You can also gain intelligence on competitors, prospects, and clients, and get insights into your company, products, and services.

With social media, the rules are constantly changing. From the algorithm used by Facebook to pick which of your posts to display, to the length of tweets, to the user interface in LinkedIn, it feels like sands are always shifting underneath our feet—all of the things that we've mentioned here are probably already outdated and old! It can easily become a full-time job just to keep up with the latest trends and best practices. New social media platforms are launched daily, and others die. You have to keep reviewing and revising your strategy on an ongoing basis in order to continue providing the best support you can.

| | |
|---|---|
| You are afforded improved networking opportunities with customers and other businesses by using social media. You have a completely different kind of relationship with your prospects and customers on social media than in any other channel: it's a two-way conversation that allows for a much deeper, quicker level of engagement. As a form of communication, it is about as close as you can get to holding a conversation with someone while not being in the same room as them. | While other forms of support allow you to tightly control the message and its distribution, making sure that only that message is communicated and nothing else, social media pushes everything out of your hands. Once you release your message you also relinquish control as it is shared, commented upon and added to. Similarly, with peer-to-peer social networking, customers, prospects, and anyone else that wants to could be talking to each other about your product, service, brand, or company and you wouldn't even know. |
| It's low cost. You do not have to pay anything to offer support on social media. Both X (Twitter) and Meta (Facebook), for example, have just started offering specific customer messaging tools, like the ones Buffer offers, that allows you to manage all social media in one place. | It's easy to mess up. Social media is more casual and more open. But, with the sheer volume of posts and constant conversation, it can be easy to take your eye off the ball and make public something you shouldn't have or post something that is open to misinterpretation. On the flip side, its very nature of informality and openness also means that it is much more forgiving. |

# Best Team Practices for Social Media Support

## Pick the Best Platform for Your Business

Navigating the vast world of social media can sometimes feel like being a kid in a candy store—you want to try everything! However, it's crucial to take a step back and really dive into some research before jumping onto every platform where you spot your customers.

Remember, engaging effectively on social media can be a real time-sucker, given the rapid pace at which customers expect responses. If you spread yourself too thin over multiple platforms, you might end up diluting the quality of support you offer. Instead, focus on fewer platforms where your presence truly matters.

By doing so, you'll be better positioned to provide those top-notch, memorable experiences that keep your customers coming back for more. Because, in the end, it's all about quality over quantity, right?

At PartnerHero, we made a decision to stop using any tools that were created by Mark Zuckerberg. This meant that our teams pulled out from Facebook and Instagram across the board. Then, when Elon Musk purchased Twitter, we also hopped off of that platform.

A few years later, we ultimately determined that in the areas where we do a great deal of our hiring, such as the Philippines, sites like Meta (Facebook) and Instagram made up even more of the internet usage than search engines like Google. We had to be able to reach that audience, and so we took a new stance.

Our hiring teams, who have the audience of our potential employees, use Facebook and Instagram to reach and respond to applicants for roles, whereas we use LinkedIn to respond to and engage with customers. Be conscious and effortful in your choices around social media.

## Monitor Social Media Mentions, and Don't Forget to Look for the Less Obvious Ones

While a good chunk of customers will give you a direct shout-out or tag you in a post when they need assistance, there's a sizable group that might take a subtler approach. When keeping tabs on social media mentions, don't just rely on exact name matches. Be on the lookout for slight variations or common misspellings of your company name. Sometimes a customer might genuinely forget to tag you or make a typo. By broadening your search criteria, you ensure that no query or concern slips through the cracks, even if they didn't tag you by mistake. It's all about staying one step ahead and ensuring every customer feels seen and heard!

That said, sometimes when you interject yourself where you're not wanted, it can be creepy. I always think about the person that stands *just* outside of the periphery of a friend circle at a social gathering because they're too timid to step in, but still want to be involved. You don't want to be a lurker, and you don't want to step in where you aren't wanted. Ensure that you practice your best judgment before getting involved, especially if you haven't been directly tagged. Everyone knows that everyone is listening, but they don't need to be reminded of it.

## Consider Setting Up a Dedicated Channel for Support

Many savvy businesses these days opt for separate social media accounts for their support and marketing teams, and there's a solid rationale behind this choice. First, it ensures that your support-related interactions don't clutter your primary feed, which for many companies serves as a dynamic advertising billboard. Second, having distinct accounts minimizes the too-many-cooks-in-the-kitchen scenario. Imagine combining the efforts of several support staff with your marketing team members, all operating within a single or a couple of social media platforms.

During high-activity times, like a product launch or a service outage, things could get a tad chaotic. So, if your brand sees a significant amount of engagement online, it might be worth giving some thought to partitioning your social media presence. It helps streamline operations and presents a cleaner image to your audience. We did this at Trello, creating a handle on X (Twitter) for the Trello brand and thought leadership, while maintaining a second account that tweeted about status updates, and responded to specific support inquiries. If someone reached out to the main-brand X (Twitter) with support questions, they were rerouted to the Support handle.

## Build Best Practices About Responding

When working for a big company, it's essential to have clear policies in place for responding to various types of messages on social media. Picture this: a customer posts something negative about a competitor but praises your brand. Do you give that tweet a thumbs up, or is it better to just scroll past? And then there's the inevitable encounter with online trolls. Do you engage in a dialogue, or is silence the best strategy? Setting these guidelines early on isn't just about damage control; it's about establishing the personality and public image of your brand on social platforms.

When I crafted the interview process for team members at Appcues, I specifically had a small quiz that gave a series of tweets, and then asked the taker to identify how they would respond to each. It gave a good opportunity to see the applicant's sense of understanding of the nuances of social, and also opened up conversation around their thinking behind some of their decisions.

Having a blueprint for these situations ensures that your team presents a consistent and considered face to the world, no matter what comes your way.

## Choose the Right Hashtags

Hashtags can be your best friends! It's a smart move to identify hashtags that resonate with both your brand and the support you're aiming to highlight. But here's a little heads-up: resist the urge to sprinkle all your chosen hashtags on every single post. It's like putting ketchup on everything you eat—not always the best fit! Overdoing it can be off-putting and might make you lose some of your audience, and it can also lead to unwanted attention to your brand, especially if the hashtag is too broad and ends up being co-opted for something nefarious. So, keep it relevant, and remember, sometimes #lessismore.

## Best Agent Practices for Social Media Support

Even as a manager you may be pulled into support on social media, especially if it's a particularly busy day. Here are some best practices to keep in mind and be sure to relay to your team.

### Speed Matters

Response time is of the essence for customer support agents. A swift reply not only meets the immediate expectations of customers but also establishes a brand's reputation for being attentive and proactive. To facilitate this speed, it's a smart move to have macros or snippets on standby for common queries. Leveraging such pre-prepared responses can save crucial seconds, ensuring you tackle the queue more efficiently and keep customers satisfied.

### Use the Right Tone of Voice

Mastering the right tone of voice is crucial in the world of social media customer support. Much like when you're communicating via email, it's essential to tune into the customer's emotions and tailor your responses accordingly. If you encounter a customer who is clearly frustrated or upset, it's wise to adopt a more empathetic and subdued tone. On the other hand, if they approach with humor or light-hearted banter, feel free to engage in a playful, yet professional manner. The key is to ensure that your responses not only resonate with the customer but also stay true to your brand's voice and guidelines. After all, authenticity and alignment matter!

## Take Things Offline when Necessary

Navigating the channel-switch can be a delicate part of social media customer support. While it's a powerful tool for engaging customers, it's important to recognize when certain issues are better resolved offline or via a different channel. For instance, any issue requiring the exchange of sensitive personal information or login credentials is a candidate for taking the conversation to a more secure environment like email or a phone call. Similarly, complex troubleshooting that might need to be escalated to a specialized team should also be directed away from public view. If you find yourself dealing with such situations, guide the customer to the appropriate channel—whether that's a direct email to your support team or a call to your service line. Make sure to actively monitor for their follow-up, as failing to promptly address their concern after directing them elsewhere would be a major customer service faux pas.

## Use Your Knowledge Base to Make Things Easy

Trying to condense complicated explanations on platforms like X (Twitter), which have character restrictions, can feel like trying to fit a square peg into a round hole. But hey, that's where the beauty of having a robust knowledge base comes in handy! If you've invested in creating comprehensive support articles or tutorials, don't hesitate to share those direct links with customers. Not only does this save you the challenge of truncating information, but it also offers customers a richer resource they can refer back to. Plus, while you're at it, take note of any gaps in your existing documentation. If you find yourself wishing for a specific guide or article, it's a good bet your customers would appreciate it too. Consider it a feedback loop that helps you continually refine your resources!

## Choose How You React

Armed with the guidelines set forth by your company, it's crucial to be selective about how you engage on social media. Before hitting that "like," replying, or deciding to scroll past a post, take a moment to reflect.

If there's ever a moment of doubt or if you feel the company's stance isn't crystal clear, it might just be the perfect time to spark a discussion with your team. Gaining clarity ensures everyone's on the same page. Without this shared understanding, there's always that lingering risk of making an off-brand move. Remember, on social media, any misstep can be amplified, shared, and potentially misconstrued.

## Features and Functions to Prioritize in Your Search

With customers actively voicing opinions and seeking support on platforms like X (Twitter), Meta (Facebook), and Instagram, ensuring timely and effective social media customer support is no longer just an option—it's a necessity. But with a myriad of tools out there, how do you choose the right one for your business? Here's a guide to features and functions you should consider when selecting a social media tool for customer support:

- Multi-Platform Integration: Your customers are everywhere. Your social media tool should be able to integrate with various platforms to ensure you never miss a customer query, be it on X (Twitter), LinkedIn, Meta (Facebook), or any other platform. This can show up in demos as a unified Inbox, which aggregates messages from different platforms into one central dashboard.

- Real-Time Monitoring and Notifications: The speed of response on social media can make or break your brand reputation. Real-time monitoring ensures that you respond to customer queries, concerns, and feedback promptly. In a demo, this might look like Instant Alerts or Push Notifications for new messages or mentions.

- Automated Workflows: Automation can help streamline repetitive tasks, ensuring that each customer query reaches the right department or individual without delay. As a product feature, this looks like rule-based tagging and routing to automatically categorize and forward messages.

- Collaboration Tools: Sometimes, resolving a customer query might need input from different departments. Collaboration tools ensure seamless internal communication for quick resolution. In the product, this shows up as Internal notes, shared inboxes, and assignment capabilities.

- Analytics and Reporting: Understanding the volume, nature, and resolution times of queries can help optimize your support strategy. Look for dashboard overviews, sentiment analysis, and detailed response-time metrics.

- Knowledge Base Integration: Being able to quickly reference or direct customers to articles, FAQs, or guides can expedite resolution. Keep your eyes open for the ability to use quick links or auto-suggestions linked to your brand's knowledge base.

- CRM Integration: Personalizing your customer support can make a significant difference. By having a tool that integrates with your CRM, you can have all the relevant customer details at your fingertips. This looks like customer history, purchase details, and previous interactions viewable within the tool.

- Scalability: As your business grows, so will your customer support needs. Ensure that the tool you choose can grow with you. This looks like flexible pricing tiers, add-on modules, and integration capabilities.

- Security and Compliance: Customer data privacy is paramount. Ensure the tool you opt for meets necessary security standards. Look for two-factor authentication, GDPR compliance, and data encryption.

- Customizability and Branding: Your customer support should reflect your brand. A tool that allows custom branding can provide a consistent experience. This shows up in a demo as customizable templates, branded chatbots, or response formats.

The right social media customer support tool can transform your support operations, enhance customer satisfaction, and build brand loyalty. Remember, the best tool isn't necessarily the most expensive or the most popular, but the one that aligns seamlessly with your brand's unique needs and objectives. Invest the time in research, take advantage of trial periods, and ensure your choice bolsters your brand's commitment to exceptional customer service.

## KPIs for Social Media Support

If you're aiming for unparalleled service on social media, tracking certain KPIs is nonnegotiable. Here are some pivotal KPIs that can be a game-changer for your social media customer support:

1. Response Time: In a landscape where speed is everything, the quicker you respond, the happier the customer. Tracking this ensures your team's efficiency and responsiveness. An average response time of less than an hour can set you apart from competitors.

2. Resolution Time: While response time is about initial contact, resolution time measures the average time taken to fully resolve a customer's query or complaint. The lower, the better. Depending on the complexity, aim for a few hours to a day.

3. Customer Satisfaction (CSAT) Score: It's a direct metric that gauges the customer's satisfaction with the resolution provided. A score closer to 100% is better, but at least look for regular improvement.

4. First Contact Resolution Rate: This metric indicates the percentage of customer issues resolved in the initial interaction, a testament to your team's efficiency. A higher percentage suggests fewer back-and-forths and higher customer satisfaction.

5. Query Volume by Channel: Understand which social platforms—e.g., X (Twitter), Meta (Facebook), and Instagram—receive the most support queries to allocate resources effectively. Aim for consistency in response and resolution, irrespective of the platform.

6. Issue Categorization: By categorizing issues (billing, technical, general queries), you can identify common pain points, allowing for targeted problem-solving. Fewer recurring issues in the same categories indicate effective resolution strategies.

7. Public Versus Private Resolution Rate: Some issues are resolved publicly on the social platform, while others are taken to private messages. Monitoring this can help in PR and managing brand image.

8. Social Listening Metrics: Beyond direct queries, customers often mention brands in posts or comments. Tracking these can provide insights into brand perception and areas of concern.

9. Conversion Rate Post-Interaction: A satisfied customer can often lead to a sale. By tracking conversions post-support interactions, you can measure the ROI of your support efforts. A higher conversion rate indicates efficient and profitable support interactions.

While these KPIs provide invaluable insights, it's essential to remember that they are just tools. The ultimate goal is to foster authentic connections, build trust, and ensure that every interaction adds value to your brand–customer relationship. By focusing on these metrics and continuously striving for improvement, your brand can redefine excellence in social media customer support.

## Self-Service Support

If you've ever dashed to Google to fix a minor tech hiccup before ringing up customer support, you've touched on the essence of self-service support. Personally, I *love* self-service support above all else, and for good reasons—not just because I'm antisocial and peopled out. Let's dive into what self-service support really is and why businesses (and customers) find it so valuable.

Self-service support is, essentially, a do-it-yourself solution for customer queries. Instead of waiting on hold to chat with a team member, customers can find answers on their own using tools like FAQs, how-to guides, forums, chatbots, and even step-by-step videos. It's about handing the reins to the customers and saying, "Hey, here's the info. You got this!" Here are some common examples of ways that you can implement self-service support:

- FAQs (Frequently Asked Questions): This is a section on a website where companies address the most commonly asked questions about their products or services.

- Knowledge Bases: A comprehensive library of articles, guides, and how-to's that provide in-depth information about a product or service. They might include step-by-step instructions, tips, and best practices.

- Forums and Community Boards: Here, customers can ask questions, and either company representatives or other customers can provide answers. This collaborative approach often generates a rich pool of user-generated content and solutions, but isn't for everyone—it's particularly effective for DTC products.

- Chatbots: These AI-driven tools can answer questions, guide users through troubleshooting steps, or even help users with processes like checking out on an e-commerce site.

- Video Tutorials: Visual guides that walk users through a process, from setting up a product to troubleshooting common issues. We used *tons* of these at Wistia, partially because it's a video hosting company and partially because they can be really helpful!

- Interactive Troubleshooting Guides: These are step-by-step walk-throughs that help users diagnose and resolve specific problems, often by answering a series of questions. These are super helpful for deeply technical products, or products for technical folks.
- Downloadable User Manuals: Comprehensive documents that provide detailed information about a product, its features, and how to use it.
- Self-Service Portals: For businesses, this might include portals where customers can check their account status, make payments, update personal details, or track orders without needing to contact customer support. Any SaaS product should have one of these.
- Feedback Forms: While they're primarily for businesses to gather feedback, they can also guide users towards self-help resources based on their queries.
- Interactive Voice Response (IVR) Systems: Over the phone, users can navigate through menu options to get automated solutions or information without speaking to a human agent.

While there are tons of benefits to implementing self-service support—and you should *always* have *some* measure of it implemented—there are some cons as well.

| Pros | Cons |
| --- | --- |
| Customers can access information and resolve issues anytime, without waiting for business hours. | Some issues are too complex for self-service tools and require human judgment or empathy. |
| Reduces the need for human intervention, which can save on labor costs over time. | If not regularly updated, knowledge bases or FAQs can provide outdated or incorrect information. |

| | |
|---|---|
| As your user base grows, self-service tools can handle more queries without a proportional increase in costs. | If users can't find answers easily, they may become frustrated, leading to a negative experience. |
| With users solving basic issues on their own, customer support teams can focus on more complex, specialized queries. | While they can save money in the long run, initial setup, design, and maintenance of self-service systems can be costly. |
| Some users prefer finding answers on their own rather than waiting in a queue to speak with a representative. | Automated systems lack the human touch, which can be crucial for building strong customer relationships in certain industries or scenarios. |
| Automated systems ensure consistent information is provided every time, reducing the risk of human error. | Over-reliance on automated systems can be problematic if there's a technical glitch or if systems go offline. |
| Automated systems can collect data on the most frequent issues or queries, helping businesses improve their products or services. | Automated systems might not always understand the nuances of user queries, leading to incorrect solutions. |

## Best Team Practices for Self-Service Support

### Understand Your Audience

At the heart of any effective support system, be it traditional or self-service, lies a deep comprehension of one's audience, like we noted in the second chapter. Think of your customers as unique individuals, each with their own set of expectations, preferences, and pain points. It's not just about knowing their demographics, but truly understanding the typical challenges they face when interacting with your product or service.

Use this information to tailor your self-service resources and directly address customers' most common queries and issues. This not only saves time for both the customer and the support team but also fosters a sense of connection and understanding, as users feel that their specific needs are being recognized and catered to.

## Keep It Updated

Every year, I order too many Girl Scout Cookies. Like, *way* too many boxes. I always anticipate that my whole family will go bonkers for the cookies, and that they'll just *fly* off my pantry shelves. This is never true, and every October, the month after they expire, I find myself eating stale Tagalongs, wishing that I didn't do this to myself.

Just as you would hate to bite into a stale cookie, your customers don't want outdated information. In the ever-evolving landscape of business and technology, things change rapidly. Whether it's a software update, a new product feature, or even a change in business operations, your self-service resources, particularly FAQs and tutorials, need to reflect these shifts.

Regularly reviewing and updating this content ensures that your customers always have access to the most accurate and relevant information. And trust me, they'll appreciate it! No one wants to spend time scouring a help page, only to realize the information is outdated. Keeping things fresh means fewer frustrated customers and more successful self-service experiences.

## User-Friendly Design

I am the type of person who looks at menus before I go to the restaurant. I want to know what I'm having before I get there, so I don't have to fret about figuring it out while trying to talk to friends. There are some times, though, when the menu has either changed, or it is so differently designed that I can't even find what I thought I was going to have. It drives me bonkers.

Similarly, when customers land on your support platform, they're hoping for clarity and ease. If they have to play detective just to find basic information, they're likely to leave unsatisfied. An intuitive interface is more than just appealing visuals; it's about creating a smooth and logical journey for the user. Remember, if they can't easily navigate your platform, all the valuable information you've provided won't do them much good.

## Categorize Information

Think of your self-service platform as a well-organized library. Just as books are sorted by genres and topics, your support content should be organized in a way that users can quickly pinpoint what they're curious about. No one wants to sift through "romance" when they're on the hunt for "science fiction." Clearly defined categories and subcategories make the user experience far less daunting and infinitely more productive. A user who finds answers efficiently is a happy user!

## Interactive Elements

While reading through chunks of text can be informative, there's something special about interactive support. Think of it as the difference between reading a cookbook and having a chef walk you through a recipe step-by-step. Incorporating elements like chatbots or interactive FAQs adds a dynamic layer to your support. These tools can guide users in real-time, answering questions and offering solutions based on the user's specific needs. It's like having a virtual assistant ready to jump in, ensuring that users aren't left to figure things out entirely on their own.

## Link Relevant Content

Ever gone down an internet rabbit hole because one article led to another? I know I've certainly started searching for what season to grow beets in in Stardew Valley and ended up in a rabbit hole learning about all of the specific uses that exist for a prismatic shard.

That's the beauty of hyperlinks. It's not just about providing answers; it's also about showing users where to delve deeper. If you mention a specific topic or solution, hyperlinking to related content can enhance the user's understanding and keep them engaged. It's a way of saying, "Hey, if you found this interesting, there's more where that came from!" It not only enriches their experience but also makes sure they have a comprehensive understanding of the topic at hand.

## Best Agent Practices for Self-Service Support

While you probably aren't the one creating the self-service support experience on your own, here are some great tips for your team.

### Continual Training

You know what they say: Change is the only constant! Just as the tech world sees a new iPhone every year or so, your products and services will evolve, and with them, new challenges or concerns from customers. It's not enough to set up a self-service platform and call it a day. Think of it like a garden. If left unattended, it might get overrun with outdated info or miss addressing new issues that crop up. Regularly training your team ensures that they're always on the ball, ready to update resources with fresh and relevant content. Plus, when they're in the loop with the latest solutions, they'll be more effective in helping users who still need that human touch.

### Promote Self-Service

I have never been good at self-promotion. In fact, I used to lead punk rock yoga at a local venue here in Austin, and I was so sheepish about advertising myself or this event that I almost exclusively relied on word of mouth.

Imagine hosting a fantastic party but forgetting to send out invites. You've got the best tunes, delicious snacks, and mood lighting, but no guests! It was exactly like that.

Similarly, your self-service portal could be a goldmine of information, but it's of little use if customers aren't aware of it. Make sure you're giving it the shout-out it deserves! Slip in mentions in your emails, showcase it prominently on your website, or give it a nod during live support sessions. It's like telling your customers, "Hey, before you reach out, did you know we've got this super-helpful spot where you might find instant answers?" The more you integrate and promote your self-service options into every customer touchpoint, the more empowered they'll feel to help themselves.

## Features and Functions to Prioritize in Your Search

If you are on the hunt for a self-service support tool, it's essential to zero in on features and functions that elevate the user experience while streamlining backend processes. Here's a breakdown of key features you should prioritize and look for:

1. Intuitive User Interface (UI): A clean, easy-to-navigate interface ensures that users can effortlessly find the information they need. The design should cater to both tech-savvy individuals and those who might not be as digitally inclined.

2. Search Functionality: A powerful search bar with predictive and auto-suggest capabilities can guide users to relevant content swiftly.

3. Knowledge Base/FAQs: A structured and comprehensive knowledge base is the cornerstone of self-service. This should be easily updatable with articles, guides, how-to's, and FAQs.

4. Categorization and Tagging: This allows for easy sorting and quicker access to related topics, making the user's journey smoother.

5. Interactive Tutorials: Tools like step-by-step guides, video tutorials, and interactive walkthroughs can visually guide users through processes.

6. Feedback Mechanism: Users should be able to rate and provide feedback on articles, which can offer insights into content effectiveness and areas for improvement.

7. Chatbots and Virtual Assistants: Integrating AI-driven chatbots can guide users in real-time, answering questions or directing them to the right resources.

8. Responsive Design: The tool should be optimized for mobile devices, ensuring accessibility for users on the go.

9. Community Forums: Allowing users to interact, ask questions, and share solutions can create a supportive community, reducing the pressure on your support team.

10. Analytics and Reporting: Tracking user behaviors, commonly accessed articles, search terms, and more can offer deep insights into user needs and areas to enhance.

11. Integration Capabilities: The tool should integrate smoothly with other business systems, such as CRM, ticketing systems, or e-commerce platforms, for a unified support ecosystem.

12. Content Versioning: As content is updated, keeping track of different versions ensures that the most accurate, timely information is presented to users.

13. Multimedia Support: Being able to embed videos, infographics, and interactive elements can enrich content and cater to different learning styles.

14. Multi-language Support: For global businesses, offering content in multiple languages is vital to cater to a diverse user base.

15. Personalization: If the platform can remember returning users and offer personalized content suggestions, it can enhance the user experience significantly.

16. Security: Ensure that the platform offers robust security features to protect user data and any business-sensitive information.

17. Scalability: As your business grows, the platform should be able to handle increasing amounts of content and user traffic.

18. Notifications: Automated alerts for content updates, community interactions, or any flagged issues can keep both users and admins in the loop.

19. Easy Content Creation: A simple backend editor, preferably WYSIWYG (What You See Is What You Get), can make content creation and updating a breeze for your team.

20. Workflow and Approval Processes: For larger teams, having a structured workflow where content can be drafted, reviewed, and approved before publishing ensures quality control.

By prioritizing these features, you can implement a self-service support tool that not only empowers users but also streamlines the support process, leading to improved customer satisfaction and operational efficiency.

## KPIs for Self-Service Support

Just as with any other channel, it's crucial to track KPIs to gauge effectiveness and optimize for better results. Here are some of the most important ones to consider:

1. Self-Service Adoption Rate: Measure how many customers utilize the self-service options compared to those who reach out directly for assistance. A rising adoption rate indicates success.

2. Article/Page Views: Track which articles or pages in your knowledge base or FAQ section are most viewed. This can hint at what issues or questions are most common among users.

3. Content Engagement Rate: Beyond just page views, understand how users interact with the content. Are they spending time reading it? Do they scroll through the entire piece?

4. Search Effectiveness: Monitor the success rate of users finding what they need using the search function. Track unsuccessful searches to identify gaps in your content.

5. User Feedback and Ratings: Many self-service tools allow users to rate content or give feedback. Monitor these ratings to ensure content remains helpful and relevant.

6. Case Deflection Rate: Measure how many potential support tickets or calls were avoided due to users finding answers via self-service channels.

7. First Contact Resolution Rate: Within the self-service domain, gauge how often a user's issue is resolved without needing further intervention from a live agent.

8. Content Update Frequency: Track how often you're updating or adding new content. Fresh, relevant content means a more effective self-service tool.

9. User Session Duration: Understand how long users spend in the self-service portal. Short sessions might indicate they quickly found what they needed, but very short sessions might mean they gave up.

10. Community Forum Engagement: If you have a community component, monitor the number of active users, threads, and replies. An active community can be a strong indicator of a healthy self-service ecosystem.

11. Chatbot Interaction Rate: If you use chatbots, monitor how often users engage with them and the resolution rate from those interactions.

12. Top Navigation Paths: Understanding the most common paths users take can provide insights into their behavior and potential pain points in the journey.

13. Mobile Versus Desktop Engagement: Measure user engagement across devices. If mobile engagement is low, you may need to optimize your self-service for mobile users.

14. Bounce Rate: Monitor how many users exit the self-service portal without interacting with any content. A high bounce rate can indicate that users aren't finding what they need.

15. Knowledge Gap Analysis: By analyzing search queries and page views, identify areas where content is lacking or needs updating.

16. Conversion Rate: If your self-service platform includes actionable items (like completing a form, signing up, or making a purchase), track the rate at which users complete these actions.

17. Retention Rate: Monitor how often users return to the self-service platform, indicating its value to them.

18. Feedback Submission Rate: Track how many users take the time to submit feedback or suggestions, which can provide actionable insights for improvement.

By keeping an eye on these KPIs, you'll be able to refine your self-service support platforms, ensuring they continually meet user needs and reduce the demand on traditional support channels.

# Community Support

Although it's a subset of self-service support, many businesses choose to use community support for their customers. Community support is specifically when a section of your community (or the whole thing) is dedicated to customers looking to find answers or solutions to their use-case problems. While it can feel *really* good when done authentically, it also can feel like you're forcing your customers to do work when all they want is to be helped.

| Pros | Cons |
|---|---|
| Customers often help one another by sharing personal experiences and solutions, sometimes even faster than official support channels can. | Information shared by peers might not always be accurate or in line with official guidelines, potentially leading to confusion or misinformation. |
| It can reduce the number of formal customer support tickets, as users often find answers in the community, thus lowering support costs. | To maintain a positive environment and prevent spam, trolling, or off-topic discussions, continuous moderation is necessary. |
| The discussions and solutions in the community can be a gold mine for content ideas, FAQs, and knowledge base articles. | If the community isn't active, users might have to wait longer for solutions, leading to frustration. |
| Direct feedback and discussion can quickly highlight areas for improvement in products or services. | Unresolved issues or vocal unhappy customers can turn a community into a platform for negative feedback. |
| A well-moderated, active community can foster brand loyalty and create brand ambassadors, as customers feel a sense of belonging. | Businesses might become too reliant on community support, neglecting formal support channels. |
| Since communities consist of global members, someone is always online, leading to round-the-clock potential support. | Members might inadvertently share sensitive information on public platforms, leading to potential security risks. |

| Businesses can directly engage with and solicit feedback from their most dedicated users in a community setting. | Setting up, managing, and nurturing a community requires time, resources, and a dedicated team. |
| --- | --- |
| Active community forums can improve search engine rankings as they continually generate fresh, relevant content. | Users might share solutions or ideas that don't align with the brand's official stance or messaging. |

Although communities can be an invaluable tool for fostering engagement and providing support, they require careful management to ensure they remain beneficial for both the company and its customers.

## Best Team Practices for Community Support

### Clear Identification

When I'm at a party, I'm either most comfortable when I know *everyone* or I know *no one*. If it is a mix anywhere in between that, I am very uncomfortable. Maybe this is the same for you? You want to know who's who.

To eliminate any guesswork, it's essential that official support agents stand out in the crowd. By giving them identifiable badges or distinct user names, you're essentially handing them a "microphone" in that crowded room. This not only positions them as go-to experts but also ensures that users have confidence in the guidance they receive. After all, knowing you're chatting with an expert instills a certain peace of mind.

### Encourage Peer Support

There's something incredibly valuable about getting advice from someone who has walked in your shoes. That's the beauty of community forums. Not all solutions need to come from official channels. Often, seasoned users or "power users" can offer quick fixes or unique workarounds.

By recognizing and occasionally rewarding these community champions, you're not only validating their contributions but also encouraging a collaborative spirit. It's like giving a nod to the neighborhood hero!

## Monitor and Moderate

I've never had a green thumb. I always imagine that I will, and plant a whole garden of squash and tomatoes in the beginning of the summer only to remember them in August and come out to cucumbers the size of watermelons. And weeds. Tons of weeds.

Similarly, a community space without oversight can get a bit…wild. By actively moderating content and ensuring that interactions remain positive and constructive, you're ensuring that the environment remains welcoming for all. It's all about maintaining a healthy balance, where users feel safe to voice concerns, ask questions, and share experiences.

## Collaborate and Share

Knowledge thrives when it's shared. Agents, with their fingers on the pulse of user concerns, are treasure troves of insights. These insights shouldn't be confined to the community space. By regularly sharing common queries, feedback, and discoveries with broader support and product teams, agents can influence product updates, FAQ inclusions, and even marketing campaigns. It's like connecting the dots between what users are saying and how the company can respond in real-time.

## Recognize and Celebrate Success

I can't be the only one who thrives on validation and pats on the back. In the world of community forums, it's no different. Celebrating milestones, like a user's 100th helpful answer, or highlighting a particularly ingenious problem resolution, adds a splash of positivity. It not only motivates the involved parties but also sets a standard for other members. Think of it as a virtual high-five, reminding everyone of the great things they can achieve together.

## Stay Aligned with Company Values

Community platforms might have a more relaxed vibe, but they're still a reflection of the company. It's essential that every piece of advice, interaction, or engagement echoes the company's core values and objectives. Whether it's demonstrating patience during a heated discussion or ensuring advice aligns with company guidelines, staying true to the brand is crucial. It's a bit like ensuring that every conversation, no matter how informal, still carries the essence of the company's ethos.

## Best Agent Practices for Community Support

Although you may not always be actively providing support in your community, your *team* is. Here are some best practices that you can implement for their success.

## Active Presence

I have always wanted to be a "regular" somewhere and have the workers know my name. I tip well and build relationships, all for the sake of being known.

That's the kind of vibe you want to create on your community platform. When agents are consistently present, actively listening, and chiming into discussions, it sends a clear message to users: "We're here, and we've got your back." This isn't just about answering queries; it's about being a familiar face (or user name) in the crowd. Over time, this consistent interaction lays the foundation for trust and a sense of community belonging.

### Know the Platform

I would almost always rather be a guest at a party rather than a host. But every once in a while, I get wrangled into doing it—and I always do too much. I make too much food, overdecorate, and always go unintentionally over the top. This is actually a *benefit* in community support.

As agents, it's vital to know every nook and cranny of the community platform. Whether it's tagging a relevant department, pinning important posts, or using advanced search features to pull up older threads, proficiency with the platform's tools ensures that users get swift and efficient assistance. Think of it as mastering the home turf; it makes you more resourceful and boosts users' confidence in your capabilities.

## Personalize Responses

Imagine getting the same "Thank you for your feedback" reply every time you reach out. Feels a bit cold, right? While it's crucial to maintain a consistent tone and approach, adding a sprinkle of personalization can make all the difference. Whether it's acknowledging a user's previous contributions or adding a touch of humor where appropriate, personalized interactions feel genuine, making users feel seen and valued.

## Solicit Feedback

There's always room to grow, right? And who better to guide that growth than the community itself? Actively seeking feedback from members isn't just about gauging the quality of support; it's an open invitation for users to share their experiences, thoughts on products, or even ideas for future features. It's like hosting a suggestion box, reminding users that their voice is not just heard but is actively shaping the community's future.

## Promote Self-Service

Sometimes, the answer is just a click away. Instead of reinventing the wheel with each query, guide users towards existing resources like FAQs, tutorials, or knowledge base articles. Sharing these in relevant discussions not only addresses issues swiftly but also encourages a culture of self-help. It's akin to teaching someone to fish; you're empowering users with tools and knowledge to troubleshoot on their own, fostering independence.

## Manage Expectations

My life would be way better if I had a magic wand that I could just wave away my problems with, but unfortunately, as I explain to my six-year-old, it just doesn't work that way. When faced with a tricky question or a complex issue that requires more time, it's essential to keep the user in the loop. A simple acknowledgment, coupled with a clear timeframe for resolution or further updates, keeps anxiety at bay. It's all about setting the stage, ensuring users know what to expect and when, and building anticipation rather than uncertainty.

## Features and Functions to Prioritize in Your Search

When considering a community platform for customer support, there are several crucial features and functions to keep in mind. These elements ensure that the platform not only offers a pleasant user experience but also serves as an effective support tool. Here's a breakdown:

1. User-Friendly Interface: The platform should have an intuitive design that makes it easy for both new and returning users to navigate, search for information, and participate in discussions.

2. Search Capability: A robust search feature is vital. Customers should be able to quickly find relevant discussions, solutions, or articles related to their queries.

3. Moderation Tools: The ability to moderate content, users, and discussions is essential to maintain the quality and integrity of the support provided. This includes features like banning users, pinning important topics, or flagging inappropriate content.

4. Integration with Existing Systems: The platform should seamlessly integrate with your CRM, ticketing system, or other essential business tools to streamline support processes.

5. Customization and Branding: The ability to customize the look and feel of the community to align with your brand identity helps in creating a consistent user experience.

6. Mobile Responsiveness: As many users may access the community via mobile devices, the platform should be mobile-friendly and optimized for various screen sizes.

7. Analytics and Reporting: Tools to track user engagement, popular topics, response times, and other KPIs will help in evaluating the community's effectiveness and areas of improvement.

8. Notification System: Users should receive notifications for replies, mentions, or updates relevant to their discussions, ensuring they stay engaged.

9. Knowledge Base Integration: Integrating a knowledge base or FAQ section can serve as a quick reference for common issues, reducing repetitive queries.

10. User Profiles and Badging: Allow users to create profiles and earn badges for active participation, which can incentivize helpful behavior and recognize top contributors.

11. Private Messaging: Users should have the option to discuss sensitive issues privately with moderators or official support agents.

12. Scalability: As your business and community grow, the platform should be able to handle increased traffic and content without performance issues.

13. Security Features: The platform should provide robust security measures, including data encryption, secure login methods, and protection against cyber threats.

14. Multilingual Support: If your business operates globally, consider a platform that supports multiple languages, both in content and user interface.

15. Interactive Elements: Features like polls, surveys, or quizzes can make the community more engaging and gather feedback.

16. Social Media Integration: Allowing users to share content or log in using their social media accounts can enhance the community's reach and accessibility.

17. Tagging and Categorization: The ability to tag content or categorize discussions ensures that information is organized and easily retrievable.

18. Automatic Content Archiving: Outdated or irrelevant content should be archived automatically to maintain the community's relevance.

19. Rate and Up-Vote System: Users should be able to rate or up-vote valuable content, helping others find the most helpful responses quickly.

20. Accessibility Features: Ensure that the platform complies with accessibility standards, making it usable for all individuals, including those with disabilities.

Choosing the right community platform involves evaluating your team's specific needs and ensuring that the chosen solution offers the tools and capabilities to address them effectively. You might not need all of these features, but you will surely need at least a few!

## KPIs for Community Support

When providing customer support via a community platform, you must keep track of key factors like tool efficacy, user engagement, and areas for improvement. Here are some important KPIs to consider:

1. Community Engagement: Measure the number of active users, posts, comments, likes, and shares to understand the level of engagement within the community.

2. First Response Time: Track the average time it takes for a user's question or issue to receive its first response. This could be from fellow users or official support representatives.

3. Resolution Time: Measure the average time it takes to resolve a user's issue or answer a question after it's been posted.

4. Satisfaction Rate: After an issue is resolved, survey the user to determine their satisfaction with the solution or the support they received.

5. Top Contributors: Identify users who are most active and provide helpful content consistently. These power users can be vital assets to the community.

6. Thread-to-Solution Ratio: Determine how many discussion threads lead to a successful solution or resolution. This can offer insights into the community's effectiveness.

7. Search Effectiveness: Analyze how often users utilize the search function and find relevant results. This can highlight gaps in content or suggest improvements in the search algorithm.

8. Content Quality: Monitor the up-votes, down-votes, and feedback on content to assess its quality and relevance.

9. User Retention Rate: Track how many users continue to engage with the community over time versus those who leave after their first interaction.

10. User Growth Rate: Measure the number of new users joining the community over specific periods.

11. Churn Rate: Determine the rate at which users stop participating or engaging with the community.

12. Issue Escalation Rate: Track the percentage of issues from the community platform that require escalation to other support channels, such as email or phone.

13. Feedback Collection: Count how many suggestions or feedback points are gathered from the community, which can inform product or service improvements.

14. Category Popularity: Analyze which discussion categories or topics are most popular to understand users' primary concerns or interests.

15. Knowledge Base Utilization: Track how often users access integrated knowledge bases or FAQs. High utilization may indicate effective self-help resources.

16. Private Message Volume: Measure the number of private messages or direct interactions, which can indicate the need for more discrete support.

17. Security Issues: Monitor any security concerns, such as spam, unauthorized access, or data breaches.

18. Platform Uptime: Ensure the community platform has minimal downtime to provide consistent support.

19. Mobile Access Metrics: With many users accessing platforms via mobile, track mobile user engagement, page load times, and mobile-specific issues.

20. Training and Development: If the platform has official representatives, track how often they receive training or development sessions to improve their community support skills.

Regularly monitoring these KPIs will help you refine your community support strategy, ensure user satisfaction, and keep the good times rolling.

## In-Person Support

While not typically a channel that individuals consider, in-person support is something that can be extremely valuable for certain types of businesses. For instance, Uber, which is a largely in-person service business, offers "Greenlight" and an in-person support hub specifically for drivers. When asked about it, Lance Conzett, a support operations manager, stated, "Greenlight success was primarily measured by driver retention, with the idea that one in-person interaction could solve a cluster of issues and that human experience would result in drivers feeling secure and trusting in Uber's ability to solve their problems."

Depending on what metrics you are trying to drive and improve through your CX strategy, offering in-person support may be something to consider. We have chosen to get specific with the best practices around this channel, as it is so specific to the type of company and type of customer base you are trying to serve. However, we have aggregated a collection of pros and cons to help you consider if this might be right for you.

| Pros | Cons |
|---|---|
| In-person support provides an opportunity to form a deeper, more human connection with customers. Face-to-face interactions often lead to more personalized service, building trust and loyalty. | Maintaining a physical location, staffing, and other overheads can be costly compared to digital-only support models. |
| Issues can often be resolved on the spot, without the back-and-forth that might be common with email or phone support. | In-person support can't be available 24/7 in most cases, unlike chatbots or online knowledge bases. |
| Reading body language can provide cues about a customer's true feelings or level of satisfaction, allowing the support agent to adjust their approach in real-time. | As a business grows, it may become challenging to offer the same level of in-person support without significant investments in more locations or staff. |
| Direct communication minimizes the risk of misunderstandings or misinterpretations that might occur over text or voice calls. | Face-to-face encounters have the potential to escalate if not handled correctly, especially if a customer is highly upset or confrontational. |

| | |
|---|---|
| Beyond just addressing the issue at hand, in-person interactions allow representatives to showcase new products, explain services in detail, or even offer tutorials. | Especially pertinent in times of health crises (like the COVID-19 pandemic), in-person interactions might pose health risks to both staff and customers. |
| | Customers outside a specific region or those who can't travel to the physical location will miss out on this support option. |

The vast spectrum of channels available for customer support will continue to evolve. From the time-honored tradition of face-to-face interactions to the instantaneous digital methods of today, companies have never had such a plethora of options at their fingertips. Yet the fundamental goal remains the same: providing customers with timely, effective, and empathetic assistance that meets their unique needs.

Each channel, whether it's in-person, over the phone, via email, through social media, or using community platforms, offers its own set of advantages and challenges. While face-to-face interactions might build a deeper personal connection, digital channels provide accessibility around the clock. The key for modern businesses is not just to pick one, but to integrate multiple channels seamlessly, ensuring that customers always have a route to assistance that matches their comfort and convenience.

However, it's vital to remember that the channel is just the medium. The heart of excellent customer support lies in the quality of the interaction. Regardless of the method, listening actively, responding with empathy, and ensuring resolution are the cornerstones of a successful support strategy.

In embracing the multichannel world of customer support, companies should not only be led by technological advancements but, more crucially, by their understanding of their customer demographics, preferences, and behaviors. One guiding principle should remain at the forefront: the customer's voice is paramount, and finding the most effective ways to hear, respond to, and satisfy that voice is the ultimate goal.

# CHAPTER 4:
# Building Your Support Operations

The real competitive edge often lies not just in the products or services a company offers, but in the post-purchase experience. But how does one construct a team that's not only reactive but proactive, not just efficient but compassionate, and not just a unit but a cohesive force? This chapter delves deep into the art and science of building your customer support team's operations—a foundation that can make or break the customer experience.

In this chapter, we'll explore the facets of team dynamics, the importance of streamlined processes, the nuances of training modules, and the integral role of technology in enhancing operations. Building a support team is more than just filling seats; it's about crafting an ecosystem where every interaction adds value, every process optimizes time, and every team member feels empowered to make a difference. Whether you're just starting to sketch the blueprint for your support team or you're looking to refine an existing one, there will be content in this chapter for you!

## Types of Support Structures

Companies have various options when structuring their support teams, depending on factors like their size, industry, customer base, and the complexity of the products or services they offer. Here are some common structures employed:

### Tiered Support

Tiered support, often depicted as a pyramid with levels denoting expertise, is a tried and true method of managing customer service inquiries. It's not just about categorizing queries; it's about efficiency, expertise, and ensuring every customer gets the right level of attention.

## Level 1 (L1): The First Responders

Imagine walking into a clinic because you're feeling under the weather. The receptionist, who first greets you, gathers initial details and perhaps administers basic treatments. That's akin to L1 in customer support. These folks are the first point of contact, handling the most common questions, from password resets to basic troubleshooting. The great thing about L1 is its swiftness; customers often get instant answers. However, the downside is that not all problems can be solved at this level, and some customers might feel they're being passed around if their issue needs escalation.

## Level 2 (L2): The Specialists

Following the clinic analogy, if the receptionist can't address your concern, you would see a general doctor next. In the world of support, that's L2. These agents have a deeper understanding of the product or service, and are equipped to handle more intricate queries that L1 might find challenging. Their specialized knowledge is a boon for customers with unique issues. On the flip side, because they cater to more complex problems, their response time might be a tad longer than L1.

## Level 3 (L3): The Experts

Now, if the general doctor feels there's something more concerning, they would refer you to a specialist. Enter L3, the final stage in tiered support. These agents are the wizards, the aficionados, dealing with the most complex, rare, or new issues. They might work closely with the team behind the product, like engineers or developers, to find a solution. The beauty of L3 lies in its depth of expertise; they ensure that even the most complicated problems find a resolution. But there's a trade-off: their deep dive approach means they might take the longest to respond, and not every customer will have the patience for it.

In a nutshell, tiered support is like a relay race, ensuring the baton (in this case, the customer's query) reaches the right runner (support level) efficiently. Although it streamlines queries, the potential downside is the risk of customers feeling like they're being bounced between levels. The key for businesses? Ensuring smooth transitions, clear communication, and always prioritizing the customer's experience.

## Functional Support

Functional support stands out as an innovative way to address user needs. It's like walking into a departmental store: instead of one long queue, there are specialized counters for shoes, cosmetics, and electronics. The idea? Each team becomes an expert in a specific function, ensuring customers get precise and swift solutions.

Imagine you've got an issue with your latest mobile bill. Instead of explaining your problem to a generalist, who then ponders which department to send you to, you head straight to the billing department. That's the beauty of functional support: it cuts out the middleman. This system ensures that agents become specialists, deeply familiar with their domain, be it billing, technical glitches, or account nuances.

With functional support, technical issues get addressed by tech teams well-versed with the ins and outs of the product. Their in-depth understanding often means they can detect problems faster and offer concrete solutions. No more generic "turn it off and on" advice; you're getting the tech-equivalent of a surgeon.

There are also those concerns that don't fit into the usual "issue" box. Maybe a user wants to understand the advanced features of a product, or perhaps they're looking for upgrade options. Enter the account management team. Their job isn't just problem-solving; it's relationship-building. They guide users, ensuring they're making the most of the product or service.

While functional support does offer an efficient way to sort queries, there's a potential hiccup: what if a customer has multiple issues spanning different departments? In such cases, they might feel they're being ping-ponged between teams. The solution? Seamless inter-departmental communication and ensuring the customer always feels heard, regardless of how many teams they interact with.

In essence, functional support is about creating a landscape where each query finds its expert, ensuring quicker resolutions and happier customers. It's a testament to the evolving world of customer service, which constantly adapts to deliver the best experience possible.

## Skill-Based Routing

I will almost always stop and ask someone for information or directions as soon as I start to get even a *whiff* of being off track. At bookstores, I will always ask the desk folks to look up books for me. Instead of spending my precious time hunting for something that I know I want, I just go right to the source. This is the premise behind skill-based routing: directing customer queries straight to agents based on their unique skills and expertise.

The magic of skill-based routing, especially popular in sprawling contact centers, lies in its efficiency. Think of it as matchmaking for customer issues. Got a tech-related question? Boom! You're connected to the tech guru. Billing issues giving you a headache? Say hello to the finance wizard. It's all about ensuring that customers aren't just getting answers, but they're getting them from the best person for the job.

At the heart of skill-based routing is a simple yet powerful concept: Match the customer with the agent best equipped to address their specific concern. No more bouncing around between representatives. Customers speak directly to someone who deeply understands their issue, ensuring swift resolutions. This efficient approach doesn't just lead to satisfied customers; it streamlines the entire support process. When a customer's journey involves fewer touchpoints, it results in quicker resolution times, creating a seamless and less frustrating experience for the end-user.

But the benefits don't stop at the customer's end. Let's peek behind the scenes. For the agents manning the phones, chats, or emails, this approach is a breath of fresh air. By consistently handling queries they're familiar with, agents operate in their zone of expertise. They aren't flustered by unfamiliar issues or forced to pass the buck. Instead, they're empowered, offering solutions with confidence. This doesn't just make their workday smoother; it contributes significantly to job satisfaction.

However, every rose has its thorns. Let's delve into some potential pitfalls of this approach.

1. Dependency Concerns. Imagine having only a handful of agents equipped to handle a recurring issue. What happens when those agents are on leave, or there's a sudden surge in that specific type of query? Customers could face frustrating wait times, defeating the very purpose of efficient skill-based routing.

2. The Monotony Factor. For agents, variety can be the spice of life. Answering the same type of queries day in and day out might get repetitive. Over time, this could sap their enthusiasm and even lead to burnout. After all, nobody wants to feel like they're stuck in a loop.

3. Setup and Maintenance Hurdles. Implementing a skill-based routing system isn't as easy as flipping a switch. It requires an intricate setup to ensure the right matches between queries and agent expertise. And as agents develop new skills or as business needs change, the system needs tweaking, making it a continually evolving beast.

Skill-based routing offers a promise of precision, ensuring that customers are matched with the best possible agent for their needs. But it's essential to remember that it's not a plug-and-play solution. To truly benefit from it, companies need to be proactive in addressing its challenges.

It's all about striking a balance: ensuring quick resolutions for customers, while also making sure that agents aren't pigeonholed into monotony. After all, the ultimate goal is fostering meaningful, effective connections—every single time.

## Dedicated Support

Customer support has evolved in leaps and bounds over the years, and one of the strategies that's been making waves is the idea of "Dedicated Support."

Imagine this: Instead of being thrown into a vast ocean of generic customer support agents every time you have a concern, you get your own personal lifeguard. Someone who knows the depth of your needs, the tides of your challenges, and can guide you ashore safely, each time. This is the essence of dedicated support, where specific agents or even entire teams are earmarked exclusively for key accounts or VIP customers.

The beauty of dedicated support is the level of personalization it offers. With dedicated agents in play, customers no longer face the ordeal of reintroducing themselves or rehashing their history every time they reach out. Their dedicated agent is already in the loop, well-acquainted with their preferences, past challenges, and future needs. This naturally paves the way for a smoother, tailor-made support experience.

Moreover, this model allows agents to acquire a deep-dive knowledge of their assigned accounts. They're not just brushing the surface; they're delving deep. Because they focus on specific accounts, these agents can expedite problem-solving and even offer proactive support, anticipating issues before they escalate.

Beyond the technicalities, there's the human aspect. This model cultivates a stronger bond between the client and the agent. It's not just about solving problems; it's about building trust and loyalty. Having a dedicated point of contact feels like having a personal concierge. It sends a clear message to the client: "You are valued and prioritized."

However, every coin has a flip side. One pressing concern is the potential for dependency bottlenecks. Dedicated support is fantastic, but what happens if the dedicated agent is unavailable? Maybe they're out sick, on vacation, or attending a training session. There's a tangible risk of delayed response times or even a dip in service quality when issues are handed over to a backup agent.

For agents themselves, the challenges can be just as real. Continually managing high-priority or high-demand accounts can wear them down. The pressure of always being "on," especially for high-stakes clients, can be intense, leading to quicker burnout or job fatigue.

Lastly, from a resource allocation perspective, dedicated support can be intensive. Assigning specific agents to particular accounts, especially if they demand a lot of attention, can strain the system. This might inadvertently lead to other customers facing longer wait times or receiving a less personalized touch.

You don't *need* to use agents to create a dedicated support function, though. At Trello we did something similar by taking in information about all of the different touchpoints in a user's life cycle, and matching them up to the data from our help desk.

We then were able to understand when most of the common help inquiries came in, and where they were on the timeline of a user's life. From there, we ended up emailing helpful information and documentation immediately prior to when the customer *would* have theoretically reached out on their own. It wasn't human, and it was entirely automated, but it made the customer feel as though we had a crystal ball.

The allure of dedicated support is undeniable. It beckons with its promise of ultra-personalized service and the chance to cultivate strong, lasting bonds between companies and their key accounts. However, it's not without its set of challenges. Successful implementation demands foresight, flexibility, and a finger on the pulse of both the customer's and agent's needs. In the end, dedicated support isn't just about allocation; it's about creating connections that matter.

## Follow-the-Sun Model

In the age of globalization, the sun never sets on some businesses. For those operating across continents and time zones, ensuring consistent support can be challenging. Here's where the Follow-the-Sun Model steps in, promising a solution that's as elegant as it is practical. Picture a relay race, where the baton is handed off from one runner to the next, ensuring continuous momentum. Similarly, support responsibilities are transferred between teams stationed in various parts of the globe, ensuring that there's always someone available to address customer concerns, no matter the hour.

At the core of this model's appeal is its assurance of accessibility. Customers, regardless of their location, are guaranteed support during their "awake" hours. No more setting alarms to catch a company's support hours halfway across the world. This real-time responsiveness not only enhances customer satisfaction but also positions a brand as truly global, attentive, and considerate of its diverse clientele.

From the standpoint of employee well-being, the Follow-the-Sun approach boasts notable advantages. Instead of expecting agents to pull graveyard shifts or work during unsociable hours, teams can operate during their local business hours. This can significantly enhance work-life balance, reduce burnout, and subsequently lead to higher job satisfaction and retention rates.

However, no model is without its challenges. The most evident concern with the Follow-the-Sun approach is the potential for communication gaps. As tickets or issues transfer from one team to another, there's a risk of information getting lost in translation. If not managed meticulously, the customer might have to reiterate her concerns, leading to frustration and a sense of being passed around.

At Campaign Monitor, we tackled the communication gaps by implementing "hand-overs" in our internal wiki. Australia would document what had happened on their shift, and then hand it over to EMEA. Then, when EMEA was done with their shift, they would write down their details and hand it over to the United States, and the cycle continued back to APAC. We had consistent, ongoing documentation about what had happened on each shift, and could even look back on days or weeks past to get a more detailed view of trends.

However, even when solving for communication problems, consistency in service quality can be a challenge. Different regions might have varied training levels, resources, or even cultural nuances in communication. Ensuring that a customer receives a uniformly high-quality service, irrespective of which global team they interact with, demands rigorous training and standardization protocols.

Additionally, managing and coordinating between global teams can require sophisticated ticketing systems and robust operational oversight. Inconsistencies in tools or protocols between regions can complicate processes, making seamless handoffs trickier.

This model offers round-the-clock support without compromising on employee well-being. However, its seamless execution requires meticulous planning, communication, and a commitment to consistency. It's not just about being available; it's about ensuring that every sunrise brings with it the promise of consistent, quality support for every customer, everywhere.

## Hybrid Models

Many companies use a combination of the above structures to meet their unique needs.

The optimal structure largely depends on the nature of the business, the complexity of the products or services, the volume of support queries, and the company's resources. It's also essential to remain flexible and adjust the structure as the company grows and the nature of customer queries evolves.

# Channel Strategy

The avenues through which businesses engage with their customers have multiplied, bringing both opportunities and challenges to the fore. It's no longer a simple choice between email and phone; companies are now navigating a maze of live chats, social media platforms, community forums, and more. Determining your customer support channel strategy isn't just about jumping onto the latest trendy platform; it's about orchestrating a harmonious blend of channels that resonates with your customer needs, preferences, and expectations.

As we delve into this section, we'll unravel the complexities of channel selection, explore the nuances of multi-channel support, and lay down the framework for a strategy that aligns seamlessly with your brand's ethos and mission. Your channel strategy is more than just a tactical choice; it's a reflection of how you prioritize customer engagement and satisfaction in a crowded digital space. Let's set the stage.

## What Is a Channel?

At its simplest, a customer support channel is a medium or platform that facilitates communication between a customer and a company. It's the bridge that connects a customer's needs or concerns with the solutions or information a company offers. These channels can range from traditional methods like phone calls and face-to-face interactions to modern mediums such as chatbots and social media.

By offering multiple channels, your team can cater to diverse customer preferences, ensuring that everyone can reach out in a way they're comfortable with. Some customers might prefer the immediacy of a phone call, while others may opt for the convenience of an email or the informality of a social media message. For more details on this, head back and review our second chapter.

As a result of these changes, customer support channels have evolved to include the following.

- Email. Allows customers to send detailed queries and is perfect for issues that aren't immediately urgent.
- Live Chat. Offers real-time support on websites, enabling instant solutions.
- Social Media. Platforms like X, Meta, and Instagram have become hubs for customer queries and feedback.
- Self-Service Portals. Empower customers to find answers independently through FAQs, knowledge bases, or community forums.
- Phone Support. Remains a popular choice for many who prefer direct human interaction.
- Video Support. With the rise of platforms like Zoom, video support provides a more personalized touch, simulating face-to-face interactions.

While it's tempting to be present on every possible channel, quality should always trump quantity. It's better to offer excellent support on a few channels than to spread yourself too thin and offer subpar service on many. It's crucial for businesses to understand where their audience primarily resides and ensure those channels are well-maintained.

## Help Desk, Service Desk, Personal Email…Oh My!

Many businesses kick off their customer support journey using personal email services, such as Gmail or Hotmail. But as the enterprise expands and the clientele multiplies, pivoting to specialized software can become an invaluable asset.

Dipping your toes into the market, you might stumble upon terms like "help desk software" and "service desks." Though sometimes tossed around interchangeably, they're not identical twins. Grasping the nuances between them can significantly sharpen your selection process.

So, what are help desks? Think of a help desk as the bridge connecting a brand with its audience. At its core, a help desk is geared towards incident management and facilitating service requests. Its purview extends to self-service portals, intricate reporting, knowledge curation, and multi-channel interactions.

Through the help desk dashboard, your team can effortlessly craft knowledge base articles, navigate various support channels, and glean insights from comprehensive reports.

And the story with service desks? Service desks are software MVPs, typically championed by IT teams or in-house tech squads, dedicated to addressing and resolving queries.

Their domain is usually confined to singular tasks, like ticket resolution, troubleshooting technical glitches, or overseeing incident management. It's the dedicated portal where your crew converges to communicate and collaborate on specific issues.

It's common to find folks blurting out "help desk" and "service desk" as if they're synonymous. But in reality, they're distinct entities with different value propositions.

A help desk is an all-encompassing suite, rich in features and inherently customer-centric. Contrastingly, service desks sport a laser-focused approach, predominantly around incident resolutions.

In essence, a service desk is a subset within the vast expanse of a help desk. Opting for a help desk, you're essentially signing up for:

- Comprehensive ticket management
- Robust self-service options
- A dynamic knowledge base
- Detailed reporting

- Multifaceted communication channels
- User-friendly contact forms
- Smart automations

On the flip side, a service desk zeroes in on core functionality: attending to and resolving service tickets. Hence, service desks usually play the role of internal tools for employees, while help desks are externally focused.

## How to Know When to Level Up?

As you scale, you may start to wonder if it's time to change over from your personal email account to a help desk or service desk. How do you know if it's time for an upgrade, though?

1. Overflowing Inbox. If you're starting to dread opening your email because of the avalanche of unread messages, that's a pretty clear signal. An overflowing inbox isn't just a sign of growing business; it's also an indication that you need a more structured system. Help desk software can streamline these queries, assigning them tickets, and ensuring no request gets overlooked.

2. Missing out on Critical Emails. Remember that time you missed a crucial email from a customer because it got buried under less important messages or was mistakenly marked as spam? With a dedicated help desk tool, such mishaps can be minimized. Critical support queries can be flagged, ensuring they're given the attention they deserve.

3. Repetition, Repetition, Repetition. If you find yourself answering the same questions repeatedly, it's not just tedious; it's also inefficient. Help desk software usually comes with features like a knowledge base or FAQ section. This enables customers to find answers themselves, freeing up your time to tackle more complex issues.

4. Collaboration Confusion. As your team expands, you'll find that multiple people might need to address a single customer query. If you're forwarding emails back and forth or constantly CC-ing team members, things can get messy. A help desk tool provides a unified platform where everyone can collaborate on a single ticket, making the process more transparent and less chaotic.

5. Tracking and Metrics Become Imperative. To refine your customer support strategy, you need data. If you're relying on a personal email, extracting meaningful metrics is like finding a needle in a haystack. Help desk software provides essential insights—from response times to customer satisfaction ratings—helping you make informed decisions.

6. Personalization Is Becoming Paramount. Today's customers expect personalization. With a personal email, it's challenging to remember the history and preferences of every customer. Help desk tools often come with customer profiles, logging their interaction history, enabling you to tailor your responses, and making customers feel valued.

Switching from a familiar tool, like your personal email, to a new system can feel daunting. But remember, it's all about scalability and efficiency. As your business grows, so should your tools. If any of the signs above resonate with your current situation, it might be time to explore the world of help desk software. The initial setup may take some time, but the long-term benefits in terms of time saved, increased customer satisfaction, and business insights are well worth the effort.

## Should I Offer Multichannel or Omnichannel Support?

The concepts of multichannel and omnichannel support are gaining traction. But while many businesses are hopping on the bandwagon, it's essential to pause and ask, "Is this right for my business? How do I know?" Here's a guide to help you decide.

## Multichannel Versus Omnichannel

Multichannel support refers to offering customer service across multiple platforms or channels. This can include email, phone, chat, social media, and more. The idea is to be where your customers are, catering to their preferred mode of communication. For instance, while a millennial might prefer reaching out via X or live chat, another customer might be more comfortable with a good old-fashioned phone call.

| Pros | Cons |
| --- | --- |
| Wider reach, as you're present across multiple platforms. | Customers can choose their preferred method of communication. |
| Can lead to inconsistent customer experiences if not managed well. | Requires resources to maintain quality across all channels. |

Omnichannel support takes multichannel to the next level. Instead of just being present on multiple channels, omnichannel support emphasizes a seamless and consistent experience across all these platforms. The focus is on providing an integrated experience where information and data flow freely between channels. For example, if a customer starts a conversation on chat and then moves to a phone call, the support agent on the call would already have all the chat information, ensuring a smooth transition.

| Pros | Cons |
| --- | --- |
| Provides a consistent and seamless customer experience. | Higher customer satisfaction due to integrated support efforts. |
| Can be resource-intensive to set up and maintain. | Requires sophisticated systems to ensure smooth data transition between channels. |

While both multichannel and omnichannel involve multiple channels of communication, the primary difference lies in the integration and consistency of the customer experience. With multichannel, each channel may operate in its silo, whereas omnichannel is all about offering a unified and harmonized customer experience across all channels.

Total transparency: I have *never* worked at a company where omnichannel support was something that we needed. For large corporations, such as Disney and Capital One, omnichannel support is almost a must-have. For smaller companies, the support experience has less at stake and requires less focus on omnichannel.

I'm not just telling you to be lazy, though. Rather than putting your attention into omnichannel support, which you may not have the bandwidth or resources to do well, focus on the things that your customers actually care about.

## Listen to Your Customers

The first and most crucial step is to actively listen to your customers. Their needs, preferences, and feedback can be a goldmine of information. Conduct surveys, gather feedback, or simply engage in conversations. Which platforms or channels do they frequent the most? Are they more comfortable sending an email, making a phone call, or reaching out via social media? By identifying where your customers are and how they prefer to communicate, you can tailor your support channels accordingly. Remember, the customer's voice should always be the loudest, even if they aren't always right.

## Less Is More

In a world where "more" is often thought to mean "better," it's easy to assume that offering support across numerous channels is the way to go. However, spreading oneself too thin can lead to diluted quality and inconsistent customer experiences. Instead of diving headfirst into multiple channels, start small. Perfect your presence and service quality on a few key channels that matter most to your audience. It's always better to be excellent on a few platforms than mediocre on many. As the saying goes,

"Jack of all trades, master of none." Ensure you master each channel before considering expansion.

If you're on the fence about whether or not to add another channel, always default to doing less. Quality over quantity should be your mantra. Every added channel requires resources, training, and continuous maintenance. Before expanding, ask yourself:

- Do I have the necessary resources to manage this new channel effectively?
- Can my team handle the additional workload without compromising quality?
- Will this channel truly add value for my customers?

Remember, it's not about being everywhere; it's about being where it matters most and delivering top-notch service there.

Deciding on whether to offer multichannel support is not a one-size-fits-all answer. It's a business decision that should be made after careful consideration of your capabilities, resources, and most importantly, your customers' needs. By tuning into your customers' voices, embracing the power of simplicity, and always prioritizing quality, you can chart a clear path forward in the multichannel debate.

## Setting SLAs

At the heart of the responsibility of customer support lies a simple yet profound question: "How quickly and efficiently can we address our customer needs?" The answer, in many ways, is encapsulated in three letters: SLA.

Service Level Agreements, commonly known as SLAs, are essentially commitments made by service providers to their clients. They outline specific metrics and standards, such as response and resolution times, ensuring that there's a shared understanding of deliverables. Think of them as the rulebook, setting the tone and expectations for the service a customer can anticipate.

But why are SLAs especially crucial in customer support? Because in this sphere, clarity and consistency are king. When satisfaction hinges on timely and effective problem-solving, SLAs provide customers with a clear time frame and quality of service they can expect. On the flip side, for support teams, SLAs offer tangible benchmarks to measure performance against, fostering accountability and continuous improvement.

Moreover, SLAs aren't just about timelines. They act as a trust-building tool between companies and their customers. By setting and meeting these predetermined standards, businesses convey reliability and a deep commitment to customer-centricity. Let's start with a case study from real life: Disney.

## Disney: An Unlikely SLA king

Right before my second son was born, I took my older, first kiddo to Disney. The family had never gone, and it seemed like a good opportunity to spend some quality time really prioritizing him. The problem that we ran into was that he was freshly five, and just wanted to go-go-go.

Anyone that has gone to Disney may recognize this picture: twiddling thumbs, checking watches, and a sea of slouched shoulders in a line that seems to twist into eternity. It feels frustrating as an *adult* to wait in line for what feels like hours, but when you add in the nagging and irritation of a young child, it can feel like a literal ring of hell.

Luckily, Disney has actually done a great job at setting the expectations around *when* you can expect to get on the ride, *and* keeping folks entertained and occupied in the meantime. Disney "magic" is sprinkled into every experience and, while on the face it may look like enchantment in action, it's actually a strategic, innovative, and—above all—cost-contained approach to maintaining customer satisfaction. Most folks don't know that in the 1980s they almost went bankrupt. The desire for the park was *so* high that the company ran into the experience of either needing to build more parks to keep up with demand, or figuring out a way to make the line experience more tenable.

Experience metrics, much like a good story, evolve, pivot, and unfurl with the times. Shifting customer expectations requires Service Level Agreements (SLAs) to be not just set but continually assessed to keep them relevant and effective. The goal? To nurture a positive customer experience without getting finance all up in a tizzy. Here are a few ways that Disney does this:

- Interactive Queues. Disney ensures that queues are not just lines but a prelude to the adventure ahead. My son *loved* playing with shimmering gemstones at the Seven Dwarfs Mine Train and exploring the graveyard and "ghost horses" while waiting for the Haunted Mansion. Each interactive queue is a mini-adventure, making the wait almost a ride in itself!

- Character Pop-Ins. While I've always been a little spooked by folks in character costumes, and this has changed since the pandemic, my partner and son *loved* the surprise visits from relevant characters while meandering through the line. Disney characters mingle, enchant, and pose for those treasured photos, ensuring that every moment in the queue is sprinkled with a bit of stardust and memories that linger.

- FastPass+ and Virtual Queues. Genie+ had just been launched when we were headed to the theme park, and it was a game changer. It isn't just a skip-the-line pass, though that certainly is a benefit. It's a crafted strategy to balance customer experience with park capacity, enabling guests to whisk through waits while also shaping their Disney day to their preferences. This was a game changer for us. We woke up every morning and planned our day, almost never having too long a wait.

- Play Disney Parks App. This isn't just an app, it's an interactive experience (specifically for kids, in my honest opinion)that turns wait-time into something more engaging. Using AI and VR technology, my son was able to translate galactic languages in Star Wars: Galaxy's Edge queues and find "hidden" items around the markets.

- Telling the Story. The story doesn't start at the ride; the queue is the first chapter! Take, for example, the Indiana Jones Adventure line that sweeps you through snake-filled caves and an archaeologist's haven, teasing the adventures that await!

- Snacks and Souvenirs. Ever had a Dole Whip? If yes, then you have experienced my sole obsession while at Disney. Thankfully, the park has strategically dotted snack and merchandise carts to not only uplift the waiting experience but also cleverly maximize Disney's revenue streams, crafting a dual strategy of guest satisfaction and savvy business.

- Entertaining Displays. These were one of my son's favorite experiences while queuing for "It's Tough to Be a Bug!" in the Animal Kingdom. Specifically for children's rides, and especially in EPCOT and Animal Kingdom, customer education is a huge strategy for Disney's customer time management.

Like Disney, your SLA doesn't necessarily *just* need to be a way to make customers happier. It can also be a *really* effective cost-containment strategy. Find a key customer metric and then benchmark when the experience starts to take a turn. Place SLAs and engagement, such as customer education and ticket touches in place to maximize profits just like Disney. Here are a few things to keep in mind:

- Innovate. Just like Disney, seek inventive ways to augment the customer journey without excessively straining the financial cords. It is feasible to mesh technology into wait times, making them an entertaining pause—AI has been a godsend in this regard. You could also consider crafting peak time interactions that are immersive and engaging, rather than draining and stressful. We did this at Trello, as I mentioned in an earlier example, by tracking when folks reached out about specific issues over time, and then preemptively sending future customers the documentation and information about common feature questions ahead of time.

- Regularly Iterate. Maintain a vigilant watch over customer responses and satisfaction metrics across various service levels. Be prepared to tweak SLA targets, ensuring they perpetually mirror contemporary customer anticipations and your operational prowess.

- Incorporate Feedback. Embed systems that perpetually harvest and analyze customer feedback, especially focusing on potential friction points or dissatisfaction sparks. This ensures your team can preemptively tackle issues before they burgeon into cumbersome problems or necessitate cost-intensive solutions.

## Key Components of an Effective SLA

Service Level Agreements (SLAs) serve as the foundation of any robust customer support initiative, ensuring both clarity and commitment between a business and its clientele. However, the efficacy of these agreements doesn't rest on the mere existence of an SLA; it's about the components within them that detail the promise and the process. In this section, we'll delve into the essential elements that elevate an SLA from a mere document to a dynamic tool, ensuring consistent, high-quality service. Join us as we dissect the pivotal parts of an SLA that not only set the stage for impeccable support but also fortify trust between companies and their customers.

## Response Time

Every customer who reaches out with an issue wants to be heard—and fast. But what does "fast" mean in a world where instant gratification is increasingly the norm? This is where your SLA's response time comes into play. It's the agreed-upon time-frame in which a customer can expect an initial reply from the support team after submitting their query or raising a ticket. Setting a clear response time not only manages customer expectations but also sets a standard for your team's performance. For example, if your SLA promises a response within two hours, it sends a clear message to customers that they won't be left hanging. On the flip side, it encourages support teams to prioritize and organize their workflow to meet this deadline. However, it's vital to set realistic and achievable response times. Overpromising and under-delivering can tarnish your brand's reputation and undermine trust.

## Resolution Time

While a swift initial response is crucial, what customers genuinely desire is a solution to their problem. The resolution time defines how long it typically takes to solve an issue from the moment it's reported until it's fully resolved. This metric is a bit trickier than response time because issues can range from straightforward password resets to intricate software bugs that require significant troubleshooting. Thus, it's beneficial to categorize issues and set different resolution times based on the complexity. For instance, simpler issues might have a resolution time of a few hours, while more complex problems could span days. It's essential to be transparent with customers about these timelines. If a particular ticket seems like it'll surpass the promised resolution time, proactive communication is the key. Keeping the customer in the loop about delays, and reasons for them, ensures that they feel valued and respected.

## Availability

Imagine a customer facing an urgent issue with your product in the middle of the night, only to find that your support is available strictly from 9 to 5. Frustrating, right? Availability in an SLA refers to the specific hours during which your support team is accessible. For businesses that operate locally, standard business hours might suffice. However, companies with a global customer base might consider adopting a "follow-the-sun" model, ensuring that some portion of their support team is always awake, alert, and ready to assist. Furthermore, it's crucial to communicate these hours clearly to customers, so they know when they can expect help. Posting your support hours on your website, in email footers, or even within your product interface can reduce potential friction and manage customer expectations.

## Escalation Procedures

Let's face it; not all problems are created equal. While many can be swiftly addressed by front-line support agents, some require a deeper dive. An effective SLA spells out the escalation procedure — a clear pathway detailing what steps will be taken if an issue isn't resolved within the initial SLA. This can include escalating the ticket to senior support agents, specialized teams, or even product engineers. Having a structured escalation process ensures that complicated problems don't get lost in the shuffle. It signals to customers that even if their concern isn't immediately addressed, there's a robust system in place to ensure it's eventually handled by the right experts. For the support agents, it provides clarity on when and how to seek additional help, fostering a collaborative and organized problem-solving environment.

## Reporting and Monitoring

Setting an SLA is just the beginning. To ensure its effectiveness, regular monitoring and reporting are crucial. This involves tracking key metrics like average response and resolution times, SLA compliance rates, and customer satisfaction scores. Regular reviews can spotlight areas where the support team consistently meets, exceeds, or falls short of the set standards. Such insights can inform training needs, resource allocation, and even potential revisions to the SLA itself. After all, an SLA isn't set in stone. As a company grows, its support capabilities and customer expectations might evolve. Continuous monitoring ensures that the SLA remains relevant, ambitious yet achievable, and always aligned with the ultimate goal: stellar customer satisfaction.

## Steps to Set up SLAs

Crafting an effective SLA isn't about slapping down a few arbitrary timelines. It's a delicate dance of balancing customer needs, team capabilities, and the company's overarching objectives. Let's navigate through the intricate steps of setting up SLAs tailored to the unique rhythm and requirements of your customer support team.

### 1. Assess Your Current Capabilities

Before diving into establishing new SLAs, it's crucial to have a solid understanding of where your support team currently stands. Start by evaluating your current response and resolution times. This requires collecting data over a significant period to ensure you're getting an accurate representation.

Ask questions like:

- How quickly does your team typically respond to customer queries?
- What's the average time taken to completely resolve an issue?

Having this foundational knowledge is essential because it not only provides a benchmark but also highlights areas that may need improvement or reinforcement.

## 2. Understand Your Customers' Needs

Remember, the primary purpose of SLAs is to meet or exceed customer expectations. Conduct surveys, host feedback sessions, or have one-on-one discussions with some of your most significant clients. Discover what they expect in terms of response and resolution times.

It's also worth considering the different support channels you offer. For instance, expectations for response times might differ between email and live chat support. By understanding these nuances, you can tailor your SLAs to meet specific channel demands and customer needs.

## 3. Set Clear, Achievable Targets

SLAs should challenge your team to deliver top-notch service, but remember, setting unattainable goals can be counterproductive. Unrealistic targets may overwhelm your team and result in rushed responses, sacrificing quality.

Consider using the SMART (Specific, Measurable, Achievable, Relevant, and Time-bound) goal framework when establishing your SLAs. This ensures that you're not just setting targets, but you're setting targets that are clear, attainable, and beneficial for both your team and your customers.

## 4. Metrics to Measure and Improve Performance

Data drives improvement. Hence, having clear metrics in place is crucial to not only measure how well you're adhering to your SLAs but also to identify areas of improvement. Consider the following metrics:

- First Response Time. This measures how long a customer waits for your initial response.
- Resolution Time. Tracks the average time taken to resolve issues entirely.
- Customer Satisfaction (CSAT) Score. Post-resolution surveys can gauge how satisfied customers are with the support they received.

- Ticket Volume. Monitor the number of tickets raised within specific periods. A sudden increase might indicate larger systemic issues.

By regularly monitoring these metrics, businesses can actively seek areas to improve and ensure that their SLAs remain relevant and beneficial.

### 5. Communicate SLAs to Your Team

Once you've established your SLAs, it's imperative that your entire support team is in the loop. Schedule a team meeting or workshop to introduce the new SLAs, explain the reasoning behind them, and discuss their importance.

Open the floor for questions and concerns. Some team members might have insights or feedback that could lead to refining your SLAs even further. Remember, buy-in from your support team is crucial—they're the ones on the front lines, ensuring these SLAs are met day in and day out.

### 6. Monitor and Adjust

The business landscape, as well as customer expectations, are ever-evolving. What works today might not be as effective tomorrow. Therefore it's vital to continuously monitor performance against your SLAs and be prepared to make adjustments as necessary.

Schedule regular check-ins, perhaps quarterly, to review SLA performance. During these reviews, consider:

- Performance Data: Are response and resolution times within the set targets? If not, why?
- Team Feedback: Are there any challenges or obstacles the team faces in meeting the SLAs?
- Customer Feedback: Are customers generally satisfied, or are there recurring complaints?

Setting up SLAs for your customer support team isn't just about laying down rules. It's about creating a framework that ensures customers receive the best possible service, teams have clear guidelines and goals, and businesses can continually evolve and improve. With the right approach, SLAs can be a powerful tool that drives excellence in customer support, fosters trust, and enhances overall brand loyalty.

## Challenges in Implementation

The road to perfecting SLAs is not without its challenges. If not carefully managed, SLAs can sometimes have unintended consequences that can influence the overall efficiency and effectiveness of the support team. Let's delve into some of the challenges organizations may face when implementing SLAs and how to address them.

### The Speed–Quality Conundrum

The most common metrics in SLAs revolve around speed—how quickly a customer can expect a response or a resolution. While these metrics are undoubtedly vital for ensuring timely support, they can inadvertently create a bias toward speed over quality.

Imagine a situation where an agent, aware of the ticking SLA clock, rushes to close a ticket to meet the resolution time, but in the process, provides a solution that's only a temporary fix. The customer may have to come back with the same issue, leading to increased frustration and potentially more work in the long run. Or consider an agent who quickly replies to meet the response time SLA but doesn't take the extra minutes to fully understand the customer's query. The result? Potentially irrelevant or inaccurate advice.

To navigate this challenge, it's essential to balance speed metrics with quality metrics. For example, alongside resolution time, consider tracking first-contact resolution rates or customer satisfaction scores. This approach ensures that while agents are encouraged to work promptly, they're also incentivized to get things right the first time.

## The Fine Line of Flexibility

While SLAs set clear expectations, they can sometimes be perceived as too rigid or limiting, especially if they're too stringent. Support agents are on the front lines, interacting with a diverse set of customers and issues. If they feel boxed in by strict SLAs, they might feel they lack the flexibility to handle unique or complex cases that don't fit the "standard" mold.

Furthermore, too stringent SLAs can inadvertently promote a "check-the-box" mentality, where agents focus more on technically meeting the SLA criteria rather than genuinely resolving the customer's issue.

Addressing this requires a two-fold approach. First, while setting SLAs, involve the agents in the process. Their on-ground insights can be invaluable in determining what's realistically achievable. Secondly, ensure that there's a mechanism in place for agents to flag and discuss unique cases that might require deviation from the set SLAs. This way, you foster an environment where SLAs serve as guidelines, not chains.

## The Evolution Dilemma

What is the only constant in business? Change! As products evolve, services expand, or customer bases grow, the nature of customer queries and issues will change, too. An SLA that was perfect a year ago might be utterly out of sync with the current reality.

For instance, whenever we released a new product or feature at Trello, the support team would almost *always* get a bump in volume as the millions of users got in there and started using it. There was always a learning curve for the team to understand and use the new feature as well, no matter how good the pre-launch education was. Had we relied on outdated SLAs in such scenarios, it would have led to inefficiencies and customer dissatisfaction.

To stay ahead of this, companies need to institute regular SLA reviews. This doesn't mean changing SLAs every month, but rather having a periodic check (maybe quarterly or bi-annually) to assess if they still align with the ground realities. Engage with different stakeholders during these reviews, from agents to product teams, to get a comprehensive view of what's changed and how SLAs need to adapt.

SLAs, when crafted and managed well, can be powerful tools in a customer support team's arsenal. They set clear expectations, drive efficiency, and ensure accountability. However, like all tools, their efficacy depends on how they're used. Being aware of the potential pitfalls and challenges, and proactively addressing them, ensures that your SLAs serve their intended purpose: enhancing customer satisfaction and trust.

## Best Practices in SLA Implementation

Service Level Agreements (SLAs) stand as a testament to a company's commitment to its customers. These aren't mere documents—though they are often treated that way—they're pledges, affirming a business's promise to deliver a defined level of service. But, while SLAs set the stage, it's the consistent performance that truly matters. Successfully implementing and managing SLAs requires a thoughtful approach. Here are some best practices that can guide businesses on this journey.

### Be Adaptable

When it comes to *any* process in CX, rigidity can be a detriment. While SLAs set benchmarks, they shouldn't be so fixed that they resist evolution. The key is to permit alterations in the agreement based on real-time data, insights, and experience.

For instance, suppose an unforeseen challenge, like a software glitch, extends resolution times. It might be more reasonable to adjust SLAs temporarily while addressing the root cause. Such adaptability ensures that SLAs remain both realistic and challenging.

## Empower Your Team

Your customer support team stands on the front-line, interfacing directly with clients and shouldering the responsibility of meeting SLA standards. Hence, it's paramount that they are well-equipped for the task.

Regular training sessions can bridge knowledge gaps, improve efficiency, and keep the team updated on evolving best practices. Whether it's mastering a new support tool, understanding product updates, or refining communication skills, continuous learning ensures that the team can confidently and competently uphold the promises made in the SLA.

## Listen to Your Customers

The true measure of an SLA's effectiveness lies in customer satisfaction. And who better to provide feedback on SLA performance than the customers themselves? Regularly soliciting their input can offer invaluable insights.

Perhaps they value a detailed solution over a quick one? Or maybe they prefer immediate acknowledgments, even if full resolutions take time? By tuning in to such feedback, businesses can align their SLAs more closely with customer expectations. Surveys, feedback forms, or even direct conversations can act as channels to gather these insights. The goal is to ensure that SLAs aren't just internal benchmarks but truly reflect the service level customers desire.

> **Case Study: StellarTech's Journey to Enhanced Customer Support with SLAs**
>
> **Background**
>
> StellarTech, a mid-sized SaaS company, had built a reputation for its innovative suite of productivity tools. However, as its customer base grew, so did the influx of support requests. While the product was commendable, customers began expressing concerns over inconsistent support experiences. Response times varied, and there was no clear commitment on how quickly issues would be resolved.

**Challenge**

StellarTech faced two primary challenges:
- Addressing the growing volume of customer support requests.
- Providing consistent and reliable support experiences to all users, regardless of the nature of their queries.

**SLA Implementation**

Recognizing the importance of clear and consistent service commitments, StellarTech decided to implement a comprehensive SLA for its customer support. The SLA had clear stipulations:
- Response Time: All queries would receive an initial response within 2 hours.
- Resolution Time: Depending on the complexity, issues were categorized into three tiers, each with its own resolution time—ranging from 24 hours to 5 business days.
- Availability: Support would be available 24/7, with a dedicated team for each major time zone.
- Escalation Procedure: If an issue wasn't resolved within the stipulated time, it would be escalated to a senior support agent.
- Feedback Mechanism: Post-resolution, customers would be encouraged to provide feedback on the support experience.

**The Results**
- Improved Customer Satisfaction: With clear expectations set and met, customer satisfaction scores saw a significant uptick. Knowing when they would get a response or solution reduced customer anxiety and built trust.
- Enhanced Team Accountability: The support team now had clear guidelines and targets. This led to a more organized approach to addressing queries and a significant reduction in backlog.

- Informed Workforce Allocation: By categorizing issues into complexity tiers, StellarTech was better equipped to allocate the right resources, ensuring that more complex issues were immediately routed to senior team members.
- Proactive Problem-Solving: The feedback mechanism highlighted recurring issues, allowing the product team to address root causes and reduce the influx of similar queries.

**Conclusion**

By introducing and sticking to well-defined SLAs, StellarTech not only improved its customer support efficiency but also enhanced customer trust and loyalty. The SLAs served as a commitment to their users, showcasing StellarTech's dedication to ensuring a seamless experience. This case underscores the transformative power of customer support SLAs when appropriately implemented and managed.

By striking a balance between ambition and feasibility, organizations can pave the way for enhanced customer satisfaction and operational efficiency. As businesses continue to evolve and the landscape of customer support undergoes inevitable changes, SLAs will remain a beacon, guiding teams toward consistent and high-quality service.

## Support Levels and Tiering

As products and services grow increasingly complex, so does the necessity for businesses to offer comprehensive, tiered support. Gone are the days when a single helpline sufficed for all queries. Today, customers demand quick, efficient, and tailored solutions to their issues. Enter the concept of support levels and tiering: a structured approach that not only streamlines the support process but also ensures that each customer gets the right help at the right time.

Tiered support, at its core, is about directing customers to the best resources based on the complexity of their issue. This ensures efficient use of company resources and provides customers with specialized assistance. The structure typically starts with Level 1 (L1) and can proceed to Level 2 (L2), Level 3 (L3), and so on. Each level represents a deeper degree of expertise and specialization.

Imagine customer support as a multi-story building. The ground floor or L1 is where most visitors enter. It's bustling, generalized, and designed to handle a high volume of common, simpler inquiries. As we ascend, each floor (L2, L3, etc.) becomes more specialized, catering to specific, more complex problems that couldn't be addressed on the floors below.

## Level 1 Support: The Front Line

Level 1 (L1) support acts as the gatekeepers of this support edifice. They're the first point of contact for customers, tackling basic queries that often have predefined solutions. Think password resets, general product questions, or straightforward troubleshooting. The challenges here revolve around handling a high volume of tickets and providing swift resolutions.

The benefits of a strong L1 team are manifold. Not only do they address a majority of customer issues, freeing up specialized teams to focus on more complex problems, but they also set the tone for the entire customer experience. A positive interaction at this level can shape the customer's perception of the brand, fostering trust and loyalty.

## Level 2 Support: Diving Deeper

While L1 is about breadth, Level 2 (L2) support is where depth comes into play. L2 agents have specialized knowledge, diving deeper into product intricacies or more involved troubleshooting. When a customer has an issue beyond the expertise of L1, it's escalated to L2.

At this level, agents often possess a deeper understanding of the product or service. They might handle issues like advanced technical troubleshooting, software bugs, or more complex service adjustments. Their expertise bridges the gap between front-line support and the most specialized support tiers, ensuring that customers get detailed, knowledgeable assistance.

## Level 3 Support: Experts and Problem-Solvers

Level 3 (L3) is where the true experts reside. These agents usually have a robust technical background, potentially liaising directly with product engineers, developers, or other specialized departments. They handle the most complex and challenging issues—problems that L1 and L2 cannot resolve.

L3 support is critical for maintaining customer trust, especially with major accounts or intricate technical products. Their deep dives can lead to identifying and rectifying product flaws, informing future updates, and ensuring that customers receive solutions to even the most perplexing challenges.

## The Pros and Cons of Tiered Support

The advantages of a tiered support system are profound. For one, it leads to faster resolution times. Customers aren't stuck waiting in long queues; they're quickly directed to the appropriate level of support. Moreover, it streamlines operations. By categorizing issues, companies can allocate resources efficiently, ensuring that specialized teams aren't bogged down with basic queries. This structure also fosters a sense of expertise and specialization, enhancing both the customer experience and agent job satisfaction. In essence, tiered support is a win-win, benefiting both the business and its customers.

All that said, tiered support is not without its challenges. Clear communication between tiers is essential to avoid redundancy and ensure smooth escalations. Companies must also strike a balance to prevent over-complicating the support process. Training becomes paramount, as agents at each level must be well-equipped to handle their specific range of issues. And as businesses grow and evolve, so must their tiered structures, ensuring they remain aligned with changing products, services, and customer expectations.

## How Does Technology Help?

Modern tiered support isn't just about human resources; technology plays a pivotal role. Advanced help desk and ticketing systems can auto-route issues based on complexity, ensuring that customers reach the right level quickly. Knowledge bases, accessible by both agents and customers, provide a wealth of information to aid in quick resolutions. And as artificial intelligence and chatbots become more sophisticated, they offer potential avenues to streamline L1 support, answering basic queries and escalating more complex issues as needed.

## How to Transition to Tiered Support

Transitioning into offering tiered customer support is a significant shift that requires planning, training, and effective communication to ensure success. Here's a step-by-step guide to help you navigate this transition:

1. Assess Your Current Support System: Begin by understanding your current support metrics. What's the volume of queries you handle? How complex are they? How are they currently resolved?

2. Determine the Need for Tiers: Not every organization needs a multi-tiered support system. However, if your products or services are complex, or if you have a high volume of customer interactions, tiering can help streamline resolutions. Make sure that you define the tiers clearly and what their responsibilities should be.

3. Train Your Team: Once you've defined the tiers, train your team accordingly. L1 agents should be trained to resolve basic queries efficiently and know when to escalate. L2 and L3 agents will

require deeper product training and might also need skills like problem-solving or even coding, depending on your product.

4. Implement Advanced Helpdesk Tools: Modern ticketing systems can automatically route issues based on their complexity. This technology ensures that customers reach the right level of support quickly, reducing resolution times.

5. Communicate Internally: Ensure all teams, not just customer support, understand the new tiered system. This is essential for smooth internal escalations and inter-departmental collaborations.

6. Inform Your Customers: Transitioning to a tiered system may affect how customers interact with your support. It's vital to keep them in the loop. Inform customers about potential changes in response times or procedures.

7. Monitor and Adjust: Implementing a tiered system is not a "set it and forget it" process. Monitor key performance indicators like first response time, resolution time, and customer satisfaction scores. Use this data to adjust your tiers, training, or even the technology you use.

8. Feedback Loop: Encourage feedback from both agents and customers. Agents on the front line will have invaluable insights into the challenges and advantages of the new system, while customer feedback can help pinpoint areas of improvement.

9. Continuous Improvement: As your product or service evolves, so will the nature of customer queries. Regularly review and adjust your support tiers to ensure they align with your customers' needs and your team's capabilities.

Transitioning to a tiered customer support system can significantly enhance the efficiency of your support team and improve customer satisfaction. By ensuring that agents with the right expertise handle queries, you not only speed up resolutions but also ensure that customers always get accurate and helpful responses!

# Ticket Escalation

When doing customer support, you want your team to strike a balance between efficiency and empathy. One essential tool in achieving this balance is ticket escalation. While it might sound like a buzzword, understanding this key practice is super important to CX success!

## What Is Ticket Escalation?

Ticket escalation is a process in customer support where an issue, query, or complaint is transferred from one support level to a higher (or more specialized) one to ensure that it is resolved effectively. This typically happens when a front-line agent recognizes that an issue is either too complex or outside their expertise.

## The Benefits of Ticket Escalation

- Improved CSAT: Efficiently escalated tickets ensure that customers don't languish in support limbo. When their complex problems are swiftly handed over to specialists, resolution times decrease and satisfaction goes up.

- Efficiency in Problem-Solving: By transferring a ticket to someone with specific expertise, issues are resolved more quickly and effectively. This means reduced back-and-forths and faster solutions.

- Empowerment of Front-Line Agents: When front-line agents know they have a reliable escalation process to lean on, they can confidently tackle the majority of queries, safe in the knowledge that complex issues can be passed on to more experienced colleagues.

- Feedback Loop and Continuous Improvement: Regularly reviewing escalated tickets can offer insights into recurring problems or potential product/service improvements.

## How to Think About Ticket Escalation

1. Define Clear Escalation Criteria: It's crucial to have clear criteria on what constitutes an "escalatable" ticket. This can be based on:

- Technical complexity
- Sensitivity (e.g., high-value customers)
- Recurring issues that front-line agents can't resolve

2. Provide the Right Training: Empower your team with the right knowledge. Front-line agents should be trained to recognize when a ticket needs escalation and how to initiate the process seamlessly.

3. Communication Is Key: Always keep the customer in the loop. If their ticket needs to be escalated, explain the reasons and reassure them that they are being directed to someone who can best address their concerns.

4. Efficient Handoffs: Ensure that all relevant information collected from the customer is passed on to the next level. This avoids the frustration of customers having to repeat themselves.

5. Regularly Review the Escalation Process: Just like any other process, the ticket escalation workflow should be periodically reviewed and refined. Analyze outcomes, solicit feedback from both agents and customers, and adjust accordingly.

6. Emphasize Resolution, Not Escalation: Although escalation is a useful tool, the ultimate goal is ticket resolution. Ensure that the escalation process doesn't become a crutch or a way to avoid dealing with difficult issues.

Ticket escalation, when handled right, can significantly enhance customer support; and when done wrong, it can be a drain on your team and the customer. It ensures that customers' issues are handled by the most capable hands, resulting in swift and satisfactory resolutions. By integrating an effective escalation process, you can improve customer loyalty, boost team morale, and gain invaluable insights for continuous improvement. So, next time you encounter a tricky customer ticket, remember to think of escalation not as a last resort, but as a strategic step towards resolution and customer satisfaction.

## Tone and Style Guides

Picture this: You've just launched a top-notch product or service and customers are flocking in. However, after a few interactions with your support team, some of them feel confused, frustrated, or even downright ignored. Why? It might just be a tone and style inconsistency in communication.

Enter the Tone and Style Guide, an often overlooked but crucial component of effective customer support.

### Why Do You Need a Tone and Style Guide?

Consistency in communication is paramount, especially when multiple agents interact with customers. Individual styles can vary significantly between agents, leading to a myriad of customer experiences. By implementing a unified tone, customers are ensured a consistent experience regardless of who they're speaking with.

Beyond consistency, it's crucial to remember that customer support serves as an extension of your brand. This interaction can determine if your brand is perceived as professional, quirky, or even super-friendly. Having a tone and style guide not only ensures that your brand's unique personality stands out, but also acts as a vital reference point for both new and seasoned team members. It guides them to communicate in a manner that perfectly resonates with your company's values.

This consistency in communication doesn't just elevate the brand's image; it also fosters trust and loyalty. When customers know what to expect and receive clear, consistent responses, their trust deepens, making them more likely to stay loyal and return in the future.

Creating Your Tone and Style Guide: A Step-by-Step Approach

A disclaimer: Much of this should be done in collaboration with your marketing team. It's possible that they already have things like personas identified, or have some ideas around personality and tone. Make sure to work with them rather than going rogue.

1. Define Your Brand Personality. Before diving into specifics, understand your brand's core personality. Are you a fun-loving, quirky startup, or a serious, solutions-focused enterprise?

2. Choose Your Tone. Based on your brand personality, decide on the tone of communication. Should it be formal, friendly, humorous, or empathetic? Maybe a combination?

3. Specify Writing Style Elements. Detail out grammatical and formatting preferences. Do you prefer bullet points over paragraphs? Do you use the Oxford comma? It might seem nitpicky, but these details matter. An example from our own experience: do you want to say "help desk" or "helpdesk?"

4. Use Real-life Examples. Provide examples for common scenarios. Instead of just saying "Be empathetic," illustrate with a sample response to a frustrated customer.

5. Incorporate Feedback Mechanisms. Encourage your support team to provide feedback on the guide. They're on the front line, and their insights are invaluable.

6. Train Your Team. A guide is only as good as its implementation. Ensure that the team is familiar with it and understands the importance of adhering to it.

7. Review and Revise Regularly. As your business evolves, so will your communication needs. Periodically review and adjust your tone and style guide to stay current.

## A Few Additional Tips

In the pursuit of a harmonized customer experience, it's easy to lean into standardizing every little interaction. Yes, consistency is crucial, but there's a magic in letting authenticity shine through. Think about it. Personal touches, the kind that make customers feel they're chatting with a real person and not an automated bot, can turn a routine interaction into something memorable. It's all about ensuring that customers feel seen and heard, rather than just another ticket number.

Now, let's chat about the global perspective. As your business grows, your communication demands an added layer of sensitivity. Cultural awareness isn't just about speaking multiple languages; it's about understanding and respecting the myriad of cultural nuances and expectations. Something as simple as a casual greeting that's considered friendly in one culture might come off as too informal or even unprofessional in another. Thus, while shaping your Tone and Style Guide, it's imperative to equip your support team with the insights they need to navigate these cultural subtleties with grace and respect.

While we're on the topic of flexibility, let's remember that our customer support agents need room to breathe. Sure, clear guidelines are like gold. They help navigate most situations. But every now and then, an agent might need to color outside the lines, adapt, and respond based on the unique flavor of the situation. Let's make sure they feel empowered to do that, and not just boxed into a rigid script.

All that to say: a Tone and Style Guide isn't just a bunch of words on paper (or a screen). It's kind of like the voice of your brand, especially when we're talking customer support. It's a compass, making sure every chat, email, or call strengthens that bond with the customer. So, as we gear up with all the latest tools and training sessions, let's not forget the power of genuine, impactful communication. Because sometimes it really is all about finding the right words.

# Budgeting

Customer support, often seen as the front line in customer interactions, plays a crucial role in shaping brand perception. Although its importance is widely recognized, getting approval to spend *anything* on customer support can sometimes seem impossible. Budgeting accurately from the beginning means that you'll be empowered to argue for the things that you need, and be able to predict whether you'll be able to afford them.

## Common Oversights in Budgeting for Customer Support

- Training Costs. An efficient support team is a trained one. It's not just about onboarding; ongoing training for new tools, policies, or industry shifts is vital.

- Technology and Software Upgrades. As your business grows, your existing software may become obsolete. Budgeting for necessary upgrades can prevent future headaches.

- Seasonal Volume Changes. Some periods might see a surge in customer queries (holidays, sales seasons). Preparing for temporary staff or overtime costs is crucial.

- Feedback Mechanisms. Tools to gather and analyze customer feedback can be an investment. However, they provide valuable insights that can improve the support experience.

## Useful Tools for Budgeting

- Microsoft Excel or Google Sheets. These traditional tools, when used with proper templates, can be highly effective for creating and managing budgets.

- QuickBooks. This is a versatile tool that not only assists in budgeting but also integrates financial data for holistic financial planning.

- Trello or Asana for Budget Tracking. Surprisingly, project management tools can be handy in setting and tracking budget milestones.

- SaaS Budgeting Tools. Platforms like SaaSOptics or Adaptive Insights cater to businesses reliant on software solutions, making budgeting in those areas precise.

Ultimately, using what other teams within your organization are using for budgeting is going to be the smartest idea. Having the ability to collaborate and cross-reference, especially with finance, will be extremely valuable moving forward.

## Tips for Those New to Budgeting

If you're embarking on the journey of budgeting for your customer support team or looking to refine the process, here are some foundational principles to keep in mind.

Starting simple is the key, especially if budgeting isn't your forte. Diving into the deep end with complex software can be overwhelming. Instead, get your feet wet with a basic spreadsheet. It's intuitive, user-friendly, and honestly it's sometimes all you need. As you get a grip on things, that's your cue to venture out and explore more advanced tools that can offer detailed analytics and projections.

Now, if there's one thing to remember about budgeting, it's that it's never static. Treating your budget as a "set it and forget it" item on your checklist is a rookie mistake. The business landscape is always shifting, as are the needs of your customer support team. Regular reviews of your budget can catch any discrepancies, allowing you to make adjustments before they snowball into bigger issues. It ensures your budget remains relevant and aligned with your team's evolving needs.

Speaking of your team, they're your gold mine. When drafting or reviewing a budget, always involve them. These are the folks in the trenches, handling customer queries, using the tools you budget for, and attending the training sessions you finance. They possess insights that can be invaluable in shaping a realistic and efficient budget. They might be aware of new tools, training, or resources that could optimize operations. So, make it a collaborative effort!

But, as with everything in business (and life), surprises happen. Those little unforeseen expenses can sneak up on you. A sudden software upgrade or an unexpected training need can throw a wrench in your budget if you're not prepared. That's why it's wise to always allocate a portion of your budget for unexpected expenses. This contingency fund can be a lifesaver, ensuring that unforeseen costs don't derail your operations.

Lastly, don't limit your insights to just your team. The broader industry can be a treasure trove of wisdom. Joining industry forums or groups can connect you with peers in similar roles. Sharing experiences, challenges, and solutions in these spaces can offer valuable insights or recommendations for budgeting that you hadn't considered.

Budgeting for customer support, or any department for that matter, isn't just about crunching numbers. It's a blend of strategic planning, collaboration, and adaptability. With these principles in your toolkit, you'll be well on your way to crafting a budget that's both efficient and resilient. If you're looking for more detail on this topic, please review Chapter 7: Finances in CX.

# QA

Quality assurance (QA) is not just a procedure; it's a commitment to excellence. It encompasses a systematic process and a series of actions specifically designed to ensure that products and services not only fulfill but potentially exceed customer expectations and adhere to defined quality benchmarks. When placed within the sphere of customer support, QA becomes the guardian of excellence, a vital tool ensuring that every customer interaction shines and consistently measures up to, if not surpasses, the expected service levels.

The incorporation of QA within a team brings a multitude of benefits. First and foremost, it's about fostering trust; maintaining a consistent standard of customer support is paramount to guaranteeing a gold-standard level of service. This consistency is the cornerstone of building trust and upholding the integrity of your brand's reputation. It goes beyond mere satisfaction, offering insights that could propel your business to new heights. QA doesn't just uphold standards; it has the power to elevate your offerings and, by extension, your customer's experience.

For sectors bound by regulations, such as finance and healthcare, QA is the watchdog ensuring adherence to legal standards and specific industry compliance requirements. It's a critical component that safeguards not just quality but also regulatory conformity.

Efficiency, too, is a byproduct of effective QA. By spotting and fixing issues proactively, processes become more streamlined, diminishing the time and energy expended in resolving customer concerns. It's a cycle of continuous improvement; as agents receive regular, constructive feedback, they gain clarity on performance expectations and areas for improvement, paving the way for enhanced service delivery.

Through trend analysis, QA may uncover that certain queries consistently result in lower scores, which could indicate the need for updated documentation, enhanced training, or process refinement. Recognizing these patterns is the first step toward remedying systemic issues.

Moreover, QA isn't just about preventing errors; it's also a strategic financial tool. With improved efficiency comes cost savings. Fewer complaints and issues directly translate into reduced resources dedicated to problem-solving, which means you're not just saving money, you're also investing in customer happiness.

Data is the new oil, and QA processes are a drilling rig. The data collected serves as a wellspring of insights that inform strategic decisions, from tweaking training programs to reallocating resources and overhauling customer support strategies. With hard numbers and solid facts in hand, decision-making becomes less of a gamble and more of a calculated strategy.

Finally, QA is a risk mitigator. Customer interactions come with inherent risks—misunderstandings, miscommunications, and missed opportunities. By pinpointing potential issues before they balloon, QA helps minimize the chance of disputes and financial setbacks, protecting not just the company's assets but also its most valuable asset: its customer relations.

## How can you structure QA?

Quality isn't just a checklist or a series of tick boxes—it's a mindset, a core element of a company's culture that echoes through every level of the organization. Quality Assurance (QA) is about creating a symphony where each department, from the front-line support agents to operations managers, plays its part in harmony. Let's explore how QA isn't just about catching errors; it's about weaving a commitment to excellence into the very fabric of an organization.

At the heart of effective QA lies the spirit of proactivity. It's about nipping problems in the bud before they even graze the customer's experience. It's also about constantly reaching higher, continuously learning, and looking for new ways to delight customers and enhance their experiences.

And amidst all this, consistency is key. It ensures every customer interaction is up to par, reinforcing trust and building a reliable brand image.

Now, let's talk structure. How do we set up a QA framework that not only catches issues but enhances the overall customer experience? The blueprint varies by team size and needs, but a good rule of thumb is that a dedicated QA specialist can efficiently handle the QA needs of 20-30 agents. If your team scales beyond this, it's wise to add more specialists—and perhaps a QA team lead—to keep things running smoothly.

For smaller teams or those with niche workflows, alternatives like peer reviews or supervisor-led QA checks can temporarily fill the void. While they're not without their challenges—like potential inconsistencies and time constraints—they ensure that quality doesn't fall by the wayside when resources are limited. But be cautious: if not managed well, peer reviews can create more chaos than clarity.

Self QA is another piece of the puzzle. It can be empowering for agents to understand their performance metrics and take ownership of their progress. However, it shouldn't stand alone. Integrating self QA with other methods, such as occasional joint reviews with QA specialists, can boost engagement without sacrificing the breadth of your quality checks.

Implementing a robust QA process is about more than oversight—it's about building a culture where everyone is invested in the mission of delivering top-notch service. From in-depth reviews to constructive feedback loops, every step in the QA process is a stepping stone towards a better customer experience.

In the following sections, we'll delve deeper into each aspect of QA—from setting up the right structures to integrating self QA effectively—laying out the strategies that will help your CX team turn quality assurance from a concept into a concrete pillar of your customer experience strategy.

# Implementing Quality Assurance Processes for Service Excellence

Quality Assurance (QA) isn't just an additional step in the process; it's an integral component of service excellence, ingrained in the very fabric of customer support strategy. As we consider implementing QA processes, it's vital to lay down a strong foundation. Clarity in expectations sets the stage for a QA framework that's uniquely tailored to meet the diverse needs of different teams, with scorecards and guidelines clearly outlining every aspect of the expected standards.

KPIs are the lifeblood of performance tracking, and in the realm of QA, they are crucial for measuring success. Metrics such as the QA Score, Error-Free Rate, and Critical Error Rate, must not only be aligned with customer satisfaction indicators like CSAT, NPS, or CES but also be part of an ongoing conversation about quality and its impact on the customer experience.

The structure of the QA team itself must be designed to cater to the specific needs and sizes of the teams it supports, ranging from individual QA specialists to full-fledged teams with leads and supervisors, each configuration calibrated to provide the most effective oversight and feedback.

A robust Customer Relationship Management (CRM) system is a powerful ally in quality assurance, providing a wealth of data that, when properly mapped and accessible, enhances the QA team's ability to conduct insightful evaluations. Furthermore, the foundation of QA is built on a reliable knowledge base, ensuring that all assessments are grounded in accuracy and consistency, moving away from unreliable "tribal knowledge."

Training and development are also pivotal; after all, the individuals who carry out QA are as important as the process itself. Not just anyone with product knowledge can excel in a QA role; it requires individuals with exceptional feedback skills, an analytical mind, reporting capabilities, and an eagle eye for detail. Developing these talents is just as important as any other aspect of QA implementation.

In essence, implementing QA processes is about creating a culture of continuous improvement and rigorous standards that can elevate the customer support experience to new heights. It's a strategic endeavor that promises not just to assess but to enhance every customer interaction through diligent analysis and actionable feedback.

## Quality Processes

Consider this scenario: You're gearing up to launch a QA initiative. If your team is the size of a small village, employing a statistical approach—like a sample size calculator—will help you review just the right number of customer interactions. If you've got a cozy team, a simple approach like checking five interactions per agent per week might suffice. Don't fall into the percentage trap; if your volume skyrockets, you'll be swamped. For example, 10% of 10,000 interactions is a whopping 1,000 checks, which could be a QA nightmare.

Now, imagine your QA team is a group of judges at a baking contest. Calibration sessions are like getting them to agree on what makes the perfect chocolate chip cookie. It's essential to do this regularly to avoid any "too many cooks" scenarios. Aim for weekly, but if resources are tight, make sure you at least sync up monthly.

And when an agent questions the score they've received on their support call—thinking they delivered Michelin-star service when marked for fast food—it's crucial to have a dispute process that's fair and transparent, like a suggestion box that's actually reviewed.

QA shouldn't be the "bad cop" of the workplace. It should be more like the coach who gives a high-five for every goal scored. Take Zappos, for example, they're known for their enthusiastic celebration of customer service victories, big and small, transforming the image of QA from a watchful overseer to a supportive ally.

Then there's the art of reporting—the Monet of management, if you will. You want to paint a clear picture without overwhelming anyone with details. Think of using charts like the pie chart that reveals customer feedback trends, or a bar graph that breaks down performance metrics, making complex information digestible at a glance.

Ensuring that the flow of feedback is like a well-oiled machine is vital. Suppose insights from QA are the ingredients; operations need to be the master chef, using them to whip up the best customer service. It could be the QA team offering one-on-one coaching or supervisors running team huddles, akin to a sports team reviewing game tape. Setting regular strategy sessions across teams can keep everyone in sync.

Finally, don't underestimate the maestro of this orchestra: the Quality Manager. They're the ones ensuring the QA team isn't just going through the motions but providing the insights that make a real difference to the customer service symphony.

In essence, QA is about making sure the service we provide isn't just good—it's memorable. It's about fine-tuning the complex machinery of customer service to ensure that every interaction is as good as your customer's favorite coffee shop where the barista knows their order by heart.

## Managing QA

Managing a QA team is a nuanced art that blends vigilance with strategy. At the foundation of successful QA management is the understanding that while quality is everyone's responsibility, it takes dedicated leadership to steer the ship. This section explores the core responsibilities and best practices for an effective QA Manager within a CX team.

Responsibilities of a QA Manager

The role of a QA Manager is multifaceted, especially in large teams where several QA specialists report to different supervisors. It becomes the QA Manager's task to ensure cohesion and consistent application of quality standards across the board. In smaller teams, one QA Manager might oversee multiple groups, balancing their attention to maintain quality at a macro level.

A pivotal part of the QA Manager's role is to forge strong connections with operations, serving as a bridge that conveys insights from the quality assurance team to the front lines of customer engagement. It is through this partnership that the quality initiative finds its footing, impacting every customer interaction. Unlike other team members, QA Managers may not engage in product training; instead, they focus their expertise on process and people management, honing the ability to see the larger customer service landscape.

## Best Practices for QA Management

Development Plan: QA Managers must prioritize the growth and development of their team. This involves identifying gaps in skills and crafting tailored plans that not only elevate the abilities of each QA Specialist but also strengthen the team as a whole.

Performance Monitoring: The balance between oversight and autonomy is delicate. It is not about micromanagement but rather about setting clear goals and empowering QA Specialists to meet them. A scorecard is an indispensable tool in this endeavor. It might include:

- Completion rate of assigned reviews
- Alignment of calibration results with set expectations
- Percentage of reviews disputed by agents (a high rate may indicate a need for recalibration)
- Attendance and punctuality
- Timely and standard-compliant completion of additional tasks

Team Health: QA Managers need to constantly gauge the pulse of the team. Metrics are the lifelines here, revealing not just performance levels but also the health of the team. A dip in scores or other indicators of distress should prompt immediate action. Proactive responses to these signals can prevent minor issues from escalating and impacting customer satisfaction.

In managing a CX QA team, a QA Manager should embody the qualities of a mentor, strategist, and analyst, nurturing a culture where quality thrives. It's about ensuring that the team does not just follow protocols but understands the rationale behind them, aligning with the broader vision of exemplary customer service. The role requires a mix of strategic oversight, operational know-how, and the ability to nurture a team that's as invested in the company's vision of quality as the manager leading them.

## Creating a scorecard

Creating a customer experience quality assurance (CX QA) scorecard is akin to charting a map for a treasure hunt; it's the guide that directs the team toward the ultimate prize of outstanding service. To craft a scorecard that is both effective and efficient, one must balance precision with simplicity, ensuring it caters to the team's unique needs without succumbing to the pitfalls of overcomplexity.

### Designing Your Scorecard Framework

At its core, the scorecard must be intuitive. Beginning with the scoring system, it's often wise to adopt a binary approach—met or not met—particularly for those in the early stages of QA implementation. This simplicity aids in clear scoring and reporting. However, if nuances in performance must be captured, a range system can be applied, but it should be kept to three clear-cut levels: below expectations, meets expectations, and exceeds expectations.

### Identifying Key Categories

The anatomy of a customer interaction can be dissected into four essential categories:

- Resolution: This measures whether the customer's issue was resolved effectively and is visible to the customer.
- Internal Processes: This tracks internal mechanisms like documentation, ticket categorization, and adherence to internal

service level agreements (SLAs)—the unseen cogs that keep the service machine running smoothly.
- Communication: This evaluates the soft skills, tone, clarity, and grammar/spelling—key elements of customer-agent interactions.
- Compliance: This ensures that all interactions are in line with legal requirements, such as data protection laws like GDPR, and industry standards.

## Question Quantification and Clarity

A common mistake is the bloated scorecard, crammed with 20 or more questions. This overeagerness leads to inefficiency and redundancy. The sweet spot? A maximum of 10 well-crafted questions applicable across all reviewed cases, with additional nuances detailed in accompanying guidelines.

When crafting these questions, the wording must be direct and unambiguous. For example, instead of asking if the agent was rude—where an affirmative response could mistakenly add points—the question should be phrased to reflect the desired behavior, such as "Did the agent maintain a professional tone throughout the interaction?"

## Determining Questions and Weights

To decide on the specific questions and their respective weights within the scorecard, consider the core objectives of your team:

If personalization is key, include questions that assess the customization of responses.

For teams in regulated industries, compliance will be a heavy-weighted category.

Evaluate whether meticulous documentation and categorization are critical to your operations.

Determine if the emphasis should be on efficiency or if the pendulum swings more towards customer experience—or perhaps a balance of both.

With these considerations, you can tailor your questions to reflect the areas of highest priority and impact.

## The QA Scorecard in Action

Let's take a fictional company, "Globex Tech Support," as an example. For them, compliance is not heavily regulated, but efficiency and customer personalization are equally important. Their scorecard might include questions like:

- Did the agent resolve the customer's issue within the first interaction?
- Was the customer's query categorized correctly in the support system?
- Did the agent personalize the conversation to create a unique customer experience?
- Was the response time within the agreed SLA?

Each of these questions ties back to Globex's emphasis on efficiency and personalization, providing clear direction for what the QA team should be evaluating.

## Continuous Evolution

Finally, a scorecard is not set in stone. It must evolve with the team, the customers, and the ever-changing landscape of the industry. Regularly reviewing and adjusting the scorecard ensures it remains a relevant and powerful tool in maintaining the highest standards of customer experience.

In summary, an effective scorecard is one that's streamlined, clear, and aligned with the specific goals of your customer support team. By focusing on these core principles, you can ensure that your scorecard is a beacon guiding your team toward exemplary service delivery.

## Red Flags

Quality Assurance (QA) acts as the crucial checkpoint that ensures the service delivered meets the high standards your customers expect. But sometimes, warning signs emerge—red flags that, if spotted early, can prevent minor issues from escalating into major problems.

### Persistent Negative Feedback

When customers are unhappy, they don't shy away from letting you know. A steady stream of complaints or negative reviews can't be ignored. This red flag is a clear indication that something isn't working and that there might be an underlying issue affecting the quality of service.

### Long Handling Times

While some customer queries are more complex than others, consistently high Average Handle Time (AHT) across the board can be a sign of trouble. It could point to inefficient processes or gaps in team training that need to be addressed to ensure customers aren't kept waiting.

### Repeating Problems

If certain types of complaints keep cropping up, it's a sign that solutions aren't sticking. This repetition is a red flag indicating that your team is not resolving issues effectively and that systemic changes might be necessary.

### Inconsistency in Service

When customers get different answers from different agents, it's a recipe for confusion. Consistent service is key, and when it's lacking, it usually means there's a gap in training or communication. Standardizing procedures and ensuring all team members are on the same page is essential.

### Failing to Meet SLAs

Service Level Agreements (SLAs) are promises made to customers. When these aren't met, it's more than an operational miss; it's a broken promise. Regularly missing SLAs is a significant red flag that could indicate broader issues within the support process.

### Internal QA Inconsistencies

Within the QA team, watch for signs such as varied outcomes for similar cases, a high rate of disputes, and a lack of agreement in calibration sessions. These are internal red flags that suggest a review of the QA process itself is in order.

## Managing Red Flags

As a QA manager, it's your role to monitor these warning signs and take action. This could involve delving into feedback for actionable insights, reviewing training programs, streamlining processes, or recalibrating your QA measures. The goal is to catch these red flags early and address them head-on, ensuring that they serve as signposts for improvement rather than stumbling blocks.

## Do you really need a QA Tool?

It's essential to acknowledge that while it is entirely possible to conduct QA without specialized tools, the absence of these tools can lead to time-intensive procedures, especially as your team grows. The question of scalability becomes prominent. With a small team and a modest volume of support tickets, manual methods using tools like Google Suite might suffice. Google Forms can serve as a makeshift scorecard, and Google Sheets can track QA results to a degree.

## The Limitations of Manual Processes

However, the manual approach comes with significant limitations. While Google Forms might replicate the process of scoring with a QA tool, it lacks the integration and sophistication of purpose-built tools. Meanwhile, managing QA directly in Google Sheets can quickly become unwieldy. As the volume of tickets escalates, so does the complexity of managing them through spreadsheets. This method becomes increasingly cumbersome and error-prone, potentially leading to oversight and inaccuracies.

## Scalability and Efficiency Considerations

In scenarios where the team is small and the evaluation volume is manageable, foregoing a QA tool might seem justified to avoid additional investment. Yet, even for smaller teams, the efficiency and oversight that a dedicated QA tool provides can be invaluable. As your team scales, the investment in a QA tool could pay dividends in time saved and errors reduced.

## Making the Decision

So, do you really need a QA tool to do QA on your support tickets? It boils down to a balance between scale, efficiency, and investment. If you're at the helm of a growing customer support operation, a QA tool could be a strategic investment, streamlining your processes and providing valuable insights that manual methods simply cannot match. On the other hand, for smaller operations with limited ticket volumes, manual methods might be a reasonable starting point, with the view to transition to a QA tool as the business scales.

In conclusion, while not strictly necessary, a QA tool is highly recommended for most operations due to its scalability and efficiency benefits. It is an investment in the infrastructure of your customer support, ensuring that as your business grows, your quality assurance capabilities grow with it.

Speaking of growth...

# Workforce Management (WFM)

When we think of customer support, we often visualize front-line agents answering queries, troubleshooting problems, or directing customers. However, behind those interactions lies a complex structure ensuring that the right agents are available at the right time with the right resources. Enter workforce management (WFM), the unsung maestro of the customer support orchestra.

## Why Is Workforce Management Crucial?

In essence, WFM is about aligning your resources (agents) with the demand (customer queries). Proper workforce management ensures:

- Efficiency. By matching staff availability to call volumes, you ensure minimal wastage in terms of idle agents and avoid long wait times for customers.

- Enhanced Customer Experience. No one likes to be kept waiting. Quick response times often result in more satisfied customers.

- Employee Satisfaction. Properly managed schedules mean agents aren't overworked or underutilized, leading to a more balanced work environment.

## Starting with Workforce Management

There are so many tools out there that help with WFM at the time of the writing of this book. However, because we don't want to date ourselves, we are trying to avoid mentioning them. With that, here are some key ways to consider starting up WFM for your organization if you are looking to do so without a dedicated tool (which we aren't naming so we don't seem old).

1. Assess Your Needs. Understand your call volumes, peak times, average call durations, and required service levels.

2. Choose a Tool. Based on your size and budget, select a tool that offers the features you need.

3. Engage Your Team. Involve your agents in the scheduling process to consider their preferences and constraints.

4. Regularly Review and Adapt. As your business evolves, so will your WFM needs. Periodic reviews ensure you remain on track.

## Key KPIs to Monitor

Several indicators will tell you if your WFM is hitting the mark:

- Service Level: The percentage of calls answered within a specific timeframe.
- Average Handling Time (AHT): The average duration taken to resolve customer queries.
- Forecast Accuracy: The difference between predicted call volumes and actual numbers.
- Schedule Adherence: How closely agents stick to their scheduled breaks, logins, and logouts.
- Occupancy Rate: The amount of time agents spend on calls compared to idle times.

Workforce management is more than just creating rosters. It's about crafting a harmonious balance between customer expectations, business needs, and employee satisfaction. When executed correctly, WFM becomes the backbone of a robust customer support function, setting the stage for stellar performances daily. If customer support is an orchestra, then workforce management is undoubtedly the conductor, ensuring each section comes in right on cue.

# Reporting on CX

For people who don't speak the language of customer experience, it can be difficult to convey how important and valuable certain metrics are. Here's where the lighthouse of well-crafted reporting shines, illuminating the way for stakeholders to grasp, evaluate, and improve the support journey. But how do you design these reports and, more importantly, for whom? We got you.

## Key Considerations in Crafting Reports

1. Purpose-Driven Data. Before jumping into numbers, charts, or tables, ask what's the primary goal of this report? Whether it's tracking performance, gauging customer satisfaction, or understanding resource allocation, the purpose should dictate the content.

2. Actionable Insights. A good report doesn't just dump data; it offers actionable insights. Instead of just presenting a problem (e.g., increased ticket volume), delve into the potential causes or solutions.

3. Simplicity Is King. Avoid jargon or complex visuals. Your aim is clarity and understanding, not to overwhelm or confuse your audience.

4. Timeframes Matter. Whether it's a weekly, monthly, or quarterly report, the time frame sets the context. Analyzing long-term trends? Quarterly might be your best bet. Need to be agile and respond to immediate challenges? Weekly updates can keep you on your toes.

## Identifying Your Audience

You should always try to speak the same language as the folks that you are directing your message to. Depending on who you are generating reporting for, your message should be conveyed differently.

### Front-Line Agents

When you think of the superheroes of the customer support world, front-line agents come to mind. They're right there in the trenches, fielding questions, resolving issues, and ensuring that customers leave with a smile. For these everyday heroes, feedback is fuel. Reports tailored to them should zoom in on their individual and collective metrics. By giving them a clear view of their performance, areas they shine in, and spots where they can lace up their boots a bit tighter, we empower them to evolve. It's like giving them a mirror that reflects not just where they stand, but also where they can go.

### Customer Support Managers

These folks need an overview of the entire team's performance, including detailed insights on team efficiency, the voice of the customer, areas needing a training boost, and resource availability. These insights help them fine-tune their strategies, ensuring team success.

### Higher Management and Executives

Now, let's chat about the bigwigs, the folks looking at the broader business landscape. For them, diving into the nitty-gritty details of every ticket or call might be overwhelming. They're looking for the 10,000-foot view. Reports for this audience should be crisp, focusing on the big picture: How is support driving strategy? Where are the cost implications? What's the return on investment? And, of course, how is the support symphony influencing the grand company opera?

### Other Departments

Picture this: The Sales team is crafting a pitch, and they're curious about common customer pain points. Or the Marketing squad is wondering how a recent campaign has affected support inquiries. Enter the magic of inter-departmental synergy! Sometimes, teams like Sales, Marketing, or even Product Development might knock on Support's door, seeking insights. Crafting reports for them is a balancing act. It's about cherry-picking the nuggets from customer support data that can enrich their strategies.

## Common Pitfalls to Avoid

Not everyone understands Support. Just like if you went to a financial presentation you might not understand everything they were talking about, so you can't expect folks outside of CX to come on a journey with you if you don't take the time to break down your points. Here are a few key ways that CX leaders can make their presentations more impactful and meaningful for other departments:

1. Always frame metrics in terms of overall business objectives. For instance, if your "First Call Resolution" rate has improved, emphasize how this leads to increased customer satisfaction, which in turn can boost retention and lifetime customer value.

2. Numbers in isolation might not resonate, but stories do. Use real customer examples or scenarios to illustrate what a metric signifies. Instead of just presenting the Net Promoter Score (NPS), share testimonials or feedback that encapsulate why scores might be high or low.

3. Let's face it: Money talks. Whenever possible, connect metrics to financial implications. For instance, show how reducing average handle time can lead to cost savings or how improved customer satisfaction can lead to increased referrals and sales.

4. Infographics, charts, and dashboards can make data more digestible. A trend line showing steadily decreasing ticket volumes after a product update can instantly demonstrate the effectiveness of that update.

5. Sometimes the best way to convey the significance of a metric is to show how it stacks up against industry benchmarks. Being above or below the industry average can provide context and urgency.

6. Business leaders love solutions. If a metric is flagging an issue, accompany it with potential solutions or strategies. This proactive approach not only demonstrates the value of the metric but also showcases the strategic capabilities of the customer support team.

7. Sometimes a deeper dive is needed. Consider organizing educational sessions where you can walk leaders through key metrics,

what they signify, and why they matter. This can be especially beneficial for more complex or nuanced metrics.

8. Demonstrate how support metrics can benefit other departments. For example, feedback collected by support can be invaluable for product development, while insights into common customer issues can aid marketing in crafting more effective messaging.

9. Instead of waiting for quarterly reviews, keep a steady stream of communication. Regularly share metric highlights, success stories, and insights with leaders to keep the value of customer support metrics top of mind.

10. Ask business leaders how metrics can be made more relevant or understandable for them. Their feedback can help refine the presentation and selection of metrics.

The key to making the metrics more understandable is to move beyond abstract numbers. By tying customer support metrics to tangible business outcomes, real-world examples, and strategic insights, you can make these figures resonate with leaders and underscore their inherent value. When done effectively, this not only elevates the perception of customer support but also solidifies its place as a strategic pillar within the organization.

Data Overload: It's tempting to include every metric, but resist. Bombarding your audience with too much data can lead to them shutting down rather than them gaining additional clarity.

# Automation

Picture this: It's the early 2000s, and you're on hold with customer support, twiddling your thumbs and humming along to the all-too-familiar elevator music. You're running up your parents' phone bill and your sister can't get on AOL. Fast forward to today, and a friendly chatbot greets you instantly, offering solutions before you even reach out to a human agent—that's not even the extent to which automation can help. It's just the beginning.

As we navigate this digital age, where the demand for instantaneous responses meets the magic of technology, customer support has found itself in the midst of an automation revolution. And why not? If we can order pizza with a simple emoji or ask our smart speakers about tomorrow's weather, why should customer support be any different?

This section isn't just about machines taking over; it's a celebration of how automation has amplified the human touch, ensuring support teams are more efficient, consistent, and available than ever. But as with all things tech, there's an art to getting it right.

## AI

At the risk of dating this book by the time it is even printed, we have chosen to include AI in this text. While AI is all the rage right now, it will only continue to evolve at the speed of light. So, instead of talking about specific AI technologies, we will talk about the three things that it is uniquely positioned to assist with in CX—especially because while the technologies may change, these things will not. From there, we'll dive deeper into automation as a whole.

### Enhancing the Ticket Experience

Imagine walking into your favorite coffee shop, and the barista, without prompting, starts making your usual drink. That's the magic of personalization, and it's time to bring it into customer support. Instead of going through the routine of asking for details like order numbers, why not use the data we already have to enhance our conversations? This approach positions us not just as problem-solvers, but as trusted guides who truly understand our customers, making each interaction smoother and more intuitive.

### Smart Ticket Deflection

Ever had that moment when you're about to ask a question, but then find the answer just in time? That's what ticket deflection is all about. Through tools like knowledge base articles, chatbots, and handy widgets, we can address common concerns without needing that extra human intervention. But remember, it's not about replacing the human touch. It's about making sure that when we do interact, it's for those moments that truly count. By creating insightful content and suggesting clever automation workflows, we empower our customers, making support an effortlessly seamless experience.

## Proactive Ticket Avoidance

Now, let's talk foresight. Imagine spotting a puddle in the middle of a hallway and cleaning it up before anyone slips. That's the essence of ticket avoidance. By diving deep into quarterly business reviews, reporting, and spotting ticket trends, we're in a prime position to take proactive measures. If a recurring issue is causing customer frustration, let's loop back to our partners, shine a light on the pattern, and collaboratively brainstorm solutions. This could be a tweak in the product or maybe a change in training. The goal? A smoother journey for the customer, and fewer bumps on the road for everyone involved.

If you are currently evaluating any kind of AI tooling within your organization or CX strategy, focus on these three areas first as the prime places where it will have a positive, easy to measure impact. However, there are other types of automation that you can implement outside of AI as well.

## Types of Automation

With each technological leap, businesses have been granted new ways to streamline operations, enhance customer interactions, and refine their overall support strategy.

Take chatbots and virtual assistants, for example. These digital entities have become synonymous with instant gratification in CX. Where once a customer might have waited on hold or waded through pages of FAQs, they can now receive real-time responses to their inquiries. Chatbots, equipped with machine learning (or without!), can tap into vast databases of information, answering questions in seconds. They're not just about efficiency, either; these tools allow businesses to be "present" around the clock, delivering a level of convenience that was previously unimaginable.

Then there are the innovations within ticketing systems. Gone are the days when customer queries would get lost in the shuffle or when agents would manually sort and assign issues. Modern ticketing systems come equipped with automation tools that handle everything from assignment to categorization and prioritization. By using criteria set by the business, these systems can automatically direct tickets to the right department or individual, ensuring that the customer's concern is addressed by the most capable hands in the shortest time possible.

Knowledge bases represent another massive stride in automation. These comprehensive repositories offer customers a self-service option, granting them access to information without the need for human intervention. By simply typing a query or navigating through a well-organized portal, customers can find solutions to common problems, tutorials, product details, and more. For businesses, this not only reduces the ticket volume but also empowers their users, fostering a sense of independence and competence.

Predictive support is also an exciting frontier in the automation space. By leveraging vast amounts of data and sophisticated algorithms, customer support tools can now anticipate issues before they arise. For instance, a scenario where, based on previous interactions and product usage patterns, a support tool can preemptively offer solutions or advice to a user. This proactive approach can drastically reduce frustrations, as users feel understood and catered to even before they articulate their concerns.

Lastly, the automation of feedback collection has provided businesses with an invaluable tool. In the past, gathering feedback might have involved cumbersome processes, but now, post-interaction surveys and feedback loops can be initiated automatically. Whether it's after a chat session, a product purchase, or any other touchpoint, these automated systems can glean insights from users efficiently. For businesses, this feedback is gold, offering direct insights into areas of improvement, user satisfaction levels, and potential avenues for growth.

Whether you use these tools with or without a component of AI (though finding them without AI may be difficult, as it continues to proliferate in the space), there are numerous benefits to implementing *some* kind of automation for your team.

## Benefits of Automation in Customer Support

The first and perhaps most immediate benefit we notice with automation is the sheer efficiency it brings to the table. Gone are the days of prolonged wait times, where customers sip their tea in frustration as they hold for the next available representative. Automated tools, like chatbots, ensure that clients get faster responses, regardless of whether it's peak business hours or the middle of the night. The beauty of automation? It doesn't need coffee breaks or sleep. It's on the job 24/7, ensuring customers always have a touchpoint.

Now, consider the myriad of questions that flood a customer support inbox daily. While each customer is unique, many of their queries can be quite similar. This is where automation shines in providing consistency in service. Instead of crafting replies from scratch each time, automated systems can offer uniform, accurate responses for those frequently asked questions. This not only speeds up the process but ensures that each customer receives a standard level of quality in the information they're provided.

As businesses grow and scale, so do their customer bases—and with that, the volume of support tickets. This is where automation becomes a game-changer in terms of scalability. Traditional systems might crumble under the weight of thousands of queries, but automation stands steadfast. By managing, categorizing, and even resolving a large chunk of tickets, it ensures that businesses can handle their growth without compromising on customer service quality.

But what about our human agents? Does automation render them obsolete? Far from it. In fact, automation plays a pivotal role in empowering agents. By taking over repetitive and mundane tasks, it allows human reps to focus on more complex issues, training, and personal development. Imagine a world where agents are free from the drudgery of answering the same questions over and over. Instead, they're diving deep into unique challenges, honing their skills, and offering the kind of empathetic support that machines can't replicate.

Lastly, we can't talk about automation without touching upon its capability for data collection and analysis. Every interaction, every click, every query processed through automated systems becomes a data point. These aren't just random numbers; they're insights waiting to be explored. With sophisticated analytics tools, businesses can understand customer behavior, detect emerging patterns, and continuously refine their support strategies. It's like having a crystal ball that shows not just the present but offers glimpses into future trends and areas of improvement.

It's clear that automation isn't just a tech upgrade; it's a paradigm shift. Automation doesn't just "support" customer support; it elevates it, merging the efficiency of machines with the warmth and adaptability of the human touch. As businesses continue to grow and customer expectations evolve, automation ensures we're always a step ahead, ready to offer exceptional service with a smile (or a friendly chatbot message).

## Combining Human and Machine

The line between automation and human interaction, especially in CX, is often blurred. Striking the right balance between the two is pivotal to providing a stellar customer experience. While automation offers speed and efficiency, there's an irreplaceable value in the warmth and nuance of human communication.

## Know When to Automate

The digital revolution has made automation an indispensable tool in our arsenal. However, it's vital to discern the right moments to deploy it. Consider automation your reliable, always-on teammate, adept at handling tasks that are routine and repetitive. Queries like "What's my account balance?" or "How do I reset my password?" are prime candidates. By letting automation take the reins here, we not only ensure prompt responses but also free our human agents to tackle more nuanced challenges.

## Where Humans Add Value

Beyond codes and algorithms lies the heart of our operations: our human agents. There are moments, laden with complexity or emotion, where machines might stumble, but humans shine. These are the instances, be it a complex query or a customer seeking empathy, that the genuine human touch becomes paramount. It's these human-driven interactions that make a customer feel truly understood and valued.

## Strike a Balance

The art of harmonizing automation with human involvement isn't always straightforward. It requires a keen focus on the customer experience. Each strategic shift should stem from one central query: Are we enhancing the customer's experience? While automation streamlines operations, it's the genuine human encounters that build trust, loyalty, and deep connections. The ultimate aim is for every customer to sense that they're not just another query but an esteemed individual.

The dance between automation and human interaction in customer support is both intricate and beautiful. As we keep pace with evolving technology, let's not forget the timeless charm of genuine human connection. By melding the two, we're set to offer a customer support experience that's nothing short of exceptional.

## Best Practices for Implementation

Automation promises efficiency and consistency, but its implementation requires thoughtfulness. When done right, automation can revolutionize the way support is delivered. Let's delve into the best practices to make this transition smooth and effective.

1. Start small. It's tempting to dive deep into automation from the get-go. However, just as Rome wasn't built in a day, automation in customer support needs a phased approach. Begin by identifying key areas where automation can offer the most significant benefits. Perhaps it's sorting and categorizing incoming tickets, or maybe automating responses to the most frequently asked questions. By starting small, you set the stage for bigger wins down the road. This approach not only allows for tangible benefits early on but also offers a chance to understand the nuances of integrating automation within the existing workflow.

2. Always be learning. Automation isn't a "set and forget" strategy. As with all things in customer support, it thrives on feedback and iteration. Regularly collect insights from both your support agents and customers. Are the automated processes meeting their needs? Are there any hiccups or points of friction? By incorporating this feedback, you can continuously refine your automation, ensuring it stays relevant, efficient, and in tune with evolving needs.

3. Don't drop the ball on integrations. In the intricate puzzle of customer support, numerous tools come together to paint the bigger picture. When integrating automation, it's crucial to ensure that it doesn't function in isolation. Whether it's your CRM, ticketing system, or any other support tool, seamless functionality across platforms is crucial. Proper integration reduces the risk of data silos, ensures the consistency of information, and elevates the overall efficiency of your support ecosystem.

4. Don't neglect your people. At the heart of every great automation strategy are the humans that use it. As you bring in new tools and processes, it's imperative to invest in training and onboarding. Your team should not only understand the technical aspects of the tools but also the larger vision behind their adoption. Effective training ensures that your team leverages automation to its full potential, making it an ally rather than just another tool in their kit.

Like all powerful tools, automation's true potential is unlocked when wielded with knowledge, strategy, and a touch of human insight. By adopting these best practices, you pave the way for an automation journey that is both impactful and seamless.

## Common Pitfalls

As with any transformative tool, there's a thin line between judicious use and over-dependence. Let's explore some common pitfalls that teams may encounter and the ways to gracefully sidestep them.

One significant trap is the allure of over-automation. The promise of consistent and efficient responses can sometimes overshadow the core essence of customer support: the invaluable human connection. Although automation is a powerful ally, over-relying on it can lead to sterile exchanges that lack the personal touch.

The fix? Prioritize the customer experience. Recognize moments where empathy, understanding, or a tailored response can turn an interaction around. Use automation to enhance these pivotal exchanges, not replace them.

Another challenge emerges with the use of scripts. These predefined responses can be invaluable in offering quick, standardized answers. Yet an over-reliance can make interactions feel robotic or even out-of-touch. After all, not every query will fit neatly into a predefined box.

The fix? Scripts should act as a foundation, not the entire structure. Ensure that customers have an easy pathway to transition from automated to human interactions when needed. And, of course, regularly updating scripts to remain conversational and relevant is key.

Lastly, there's the pitfall of stagnation. With the dynamic nature of customer needs, products, and market shifts, allowing automated systems to become outdated is risky. It's not just about efficiency but also about maintaining customer trust.

The fix? Dedicate time to periodically review and refresh automated systems. Stay updated on product changes, feedback, and emerging customer preferences.

## Case Study: Brew & Beans. Revolutionizing Customer Support Through Automation

**Background**

Brew & Beans, a burgeoning online coffee retailer, was witnessing a rapid ascent in its customer base. With artisanal blends sourced from across the globe, their platform was buzzing with both casual coffee drinkers and aficionados. However, with growth came the challenge of managing an increasing number of customer inquiries, complaints, and feedback.

**Challenge**

The small yet dedicated customer support team of Brew & Beans found itself overwhelmed. The influx of order-related queries, blend recommendations, and delivery questions meant long waiting times and occasionally missed responses. The team was stretched thin, and there was an increasing concern about maintaining their reputation for exceptional customer care.

**Solution**

Understanding the need to innovate, Brew & Beans decided to embark on a journey into automation. Here's how they transformed their customer support.

Chatbots for Basic Inquiries. They introduced "BeanBot," an AI-powered chatbot designed to handle routine questions about order statuses, delivery timelines, and basic product details. This allowed customers to receive instantaneous responses at any hour.

Automated Ticketing System. Brew & Beans implemented an advanced ticketing system that automatically categorized and prioritized incoming queries. This ensured that urgent issues were immediately flagged and addressed, streamlining the workflow for human agents.

Knowledge Base Creation. To empower customers to find answers on their own, Brew & Beans set up a comprehensive knowledge base. It included FAQs, brewing guides, and product details. This self-service portal drastically reduced the number of basic queries reaching their support team.

Predictive Support. Utilizing machine learning, Brew & Beans started analyzing buying patterns and preferences. This allowed them to anticipate common questions and provide preemptive assistance, further reducing the volume of queries.

Feedback Loop. Post-interaction surveys were automated to gauge customer satisfaction, providing the team with insights to continuously refine their automated processes.

**Results**

Post-implementation, Brew & Beans saw a dramatic 40% reduction in the average response time. The number of missed or delayed replies plummeted by 85%. The knowledge base was a hit, with over 60% of customers finding the answers they needed without reaching out to an agent. BeanBot, with its quirky persona, became a customer favorite, handling 50% of all inquiries.

Moreover, the company's NPS (Net Promoter Score) saw a surge, reflecting higher customer satisfaction. Human agents, no longer inundated with routine questions, were now able to focus on complex issues and relationship-building, further enhancing the brand's reputation.

**Conclusion**

Brew & Beans showcased how the strategic application of automation in customer support can yield substantial benefits. By blending technology with their core ethos of customer-centricity, they not only managed their growth challenges but set a new standard in online retail customer care.

# Moderation and Trust and Safety

In the age of digital platforms and online communities, there's an underlying social contract that companies enter into with their users: to provide a safe environment for engagement. Whether it's a bustling social media platform or an intimate customer feedback forum, establishing trust and maintaining safety is paramount.

Let's dive into the intricacies of Trust and Safety, understanding its importance and practical execution.

## Understanding the Need for Trust and Safety

Any online community or platform acts as a melting pot of diverse voices. However, as platforms grow, so does the potential for misuse. Spam, harassment, scams, or even more severe illicit activities can tarnish the user experience, deter new users, and even cause legal headaches. This calls for a robust Trust and Safety practice that serves as a guardian of both platform integrity and user welfare.

A few negative incidents, especially if repeated or high-profile, can create a pervasive atmosphere of mistrust. There's the conundrum: how does a platform continue to trust the larger user base when a specific cohort consistently disrupts the harmony?

It's vital to remember that the actions of a minority shouldn't dictate the approach to the majority. Offering clearer guidelines to users, emphasizing the importance of community values, and employing automated monitoring tools can help segregate genuine users from those with potential ill intentions.

## Establishing Trust and Safety and Risk Teams

As platforms mature and user bases expand, the challenges of maintaining safety and trust evolve. Recognizing the signs that hint at these shifting challenges becomes critical in ensuring a thriving community:

- Growth in User Numbers. With an increasing number of users, managing content becomes an intricate task. As the crowd grows, diverse interactions and potential pitfalls follow suit.

- Rising Incident Alerts. An uptick in user-reported issues or flagged content signals an emerging need for a structured approach to address these concerns.

- Legal Ramifications. Addressing potential legal risks linked to content or user behavior becomes paramount. This could span from hate speech to copyright issues.

- Public Perception. A surge in negative publicity due to incidents on your platform emphasizes the need for a dedicated team to both preempt and manage such scenarios.

- Evolving Challenges. Platforms in their infancy grapple with organic issues, like random spam. However, as challenges grow systematic, with organized attempts to exploit the system, a specialized approach is necessary.

- Serving a Global Crowd. As you cater to users from different corners of the globe, the need to respect cultural subtleties and legal diversities grows.

- Moderation Scalability Issues. If existing systems, whether AI-driven or community-based, falter under the volume or complexity of tasks, it signifies the need for a more specialized approach.

- Financial Moves and Collaborations: Introducing revenue models like advertising or partnering with brands necessitates a pristine, user-friendly environment.

- Feature Rollouts. New additions, such as live streams or user-generated content platforms, come with their unique set of challenges.
- User Loyalty and Confidence: A dip in engagement rates or waning trust, triggered by safety concerns or irrelevant content, is a wake-up call for reinforced measures.

The birth of a Trust and Safety team becomes inevitable when the core values of community and brand integrity are at stake. This strategic move signifies a pivot towards ensuring an inclusive, positive user space.

Such dedicated teams are masters in tackling gray areas where clear intentions blur. Their playbook includes:

- Real-time content reviews in line with platform ethos.
- Deep-diving into reports of dubious activities.
- Collaborating with legal experts when the situation calls for it.
- Adapting platform norms in tandem with emerging risks or behavioral shifts.

And if you're charting the course for a fresh Trust and Safety team, here's a primer:

1. Tailor-Make for Your Platform. Each platform sings a different tune with its unique set of challenges.
2. Craft Concrete Community Standards. Draw the line clearly—establish what's in tune with your platform's spirit and what's off-key.
3. Leverage Tech. Embrace AI and other technologies to spot potential safety breaches.
4. Assemble the Crew. Marry technology with the irreplaceable human touch. Assemble a crew that's trained to safeguard Trust and Safety.

5. School the Community. Keep your user base in the loop. Share guidelines, updates, and safety pointers consistently.
6. Stay Agile. In the face of new-age challenges, the mantra is to adapt, evolve, and fine-tune your strategies.

## KPIs for Trust and Safety

You can't manage what you can't measure. Here are some KPIs that you can track to ensure that what you're trying to achieve with your Trust and Safety team is being met.

- Incident Rate. The frequency of reported or detected trust and safety incidents.
- Resolution Time. The average time taken to address and resolve an incident.
- User Feedback. Post-incident surveys to gauge user satisfaction with the resolution.
- Repeat Offenders. Tracking users who consistently violate guidelines despite interventions.
- Escalation Rate. Incidents that require involvement from higher authority or legal intervention.

Trust and Safety isn't just a functional requirement for online platforms; it's an ethical one. Protecting users, maintaining platform integrity, and fostering a positive community atmosphere are not just goals but foundational necessities. With a balanced mix of guidelines, technology, and dedicated teams, platforms can nurture a thriving, safe, and trustworthy digital environment.

Alright, let's take a step back and look at the big picture. Setting up a customer support operation is kind of like assembling a massive jigsaw puzzle. It might seem daunting at the beginning, but piece by piece, it all comes together. And remember, it's not just about the tools and processes, but also the vibe and energy you bring into it. At the heart of it all? Making sure your customers feel heard and valued. It's a dynamic process—there's no one-size-fits-all blueprint. Instead, it's about being nimble, learning on the go, and being open to tweaking things based on what works best for your business and your customers.

And so, as you wrap up this hefty chapter and gear up to dive into building your support squad, just remember: Every big success story starts with that first, small step.

# CHAPTER 5:

# How to Hire (and Keep) a High-Performing Team

Constructing a team, in many ways, mirrors the intricacies of constructing a building. Aesthetics alone won't suffice; a slight misalignment in the foundation can lead to cracks in even the most elegant of skyscrapers. Similarly, in customer support, there's a delicate balance of emotional intelligence and skill required. These agents are empathetic to the core, absorbing the sentiments of everyone they interact with. It's no surprise that such teams, brimming with emotions, can be challenging to coordinate, especially in bulk.

Think of piecing together a customer support team as arranging a meticulously crafted mosaic. Each tile, representing a role or a skill, must seamlessly fit into the larger picture. Beyond the core team, there are other external elements to ponder over, like ensuring 24/7 support across diverse time zones. Contrary to popular belief, there isn't an endless queue of ready-to-hire candidates possessing the ideal blend of talent and temperament. Hiring such a proficient battalion of support champions requires a strategic approach to recruitment, interviews, and onboarding.

Fear not, for this book is here to guide you through every facet of the process. From identifying the "right fit" to nurturing their growth within the company, we'll shed light on every step of the journey. Buckle up and let's navigate this together!

## Defining the DNA

Before you get started hunting for great team members, you need to understand what you want your team to look like and how you want it to behave when it is *much* larger. Here are a few steps to follow to gain clarity in that space:

1. Qualities of Your Company

Every successful company has a unique DNA that sets it apart. This DNA is primarily made up of the company's core values. These values are not just buzzwords that look good on paper; they are the essence of the company's identity. They're what drives every decision, shapes the culture, and instills a sense of purpose.

2. Positioning Customer Support Within the Value System

Before embarking on the hiring process, it's crucial to determine where Customer Support fits within this value system. Ask yourself how does the support team embody our core values? Perhaps "Customer First" is one of your primary values, indicating that the support team is the front line in ensuring this value is upheld every day. Or maybe "Continuous Learning" is a pillar, suggesting that your support team should always be looking for ways to evolve and improve the customer experience.

3. Determining Candidate–Value Fit

Now, as you delve into the hiring process, the big question arises: How do you ensure that a potential hire not only understands but also resonates with these core values? The answer lies in a well-structured interview process.

During interviews, craft questions that aren't just about the candidate's experience but also about their beliefs and attitudes. For instance, if Integrity is one of your core values, you might ask, "Can you recall a time when doing the right thing was challenging, and how did you handle it?" Or, if Team Collaboration is vital, ask, "Tell us about a time you had to work closely with a team member you disagreed with. How did you navigate this situation?"

4. Identifying a Cultural Cohesion

Beyond the specific answers, observe how candidates react to these questions. Their level of comfort, their anecdotes, and even their body language can provide insights into whether they truly share the company's values. Remember, while skills might be taught, alignment with core values is often intrinsic.

5. Qualities of a Great Support Rep

Understand what traits you *really* want in your ideal support rep. This is going to be specific for your team, and should not be the same list that other companies use.

6. Recognizing Red Flags

Lastly, while every individual is unique and might bring a fresh perspective, there are certain characteristics that could be detrimental to customer service. Identify what the traits that you couldn't have on your team would be. The "instant no," as it were.

# Building the Hiring Process

Building a solid team starts with hiring the right people. But how do you find the best fit? Embarking on this hiring adventure is just your first step in shaping a remarkable team. To make sure that you're not doing double work, here are a few tips and tricks to make sure that your hire is great the first time.

Want top-notch talent for your support team? It begins with an enticing job description. Even seasoned managers sometimes miss the mark, focusing too much on job duties or requirements and forgetting they're essentially writing an ad to woo the best candidates. But there are must-haves for every job post.

## Creating a Job Post

Regardless of how jazzy or straightforward your description is, some non-negotiables should be present in every job post. This ensures potential candidates know exactly what they're signing up for and whether they fit the bill. Always include:

- Job Title
- Quick Role Overview
- Tasks and Objectives
- Work Hours and Location
- Must-Have Skills and Qualifications

Of course, while you cover the essentials, toss in some flavor. Give it a personal touch that resonates with your company culture and the team you're sculpting.

## Choose Your Language Wisely

The devil is in the details. Are your team members "agents" or "representatives"? Are they just "doing" tasks or "achieving "milestones"?

Let's put it this way. Instead of stating, "Handle customer queries in our inbox," why not jazz it up with "Empower customers by addressing their concerns via email, chat, and video." Sounds more engaging, right?

The way you talk about what you do is important. While companies like FullStory have "Huggers" on board, Wistia boasts of "Customer Champions." If those don't fit your team, perhaps a classic "Customer Support Representative" à la Trello will do the trick.

A great example of choosing phrasing that is reflective is this job description from Figma:

- Work with our Product Education Specialist on drafts of new help center articles.

- Write scripts for new video tutorials and work with our small production team.
- Do you have SQL skills? Write queries and create dashboards for monitoring our support KPIs.
- Help us compile and organize an internal knowledge base.
- Aspiring author? Design a new onboarding manual for future Product Support Team members.
- Are you a natural-born teacher? Lead Figma 101 sessions for new hires to get them up to speed on Figma's features and functionalities.

You can really get an understanding of what type of team you would be joining, looking at this listing.

Lastly, while creativity in language is commendable, authenticity trumps all. If your job description is all fireworks but the real deal feels lackluster, candidates will notice the disconnect. So, let your description vibe with the genuine spirit of your company.

## Highlight Your Culture

You're probably nailing this already. Your marketing squad has been championing your company culture in every nook and cranny of your marketing materials and product showcases. Similarly, your support team effortlessly weaves it into every email, tweet, chat, and social message they draft. Now, the baton's in your hand to ensure that your job descriptions reflect that same cultural spirit.

As you detail the attributes of your dream candidate, sprinkle in links to relevant blog posts or suggested reads. This not only paves the way for potential hires to delve deeper, checking if they've found their ideal workplace, but also grants them a tangible sense of your cultural essence, be it in your blog entries or customer-centric product pages.

For instance, GitLab seamlessly incorporates a link to their culture page within their job descriptions, offering candidates a chance to know the company's heartbeat before taking the plunge:

> About GitLab
>
> GitLab Inc. is a company based on the GitLab open-source project. GitLab is a community project to which over 1,000 people worldwide have contributed. We are an active participant in this community, trying to serve its needs and lead by example. We have one vision: everyone can contribute to all digital content, and our mission is to change all creative work from read-only to read-write so that everyone can contribute.
>
> We value results, transparency, sharing, freedom, efficiency, frugality, collaboration, directness, kindness, diversity, boring solutions, and quirkiness. If these values match your personality, work ethic, and personal goals, we encourage you to visit our primer to learn more. Open source is our culture, our way of life, our story, and what makes us truly unique.
>
> Top 10 reasons to work for GitLab:
>
> 1. Work with helpful, kind, motivated, and talented people.
>
> 2. Work remote so you have no commute and are free to travel and move.
>
> 3. Have flexible work hours so you are there for other people and free to plan the day how you like.

Another thing you may include as a clever way to showcase your culture without spelling it out is a stellar email or interaction (with the customer's green light, naturally). This not only radiates your cultural vibes but also highlights how support staff add their unique touch in customer conversations. Potential hires can then gauge if your brand's support style resonates with their own.

## Use an Assignment

Assignments are a great way to see how an applicant would actually perform tasks associated with the job. That said, when creating your assignment, consider how much of the applicant's time you are asking. If it's a really long time, consider financially compensating them for the time and effort.

A project could be anything from a short six-question assignment to an hour-long project that they take and complete on their own time. The most important thing is that it reflects work that they would actually do and is not manufactured to be especially difficult or challenging. And, just to reiterate, if you are taking a lot of their time, consider compensating them.

Zapier, for instance, includes questions right within their customer champion application form, including setting up a "zap" in their product and questions about APIs. Here's an example:

> How to Apply
>
> We have a non-standard application process. To jumpstart the process we ask a few questions we normally would ask at the start of an interview. This helps speed up the process and lets us get to know you a bit better right out of the gate. Please make sure to answer each question.
>
> Complete this form with answers to the below questions. Make sure each answer stands alone as we review question-by-question instead of applicant-by-applicant.
>
> 1. Tell us why you would be a good fit for this role.
> 2. Tell us why you want to work at Zapier instead of somewhere else.

3. What should our goal be when replying to users?

4. A user requests an integration with a service that we don't support yet. Compose a reply to this user.

5. Set up a zap that takes new Gmail emails from a specific sender and adds them to a Google Sheets spreadsheet. Send us the link to the zap and a share link for the spreadsheet.

6. Send us a link to an app's API docs that you think are well done, and explain why you think they are good.

One of the benefits of this approach, besides getting a deeper insight into the candidate, is that it filters out those who apply en masse. Some folks scatter their applications far and wide, not particularly connecting with any specific role or company. By adding an assignment step, either before or after they submit their resume, you're essentially sieving out the casual applicant. Sure, you might lose a few good ones, but the ones who stay are truly invested and eager for the shot.

Another plus? It offers a sneak peek into their real-world approach to customer service. A polished resume is great, but an actual project showcases their hands-on style. You get to gauge how they would interact with your clientele, and how much (or little) coaching they might need.

## Prioritize the Role, Sprinkle in the Extras

While job perks are enticing and can grab the attention of potential candidates, they aren't the be-all and end-all. You wouldn't want applicants who only recall the allure of your seven ping-pong tables and charismatic debate squad but are clueless about their actual job responsibilities.

So, as you write down your job description, let the core responsibilities shine, subtly blending the perks within. Consider framing it like this:

> Gear up to manage about 60 email interactions with our valuable customers daily. Sounds intense? We've got you!

To decompress, you might fancy a game at one of our seven ping-pong tables or perhaps take a refreshing nap in our designated snooze lounge.

Our support squad is tightly knit with our product and tech units, bridging customer feedback, bugs, and product nuances. If being a stellar communicator is your thing, you'll excel here.

More of an introvert? No worries! Hone your mingling skills at our relaxed, optional game nights where we shuffle teams, giving everyone a chance to bond with new faces.

If you're leaning towards a concise style, keep the role details upfront and list the perks later, maybe in bullet points. These clear, quick-to-scan lists are reader-friendly, helping candidates gauge compatibility in a jiffy. Mixing some detailed content with bulleted highlights can strike a good balance.

With your crafted job description in hand, the next step is to get those applications rolling in.

# Finding Applicants

There are so many great places to find applicants, and many great websites where you can post your job listings. As we know, though, the internet moves at a million miles a minute. So, rather than including specific websites where you can go to post roles, we wanted to mention some *non*-traditional places where you might look for your next hire. Here are some nontraditional methods to consider:

1. Referral Programs. Encourage current employees to refer friends or acquaintances who might be a good fit. Offering incentives can make this even more appealing.

2. Networking Events. Attend or host industry meetups, workshops, or other networking events where you can meet potential candidates in person.

3. Social Media. Use platforms to search for and reach out to potential candidates. Regularly share content about your company culture to attract like-minded individuals.

4. Online Communities. Engage in online forums, groups, or platforms related to customer support.

5. Freelance Platforms. There are tons of websites that have many professionals looking for full-time roles. You can vet potential candidates by giving them a small project before considering them for a full-time position.

6. Internship Programs. Convert interns into full-time employees. This allows you to train candidates according to your company's requirements from the outset.

7. Local Colleges and Universities. Partner with educational institutions for campus recruitments or job fairs. They can provide a fresh pool of eager-to-learn candidates.

8. Industry Conferences. Attend or sponsor panels at conferences related to customer experience or support. It can be a great place to meet seasoned professionals.

9. Talent Pools. Maintain a database of impressive candidates from previous rounds of hiring, and reach out when new positions open up.

10. Hackathons or Innovation Days. While traditionally for tech roles, these events can be tailored for customer support challenges, allowing you to observe candidates' problem-solving skills in real-time.

11. Collaborations with Boot Camps. Some Boot Camps train individuals in soft skills or even specific support tools. Forming partnerships can offer a direct line to newly trained talent.

12. Engaging with Passive Candidates. Not everyone actively looking is on job boards. Some of the best talents might be currently employed but open to a discussion. Direct outreach can sometimes yield impressive results.

13. Employee Testimonials. Share stories of your current employees' growth and experiences on your website or social media. It can act as a magnet for like-minded individuals.

14. Customer Base. Sometimes your best supporters are your current users or customers. They already understand and appreciate your product, making them potential candidates.

Remember, regardless of the method, ensuring a seamless and respectful candidate experience is vital. It not only impacts the present hiring process but also your company's reputation in the long run.

# Interviewing

You've gathered a roster of potential game-changers for your squad—nice move! Embarking on the interview journey can often feel like stepping into a ballroom without prior dance lessons—there's a mix of excitement and uncertainty. But it's all about finding that harmonious sync. During the phone screenings, trust your intuition. Even a faint alarm bell is worth noting.

While a growing talent pool sounds comforting, it's crucial to ensure each addition is a potential fit. Aim for the standout, the one who'll not only merge seamlessly with your existing team but elevate it. Consider this: A misfit hire might cost you about 30% of their annual earnings. That's an expensive misstep!

## Create a Checklist

Initiate this during the job description phase—just like we talked about in the "Defining your DNA" section. Outline the non-negotiables and the desirable traits. Circulate this list amongst your hiring ensemble. It's vital that everyone's on the same page, ensuring a streamlined process. Design your interview questions to revolve around these core attributes. It's akin to a relay race: your teammates should effortlessly pick up from where you left, ensuring no vital point is missed.

## Questions to Strike a Chord

Selecting the right questions is like curating a playlist for a party—hit the right notes, and you'll get invaluable insights. Depending on your company's pulse, these might shift, but here's a detailed cheat sheet.

- Pose questions like, "Imagine you're tasked with spearheading our support team. How would you innovate to make it the industry benchmark?" These shed light on their strategic mindset and creativity.

- Probe into episodes like, "Narrate an instance where your perspective clashed with a colleague. What was the journey to resolution?" This can offer a window into their interpersonal skills, self-awareness, and adaptability.

- Use quirky queries such as, "You're handed an unfamiliar Lego set. Walk me through your building strategy." Such queries reveal not just their problem-solving prowess but also their comfort with ambiguity.

- Dive into their research skills and genuine interest. "What drew you to our brand, and how do you see your role evolving here?"

- Gauge their tech literacy. Questions like, "How comfortable are you troubleshooting basic HTML issues?" can help understand their technical grounding, even for non-tech roles.

## Interviewing for a Remote Hire

Remote recruitment is like exploring uncharted territory. You don't get those in-person nuances—a raised eyebrow signaling confusion or those stealthy glances towards their phone. Here's how you can demystify a remote candidate's potential.

- Initiate with, "Describe your journey with remote work. What about it appeals to you?" Their answer might offer a deep dive into their work preferences. For instance, you'll learn if they like remote work because they want to veg out with their partner at home, or if it empowers them to do something that they might not otherwise be able to do.

- Spark their introspection with, "Can you share the latest skill or hobby you took upon yourself to learn? What motivated it?" This unearths their proactive learning tendencies.

- Dive into their collaboration experiences. "Discuss a project where you had to collaborate cross-functionally. Were there any challenges, and how were they addressed?" Probing here clarifies their remote teamwork and communication capabilities.

- Questions like, "Recall a situation where a seemingly resolved issue resurfaced with complications. How did you manage and resolve it?" showcase their crisis management and conflict resolution skills.

- Pose a fun challenge. "If handed a complex, abstract puzzle, how would you approach it?" Their response will unravel their strategic thinking and perseverance.

Remember, the essence of interviewing extends beyond evaluating the candidate—it's a two-way street. While you're gauging their fit, they're assessing your company's culture and potential. So always keep the communication transparent, and genuine.

## Onboarding Your New Hire

The onboarding phase is much like a dancer's debut performance—filled with anticipation, nerves, and the hope of making a lasting impression. This initial phase offers companies a golden window to set the stage, illustrating their ethos and culture. For the fresh recruit, it's the time to soak in the ambiance and decide if this is where their heart truly belongs. Why is this important? About one in every three employees decide their long-term commitment within the initial 30 days.

Given the weight those initial 30 days carry, how can you ensure the ship sails smoothly? Read on!

1. Reach out before the actual first day. Pioneers like Campaign Monitor and Help Scout have already tapped into the power of pre-start date engagement. Consider an email sequence that paints a picture of the journey ahead, from logistics like workstation readiness to company culture insights, even extending to apparel pointers and mealtime cues. It's not just about the specifics; it's a gesture that screams, "We can't wait for you to join!"

2. Have all their tools prepared. Nothing dampens the spirits like a disorganized first day. To paint a picture of efficiency and care, have their workstation, tech, and accounts set up before they step in. Their focus should be orientation, not hunting down login credentials.

3. Make the first day special. Think of the first day as a grand carnival. Introduce them to the grandeur of your brand, the vibrant culture, and the promising journey ahead. Schedule team interactions, head of department introductions, or even a fun team-building escapade. Save the detailed training for day two and beyond. Let day one be a memorable melody they hum.

4. Have an organized, prepared schedule. An efficient onboarding calendar is like a well-composed symphony—deliberate and harmonious. Ensure every event, every meeting, has its rightful

place, and purpose. Keep the timeline tight; it fosters focus. The magic? Brandon Hall Group's study unveils that such meticulous planning can amplify retention by 82% and surge productivity by a staggering 70%.

5. Get the whole company involved: Onboarding isn't a HR-only show; it's a collective performance. Enlist department heads for sessions, ensuring the newbie recognizes faces and understands inter-departmental dynamics. This doesn't just familiarize them but prepares them for cross-functional endeavors in the future.

6. Bring in culture. Culture isn't just a buzzword; it's the heartbeat of your organization. Bring it center-stage during the onboarding saga. With a mere one-star spike in culture rating potentially retaining employees longer, this is an investment you would want to make. Anchor the cultural lessons with real-life tales, ensuring they resonate and linger.

7. Make sure they can give feedback. Cultivate a culture where the newcomers feel empowered to voice their observations. Encourage peer insights, making it clear that every perspective is valuable. Echo this sentiment by showcasing constructive feedback in action.

8. Set realistic expectations. Anticipate a learning curve. While we all wish for a rock star recruit who's instantly on fire, most need time to warm up. Understand that they're navigating unfamiliar waters, mastering new tools, and adjusting to fresh dynamics. Gift them patience and guidance.

9. Map the 30/60/90. Think of these check-ins as milestones, guiding them through their journey. Each checkpoint illuminates the path ahead, establishes performance expectations, and reaffirms their trajectory.

10. Institute the Buddy System. Starting fresh can be a cocktail of excitement and jitters. Offer them a guiding star, a mentor or buddy, someone they can turn to, confide in, and learn from. Whether it's a teammate or someone from a different department, ensure they have a companion to lean on.

11. Consistent interactions with their boss. Regular touchpoints with the manager ensure that the newcomer never feels adrift. These interactions serve as anchors, providing clarity, answering queries, and ensuring alignment. Start with a high-frequency cadence and adjust based on the recruit's comfort and needs.

Remember, onboarding is your symphony's opening note. Make it resonant, make it memorable, and you'll have an ensemble ready to create harmonious success stories.

# Starting 24/7 Support

Companies are increasingly finding their customer base scattered across different time zones. While it might be fine to start out with just offering support during your business hours in your home time zone, if you are growing and scaling it might not be something that lasts forever. But when should you consider hiring a customer support team across various time zones? And how do you discern if your current setup needs a revision? Let's dive in.

## Understanding the Need

Before diving into the strategies, it's vital to understand why you might need a 24/7 support system. Assessing this necessity entails an in-depth look into two primary factors: data patterns and global market influence.

### Data Patterns

Begin your assessment by analyzing the volume of support requests and, importantly, their timing. Leveraging data analytics tools can help in recognizing patterns. For instance, if a high number of support tickets originate from Asia during its daytime, but it's nighttime in your region, you have an untapped support demand. This imbalance can lead to delayed responses and lower customer satisfaction.

## Global Market Influence

If you're pushing marketing efforts or launching products in specific global markets, anticipate a rise in customer interactions from those areas. Being proactive about offering timely support can make a significant difference in customer adoption and retention in new markets.

## Customer Feedback

One of the most authentic indicators of your support effectiveness is direct feedback from customers. Pay close attention to complaints or comments about slow response times or the unavailability of support agents during specific hours. Such feedback is a clarion call for recalibrating your support model. Periodically surveying your customers can offer a goldmine of insights. Simple questions about their experience with your support timing can offer a clear picture of where gaps might exist.

# Things to Be Mindful of

Embracing a 24/7 support model isn't merely about being available; it's about being prepared, sensitive, and efficient. Companies venturing into continuous support will encounter unique challenges that demand foresight and strategic thinking. As your organization seeks to seamlessly cater to global customers, there are certain intricacies that can make a monumental difference in the quality and efficiency of the support provided. Let's explore some of these crucial considerations:

## Cultural Sensitivity

Offering support that transcends time zones invariably means engaging with a diverse clientele. Each region or country comes with its set of customs, practices, and manners. For instance, greetings in Japan might differ vastly from those in Brazil. An understanding of such subtleties can enhance the customer experience and foster trust.

Similarly, while English might be a global business language, idiomatic expressions, phrases, or colloquialisms can differ. Agents must be trained not just in language but in context, ensuring they can resonate with customers authentically. If you are choosing a shift-based staffing model, rather than a "follow-the-sun" model (more in the next section!), this is particularly important to be mindful of.

## Communication Tools

Investing in tools for your team that help show time zones in a unified space (such as Google currently offers as a widget for their home screen) doesn't just help in tracking different time zones. It offers clarity, aids in scheduling, and ensures no region is unintentionally overlooked. Imagine if you hold a meeting at 9 a.m. every week because the majority of your company is based on the East Coast of the United States, but you have 20% of your staff living in Australia? That's an 11 p.m. meeting that they need to attend every week!

Beyond just tracking time, it's essential to have platforms that allow real-time and asynchronous communication. Tools like Slack, Microsoft Teams, or Trello (or whatever new and beautiful thing has been made since this book was written—looking at you, Hoop!) can keep your dispersed teams connected, fostering collaboration. Similarly, using tools that offer a centralized repository of information can ensure that team members, regardless of their time zone, have access to the same resources, ensuring consistency in support.

## Maintain Some Overlapping hours

It's vital that there's no abrupt end to a support query due to a shift change. Overlapping hours can ensure that ongoing issues are handed over seamlessly, and customers experience no disruptions.

Overlapping work hours also offer a window for teams to discuss, brainstorm, or simply catch up, promoting camaraderie and ensuring everyone feels part of the larger organization. Whether you do a follow-the-sun approach or a flexible staffing approach, this is extremely important!

Lastly, before jumping into hiring new team members, consider reevaluating your current team's schedules. Offering flexible scheduling options can reveal team members who might prefer, or even benefit from, unconventional hours. Flexible scheduling can improve job satisfaction, as it often aligns better with personal commitments or lifestyles. It can serve as an incentive and also foster loyalty.

As the adage goes, the devil is in the details. The success of a 24/7 support system isn't just in its implementation, but in the meticulous attention given to these considerations.

## Know Your Options

There is no one "true" way to offer 24/7 support, and you'll have a ton of options at your fingertips. Here are the most common ways that businesses staff 24/7 support, as well as their benefits and drawbacks.

In our always-on, hyper-connected world, businesses can no longer afford to confine themselves to the traditional 9-to-5 window. Customers are active around the clock, and they expect immediate support when issues arise, irrespective of the hour. By offering 24/7 support, companies can improve customer satisfaction, enhance their brand reputation, and capture opportunities from different time zones. But how can this be achieved efficiently and effectively? Let's explore the various ways to offer unwavering, round-the-clock support.

### Geographically Distributed Teams (Follow the Sun)

A geographically distributed support team, often referred to simply as a distributed team or a remote team, is a group of individuals who work across different geographical locations, time zones, or even countries, yet collaborate together to provide customer support. This structure is different from a traditional centralized support team where all members work from the same office or location.

**Benefits**
- Natural time zone coverage without requiring staff to work unconventional hours.
- Rich cultural insights for a diverse customer base.

**Challenges**
- Coordinating communication between dispersed teams.
- Managing and training teams remotely.

**Best Practices**
- Use tools like Slack or Microsoft Teams to maintain seamless communication.
- Set regular check-ins and virtual team-building activities.
- Employ a robust knowledge base to maintain consistency in support.

## Shift-Based Teams

A shift-based strategy revolves around organizing the support team's working hours into distinct blocks or shifts to ensure continuous coverage over extended periods. This approach is particularly prevalent in industries where constant support is crucial, such as healthcare, IT support, hospitality, and any other business with round-the-clock customer interactions.

**Benefits**
- All agents work from a central location.
- Easier coordination and training.

**Challenges**
- Shift work can affect employee morale if not managed effectively.
- Requires efficient scheduling to prevent overworking.

**Best Practices**

- Rotate shifts regularly to prevent burnout.
- Offer incentives for night shifts, such as shift allowances or additional breaks.
- Use scheduling tools to manage shifts efficiently.

## On-Call Support

An on-call support model for customer support refers to a system where specific team members are designated to be "on-call" outside of regular business hours to handle urgent issues or requests. This model ensures that critical customer concerns are addressed promptly, even if they arise outside the standard operational window. It is not an equal substitute for the support provided within the "operating hours" of a business, as traditionally on-call support folks will only handle critical situations, such as outages. For instance, at Trello we had one "on-call" support person who would handle critical issues that came up on the weekends, and notify the rest of the team if they needed back-up.

**Benefits**

- Not all agents are required to be active; only those on-call respond to issues.
- Can be cost-effective.

**Challenges**

- Unpredictable work patterns can lead to stress.
- Not suitable for businesses with high after-hours support requests.

**Best Practices**

- Set clear expectations and guidelines for on-call support.
- Rotate on-call responsibilities among team members.
- Compensate on-call agents appropriately for their flexibility.

## Outsourcing

Outsourcing for customer support refers to the practice of contracting an external company or individual(s) to handle certain customer service functions instead of managing them in-house. Companies often turn to outsourcing as a way to reduce costs, access specialized expertise, manage seasonal volume fluctuations, or expand their support coverage across different time zones and languages.

For more details on outsourcing or if it may be right for you, please have a look at our chapter on Outsourcing.

**Benefits**

- Leverage the expertise of specialized vendors.
- Cost-effective for many businesses.

**Challenges**

- Less control over customer interactions.
- Ensuring the third-party aligns with company values and quality standards.

**Best Practices**

- Regularly review performance metrics of the vendor.
- Conduct training sessions to align them with your brand's voice and values.
- Have a clear Service Level Agreement (SLA) in place.

## Hybrid Models

Combining two or more of the above strategies can sometimes provide the best results. For instance, a company might have a geographically distributed team handling most issues and use on-call support for specific high-level problems. We did this at Trello with great success. We also gave folks the opportunity to take on "optional" weekend work for an additional bonus to their weekly paycheck, or an extra day off to be used in the next month.

## Leveraging Technology

If you're not ready to offer full staffing in specific time zones, but still want to start helping larger segments of your customers, you may want to consider making use of technology. There are some great tools that either help your customers help themselves, or make it easier to offer information to them outside of hours.

### AI-powered Chatbots

Chatbots, driven by artificial intelligence, have emerged as virtual assistants that can interact with customers in real-time. They are programmed to understand and respond to user inputs, making them an invaluable asset for customer support. They are particularly useful for a few reasons:

- Chatbots can quickly respond to frequently asked questions or routine inquiries without the need for human intervention. This speeds up response times and ensures that customers get immediate answers.

- Unlike human agents, who can only handle one query at a time, chatbots can engage with multiple users simultaneously. This capability is especially useful during peak traffic times when the volume of requests is high.

- While chatbots are adept at managing standard queries, they are also designed to recognize when a problem is beyond their capability. In such instances, they can seamlessly direct the issue to a human agent, ensuring that complex problems receive the necessary expertise.

## Self-Service Portals

Self-service portals are dedicated platforms where customers can search for solutions to their problems without reaching out to customer support. These portals house a wealth of information, including FAQs, video tutorials, guides, and more. They are *also* great for a few reasons:

- By providing resources like how-to guides, troubleshooting steps, and FAQs, businesses empower customers to resolve their issues independently. This not only boosts customer satisfaction but also fosters a sense of autonomy.

- When customers find answers on their own, the overall number of queries directed to human agents decreases. This allows agents to focus on more complex and pressing issues, optimizing the overall efficiency of the support team.

## Predictive Support

Predictive support utilizes data analytics and machine learning to forecast potential issues and address them proactively. By analyzing historical data, user behavior, and other metrics, support teams can anticipate common problems before they escalate. Here are a few ways this could be beneficial for your team:

- Instead of waiting for customers to report issues, businesses can proactively reach out with solutions. This preemptive approach not only resolves issues faster but also shows customers that a business is attentive to their needs.

- Predictive support can lead to personalized customer interactions. For example, if data analytics indicate that a customer might face a particular problem, support teams can send tailored guides or tips, elevating the overall customer experience.

Offering 24/7 support isn't just a business choice; it's about genuinely caring for your customers. As people shop and seek assistance outside regular business hours, it's essential to be there for your customers, no matter where they are in the world. It's important to find a balance between what your team can handle and what your customers need. Doing this well can greatly improve customer happiness and trust in your business.

# Conducting Great 1:1s

As much as numbers like ticket resolutions and customer feedback scores matter, they shouldn't eclipse the humans behind the statistics. One-on-one (1:1) sessions are that vital bridge that connects the team leader with the individual team member. Let's dive into the art of holding 1:1s that truly resonate and foster a deeper connection:

Being on the front line, customer support professionals have their mettle tested daily. Regular 1:1s offer them an oasis amidst the hustle—a dedicated slot to express their feelings, aspirations, and concerns. This interaction isn't just about ticking a managerial box; it's about human connection. By fostering this bond, you can elevate not only an individual's performance but also their passion for their role.

## Schedule and Structure

Just like any other critical task, 1:1s should be embedded in your regular routine. Whether they're weekly or bi-weekly, maintaining a rhythm is essential. Allocate at least 30 minutes for each session. But here's a pro-tip: be flexible. For example, if a team member shares their struggles with the recent surge in support queries after a software upgrade, it's more valuable to stay and address it than to wrap up on time.

## Collaboration Over Dictation

Your 1:1 shouldn't feel like a lecture. Encourage team members to set the discussion's tone by asking them a day ahead about topics they would like to cover. As for you, come prepared with your points, which might range from their recent achievements to updates on organizational changes.

# Diving into the Discussion Points

## Performance Metrics

Kick things off with a review of their recent stats. Instead of just stating figures, spark a conversation. Ask, "I've noticed you've been closing tickets faster lately. What's your secret?" Or, "I've observed a slight drop in your customer feedback score this month. Let's brainstorm how to turn that around."

## Growth and Career Path

Pivot the discussion towards their aspirations. Pose questions like, "What's a skill you're eager to master this year?" or "Are there any side projects or roles you would like to explore?"

## Checking the Emotional Pulse

Sometimes, the most potent questions are the simplest. Asking, "How's everything going?" or "Are you finding your current workload sustainable?" can unravel deeper sentiments. Not everyone will be comfortable sharing with you right away. Continue to create space and let them know that it's okay to talk to you, and that you're ready to listen whenever they are ready.

# Mastering the Art of Listening

Being a great communicator isn't just about talking; it's majorly about listening. This means not just hearing the words but also tuning into the emotions behind them. If a team member expresses excitement about a task but sounds hesitant, dig deeper. Ask, "You sound thrilled about this project but a bit concerned, too. Want to discuss that?"

## Writing Down Key Takeaways

No, you're not jotting down minutes of the meeting. But capturing the essence of your discussion, the challenges acknowledged, and the solutions proposed ensures clarity and commitment from both ends.

## Post 1:1

A fruitful 1:1 doesn't end when you leave the room. The real testament of its success is in the follow-through. If you've promised any resources or agreed upon any changes, ensure they materialize before you meet again. Actions, as they say, speak volumes.

While dashboards and scorecards have their place, the heart of customer support thrives on human interactions. Skillful 1:1s don't just nurture your team's professional growth but also enrich the very fabric of your organizational culture. So, next time you're about to step into a 1:1, remember that it's more than a meeting; it's an opportunity to inspire, connect, and elevate. Make it count!

## Annual Reviews

Yearly reviews for your customer support staff aren't just about reflecting on past achievements, but also about paving the way for future success. They're a prime opportunity for managers and employees to align on goals, celebrate accomplishments, and identify areas for improvement. Here's a comprehensive guide to conducting outstanding annual reviews for your customer support personnel.

Annual reviews aren't mere formalities—they serve multiple purposes:

- Employee Development: Pinpoint areas of improvement and growth.
- Goal Alignment: Ensure everyone is on the same page regarding company and department objectives.

- Feedback Exchange: Provide a structured platform for bidirectional feedback.
- Preparation: The Key to a Successful Review

The foundation of a fruitful annual review lies in thorough preparation:

1. Self-Assessment First. Before the review, ask the employee to complete a self-assessment. It's a chance for them to reflect on their accomplishments, challenges, and areas they would like to focus on.
2. Gather Data. Arm yourself with statistics and data points. How many tickets did they handle? What was the average resolution time? Were there any recurring issues? Numbers provide clarity and reduce bias.
3. Feedback from Peers. Incorporate insights from team members who regularly collaborate with the employee. This 360-degree feedback can offer a more holistic view.

## Structure of the Review

1. Begin Positively

Start with a genuine acknowledgment of the employee's contributions over the past year. Maybe they stepped up during a particularly challenging product launch, or perhaps they consistently maintained high customer satisfaction scores.

2. Dive into the Data

Share the quantitative data you've gathered. Discuss the highs and lows. For example: "You managed to handle X number of tickets this year, which is a 20% increase from last year. However, I've noticed that during peak times, resolution time tends to lag. Let's discuss ways to address this."

3. Feedback Exchange

Go over the feedback from peers. Also, give the employee an opportunity to share their perspective on the feedback they've received, both from peers and from you.

4. Discuss the Self-Assessment

This part is crucial. By discussing their self-assessment, you show that you value their self-awareness and insights. Explore areas where their self-perception might diverge from the feedback, as these can be rich areas for growth.

5. Future Planning

Ask questions like, "Where do you see yourself next year? What skills would you like to develop?" This not only gives the employee a forward vision but also helps align their aspirations with company goals.

6. Address Concerns and Provide Support

Finally, discuss any concerns the employee might have and brainstorm solutions together. This might involve further training, modifying workflows, or providing additional resources.

## Additional Tips for an Effective Review

- Maintain a Constructive Tone: The review should be a balance of positive reinforcement and constructive feedback.
- Be Specific: Whether praising or providing feedback, be precise. Instead of saying "You did great," say "Your proactive approach in handling the system outage last month was outstanding."
- Stay Objective: Keep personal biases at bay. Stick to facts, data, and direct observations.
- Two-way Communication: Encourage dialogue. The employee should feel they have a voice in the process.

Post-review, provide a summary of the discussion, including key takeaways and agreed-upon action items. Set a timeline for these actions and check in periodically to ensure progress. The annual review shouldn't be an isolated event, but rather a springboard for ongoing development.

Annual reviews, when conducted thoughtfully, can be a catalyst for growth, alignment, and enhanced performance. For customer support employees, who often face the brunt of customer frustrations and rapidly changing scenarios, these reviews are pivotal in ensuring that they feel valued, heard, and equipped for success. Invest time and effort into these reviews, and you'll cultivate a motivated, aligned, and high-performing customer support team.

## How Much Should You Pay?

Compensation is a crucial topic when discussing terms with potential employees. Everyone wants to be paid fairly—totally understandable. However, an intriguing study from Northeastern University suggests that if you pay a person fairly right at the start, you are unlikely to see any kind of salary frustration from them as they grow their career within your business. So, it's super important to strike the right note from the beginning. But how do you do it?

Personally, I have always been inspired by Buffer's approach of transparent salary scales. While they've refined their method over time, the core principle of prioritizing employee fairness has been consistent.

Buffer's current model calculates the salary in this manner:

- They begin with half the standard salary for the role, referencing San Francisco's market rates.
- This figure is then adjusted based on the cost of living where the employee resides. For instance, living in an expensive city like New York would mean no adjustment (a 100% multiplier). In contrast, living in a moderately priced city like Nashville leads to an 85% multiplier. If you're in a more affordable suburb, like

those surrounding Atlanta, you would receive 75% of the San Francisco benchmark.

- Factor in the specific role and the employee's experience in that role. So, an experienced Director will earn more than someone new to support as a whole.

Think about those core tenets as you start to craft your strategy. Even if your team works in one central location, the cost-of-living adjustments can be applied based on your city's economic context. CX as an industry is tragically underpaid. If you work to break that cycle, you may see some truly delighted employees.

# Avoiding Burnout

Consistently fostering a team that offers exceptional support is both an art and science. Central to this goal is ensuring their mental and emotional well-being. Here's an in-depth exploration of strategies that can help your team remain vibrant and prevent the lurking shadow of burnout.

## Team Building

Team building often elicits images of outdated, cringe-worthy corporate exercises. However, beneath the stereotype lies an effective method for strengthening team cohesion and boosting morale. Team building is not about hasty, occasional initiatives; it's about consistently fostering an environment of trust and mutual respect.

While a portion of the workforce may roll their eyes at traditional activities, modern team-building exercises, when executed thoughtfully, have proven results. Instead of one-size-fits-all approaches, the focus should be on inclusive activities that resonate with everyone. Activities like volunteering not only unite teams for a noble cause but also elevate the team's sense of purpose beyond the daily grind.

## Follow Maslow

At first glance, Maslow's Hierarchy of Needs might seem far removed from the corporate world. However, this theory provides a profound framework to ensure your team's holistic well-being. From basic physiological needs to the pursuit of self-actualization, understanding these levels offers insights into what truly motivates and satisfies your team.

The workplace, contrary to common misconceptions, can cater to every tier of Maslow's pyramid. By ensuring a safe and comfortable working environment, recognizing achievements, fostering positive peer relationships, and supporting personal growth, leaders can help team members navigate towards self-actualization. When employees feel their needs are recognized and addressed, they are more likely to invest emotionally and intellectually in their roles.

## It's Dangerous to Go Alone! Take This!

Every professional, like an artisan, requires the right tools to craft their masterpiece. When employees are continuously making do with inadequate tools or resources, it not only affects efficiency but also chips away at morale. An employee, when empowered with the right tools, can transform from being merely functional to exceptionally productive.

However, providing tools isn't just about physical resources. It's also about being receptive to their feedback and understanding the challenges they face. If an employee suggests something that might streamline their workflow, it's worth considering. By doing so, you demonstrate that the company values their expertise and is invested in their success.

## Give them Props

Recognition is a universal motivator. When achievements, no matter how small, are acknowledged, it reinforces the individual's value within the team. Moreover, rewards, both tangible and intangible, can amplify this positive sentiment, leading to increased motivation and commitment.

But appreciation isn't just about grand gestures. Sometimes, a simple "thank you" or acknowledgment in a team meeting can make a world of difference. The key is to foster a culture where efforts don't go unnoticed. In doing so, employees not only feel valued but also share a sense of belonging and purpose.

## Don't Understaff

Strategic staffing is more than just filling roles. It's about anticipating needs, understanding workflow patterns, and ensuring that no team member feels overwhelmed. Adequate staffing can mean the difference between a team that's constantly firefighting and one that's proactive and engaged.

By employing data-driven insights, like understanding peak work times or gauging the average workload of team members, managers can make informed decisions. Proper staffing ensures that employees can comfortably take time off without leaving the team in a lurch. Such planning conveys the crucial message: the company cares for its employees' well-being.

## Provide Clarity

Clear goals are akin to a lighthouse, offering direction amidst the chaos. Ambiguity can be a silent demotivator, leading to confusion and diminishing morale. On the other hand, well-defined objectives serve as a rallying point, aligning efforts and fostering a sense of collective purpose.

Goals should not only be clear but also measurable. Instead of vague aspirations, metric-based targets provide clarity and a sense of purpose. By setting achievable benchmarks, you give the team a clear vision to strive towards and celebrate when these milestones are reached.

## Help Them Develop

For many, a static role can lead to a feeling of stagnation. Growth opportunities, both in terms of role and skills, can rekindle passion and commitment. By delineating clear career paths and growth trajectories, you empower employees to envision a future within the organization.

Moreover, it's vital to allocate time for professional development within the regular work schedule. This approach not only enhances skills but also underscores the company's investment in its employees' futures. Whether it's workshops, courses, or certifications, these opportunities can re-energize and motivate team members.

## Don't Ditch 1:1s

One-on-ones offer more than just status updates. These sessions can be platforms for genuine dialogue, feedback, and mutual growth. A well-structured one-on-one, characterized by openness and candor, can unearth concerns, aspirations, and insights that might otherwise remain hidden. Never skip a 1:1 if you can help it, and avoid rescheduling them—this *can* signal to your employee that their time is less valuable than yours, or that you don't care as much about the meeting as they do.

While it's essential for managers to guide the conversation, it's equally crucial to listen. These sessions should foster a two-way dialogue where both parties feel heard and valued. By demonstrating genuine interest in employee perspectives and challenges, managers solidify trust and mutual respect.

## Advocate for Downtime

Rest isn't merely a break from work; it's an essential component of productivity. Encouraging employees to take regular vacations is about more than just personal well-being; it's also about long-term professional sustainability. A well-rested individual returns with fresh perspectives and rejuvenated energy, ready to tackle challenges head-on.

Promoting a culture where vacations are not just a perk but a recommended practice requires leadership buy-in. At Zapier they support unlimited vacation by requiring that team members take *at least* two weeks, rather than not tracking it at all.

It's essential to dismantle the unspoken narrative where taking time off might be seen as a sign of a lack of commitment. Instead, by valuing and promoting rest, you reinforce the idea that the organization values its employees' holistic well-being.

By embracing these strategies with sincerity, leaders can create an environment where employees feel valued, understood, and empowered. The end goal is not merely to prevent burnout but to foster a vibrant, motivated, and contented team.

Alright, we've covered a lot of ground. We've laid out our support stack, picked out the essential tools, and got a game plan for building and maintaining a stellar team. That's a great start! But here's the deal: setting things up is only half the battle.

Remember the golden rule? "You can't manage what you don't measure." So, the next logical step is to get a grip on our metrics. Think of them as the dashboard of your car. You wouldn't drive without checking your speed or fuel levels, right? Metrics will show us how well we're doing and where we might need a tune-up.

As we dive into the upcoming chapters, we'll get hands-on with these metrics. We'll look at why they matter and how to use them effectively. Building is important, but measuring and tweaking based on real data? That's where the magic happens. Let's keep this momentum going and dive into the data-driven side of things.

# CHAPTER 6:

# What to Measure

Data serves as a compass guiding you towards improved service, efficiency, and customer satisfaction. It offers a clear, objective snapshot of where you are and the areas that require attention. With data, you're not just shooting in the dark; you're making informed decisions based on concrete evidence. For businesses striving for continuous improvement, it's essential to understand that every interaction, feedback, and resolution carries invaluable insights. By harnessing this data, you position your support system to be more responsive to the ever-changing needs and preferences of your clientele.

Often one of the first things that will get pushed off is creating meaningful reporting around data for your customer experience team. There are always "more pressing" fires to put out, especially in the early days. However, one of the biggest mistakes that most smaller organizations make is not taking the time to put some reporting in place to make things easier for themselves in the future.

Don't wait until you *need* informed, formalized, data-driven dashboards to start creating them. It will take you much longer to set up and organize with your now mountains of existing data than it would have been to set up guardrails when you were just starting out. You will end up in "tech debt," as we mentioned in our starting chapter.

Not familiar with tech debt? Lucky you! Tech debt isn't just a buzzword; it's a genuine concern for organizations looking to optimize their support processes. Tech debt is the accumulated costs and long-term consequences of using outdated or ineffective technology. This can hinder the collection and analysis of accurate data, ultimately limiting the growth potential of your customer support initiatives. Say, for instance, you're using a manual spreadsheet to track your CSAT and report on it. Not only does it slow down operations, but it might also not integrate well with modern analytics tools, leading to missed opportunities. By addressing tech debt, you're ensuring that your tools and systems are streamlined, efficient, and primed to handle the data-driven demands of modern customer support.

## Agent, Team, and Operational Performance

When considering what to measure for your team, it is important to take metrics that reflect on each of the different areas of your team: agent, team, and operational performance. The first, agent performance, highlights individual strengths and areas for potential training. Next, team performance provides a broader view, focusing on the collective efficiency of the team and offers insights into the team's overall effectiveness and collaboration. Lastly, operational performance offers a macro view, assessing the support ecosystem's backbone, from resource allocation and tech efficiency to overarching support strategies. Together, these three avenues provide a holistic understanding, enabling managers to make informed decisions that enhance overall support quality.

### Agent

Understanding the nuances of agent performance is crucial in CX. At the heart of this assessment lies the individual, and it's the metrics related to them that play a pivotal role. Resolution time stands as a testament to an agent's efficiency. A lower resolution time indicates a swift understanding and solving of customer queries, while a prolonged time might signify a need for more training or resources. Customer feedback is another goldmine of insights. Positive feedback celebrates the agent's capabilities, while constructive feedback provides a roadmap for improvement. Lastly, ticket volume can reveal an agent's workload. Monitoring this ensures that no agent is overwhelmed, which can otherwise impact service quality. By closely watching these metrics, managers can pinpoint specific areas of strength and opportunities for growth on an individual level.

## Team

When you zoom out from individual agents, you transition into the scope of team performance. This broad view is vital to understand the collective strength and potential areas of growth for the entire support unit. The average handle time serves as a composite measure, reflecting the team's collective efficiency in handling queries. A shorter average indicates streamlined processes and effective teamwork, while a prolonged average might highlight areas needing intervention or training. Customer satisfaction scores shed light on the cumulative impact of every interaction. High scores celebrate the team's collaborative efforts, while lower scores might signal the need for improved training or strategy. By evaluating these and other team-centric metrics, managers gain a panoramic view of the team's effectiveness, enabling them to implement strategies that bolster collective success.

## Operational Performance

Operational performance transcends individual and team metrics to offer a holistic view of the entire support ecosystem. This assessment is vital for ensuring that the infrastructure supporting the agents is optimized for success. Resource allocation is at the heart of this, as it determines how tools, training, and time are distributed among the team. Proper allocation ensures each agent has the necessary tools and knowledge to excel. Tech efficiency dives into the software and hardware in play. Are the current systems enabling agents, or are they causing hindrances? Lastly, the overall support strategy dictates how the team approaches customer queries, complaints, and feedback.

An effective strategy will be proactive, data-driven, and flexible to changing customer needs. By understanding these operational metrics, managers can ensure that both the agents and the systems supporting them are aligned for maximum efficacy.

Creating a reporting strategy that reflects each of these three facets of your team's performance is incredibly important. If you are really clued into agent performance, for instance, but not so tuned in to how your team is performing operationally, you may be taken by surprise when things like busy seasons, or outages, arise.

## Selecting the Right Metrics

Measuring the effectiveness of your customer support team goes beyond just numbers; it's about understanding the story behind those numbers and ensuring they lead to genuine service improvements. The metrics you choose act as a roadmap, guiding the team's behaviors, priorities, and strategies. Selecting the right metrics is super important.

The metrics you choose must be directly aligned with your organization's customer service objectives. If your primary goal is to increase customer satisfaction, your metrics should focus on factors that directly influence that outcome, such as first-call resolution rate or average response time. By tailoring your metrics to your strategic objectives, you ensure that your team is always moving in the direction that brings the most value to your customers and your business.

However, while it's essential to incentivize the right behaviors through metrics, there's a flip side. Overemphasizing certain metrics can inadvertently lead to problematic behaviors within the team. For instance, if you over-incentivize response time, you might find that agents prioritize speed over quality. They might rush through interactions, offering quick but ineffective solutions just to boost their numbers. This can lead to repeated customer issues, increasing dissatisfaction in the long run.

Moreover, focusing narrowly on a single metric can obscure other vital aspects of service. A team might boast excellent response times, but if those rapid responses are routinely ineffective or unsatisfactory, the customer experience suffers. It's like praising a medic for quick response times while ignoring the patients' health outcomes.

Regularly assess where your team's major areas of opportunity are. This can be done by implementing QA (see the section in Chapter 4 on QA), or by regularly reviewing your help desk tag volume and customer reviews.

Picking the right metrics is a balancing act. It's about ensuring that the metrics reflect genuine value, drive beneficial behaviors, and resonate with the broader objectives of your organization. By being thoughtful in metric selection and wary of potential pitfalls like over-incentivization, you can ensure that your customer support team remains on a path that benefits both your customers and your business.

We have tried to include key metrics and KPIs to use to measure each of the individual aspects of this book. If there is something particular that you are looking for inspiration on, please use the Index to find it! Or, better yet, read through and highlight the ones that seem particularly interesting or helpful for your team.

## Defining the Scope and Responsibilities of Your Team

The folks on support teams are used to being the Swiss army knife in the lives of their friends and family. They are the folks that people call when their iPhone isn't working, or they aren't able to forward emails anymore. In the workplace, this can show up by having support get their hands into a little bit of everything. Some companies do this intentionally with a "support embed" program, where folks from the support team sit in on other teams' meetings in order to understand and be more closely related to them. However, if you *aren't* doing this intentionally, and things just fall to your support team because they are available, you need to take some time to set some boundaries and scope around your team.

Not only does it help with keeping your team from getting dragged into work that isn't theirs, but when everyone knows their role and its boundaries, the team functions like a well-oiled machine. But how do you establish these parameters effectively?

## Start with the Customers

Before you can define the scope of your support team, you need to understand your customers. What are the common issues they face? How do they prefer to communicate? By conducting regular feedback sessions, surveys, or leveraging data analytics, you can gain insights into their needs. This will help you establish a foundation upon which to build your team's responsibilities. You'll know exactly what your customers care about, which will help you understand where you need to put most of your resources and attention.

For instance, if none of your customers care about getting quick chat responses, but they *do* care about reading useful content on your blog, you might deprioritize helping the sales team get that Hubspot bot out the door, and focus more on helping marketing write up more evergreen product content.

## Set Clear Objectives

What do you want your support team to achieve? Whether it's reducing resolution time, improving customer satisfaction scores, or increasing first-contact resolution rates, set clear, measurable objectives. With clear goals, it's easier to delineate responsibilities that align with achieving these objectives.

Many companies use frameworks like OKRs, SMART goals, MBOs, or balanced scorecards to break larger, meatier "company" goals into smaller, more attainable team or individual goals. Once you have a clear understanding of customer needs and objectives, list all the tasks required to meet them. This might range from responding to emails, handling live chats, troubleshooting specific issues, or managing feedback. Once listed, categorize them by specialization or skill set. This categorization makes it simpler to assign tasks to team members based on their strengths.

## Set (and Hold) Your Boundaries

Customer support often intertwines with other departments like sales, product development, or marketing. It's essential to set clear boundaries. For instance, while the support team can gather product feedback, it might be the product development team's responsibility to implement changes. Clearly define where one team's role ends, and another's begins, to avoid overlaps and conflicts. If you can document these processes and put them in a shared, entire-company-accessible place, that's even better.

Come to a mutual agreement rather than your team just defining the process and handing it over to the other. When there is mutual buy-in, it makes starting up a process that could certainly cause some pain in its very early stages slightly less painful.

## Regularly Review

I feel like a bit of a broken record at this point, but the business landscape, especially in the tech world, changes rapidly. As products evolve and customer needs shift, the responsibilities of your support team will also need adjustments. Schedule regular reviews of your support scope. Assess what's working and what isn't. Maybe there's a new channel of communication that customers prefer, or perhaps a set responsibility is no longer relevant. By keeping your finger on the pulse, you ensure your team remains agile and effective.

Defining the scope and responsibilities of your support team is not a one-time task but an ongoing process. It's akin to setting the rules of a game—everyone knows their part, understands the goal, and collaborates efficiently. By staying proactive and receptive to change, you can ensure your support team remains a beacon of excellence, driving customer satisfaction and loyalty.

# Integrating Support with Other Teams

The harmonious collaboration of various departments within a company is essential for success. Connecting product teams—and indeed, all other departments—with support teams stands at the forefront of importance. Working together, your CX team and other teams pave the way for seamless customer experiences and work together to refine product quality. Additionally, such interconnectedness is integral to a successful company, where teams understand and support the overarching goals and visions of the organization, and work together to achieve them.

As companies evolve and grow, identifying and implementing strategies to bridge the potential gaps between these teams becomes paramount. Here are some of the most effective strategies to ensure smooth inter-departmental operations and bolster customer satisfaction:

1. Regular cross-team meetings. Hold periodic cross-functional meetings where product and support teams can discuss feedback, share insights, and jointly plan the way forward. This encourages collaboration and fosters a better understanding of challenges and opportunities from both ends. Make sure they go both ways. While support should certainly have prioritized time to share direct customer feedback, your product team should also have the space to show off new features, get feedback, and work with your support team to make sure that team education and documentation are where they need to be.

2. Integrated feedback loop. Implement a structured process for the support team to gather customer feedback and share it with the other teams. This ensures that the product team gets actionable insights to improve product features, fix bugs, and prioritize development efforts, as well as other teams (like marketing) having resources to make their projects better and more customer-aligned.

3. Joint training sessions. Conduct sessions where product teams can train support and marketing teams on new features or changes. Conversely, support teams can educate other teams on common customer issues and challenges. Not only will everyone's education be leveled, but so will everyone's empathy. When you're forced to take a walk in somebody's shoes, it creates a deeper understanding of each other's roles.

4. Unified communication. This really goes without saying, but use tools like Slack, Microsoft Teams, or Trello to create shared channels or boards for real-time communication. This facilitates quick problem-solving, idea sharing, and keeping everyone on the same page. This is especially important if something is changing in your product, there is an outage, or your support team is just seeing a spike in volume.

5. Shared KPIs and goals. We've talked a lot about the specific metrics that teams can track, and the best ways to put them in place—but that's just at your individual team level. Consider creating shared objectives that both teams can work towards. For instance, if reducing customer complaints about a specific product feature is a goal, both teams should be accountable. Shared KPIs encourage collaboration and mutual responsibility, and open up space for more candid conversation.

6. Embed team members. We mentioned this earlier, and it certainly isn't for everyone. However, sometimes it can be really impactful to embed a member from the support team within the product team and vice versa. This "exchange program" helps both teams gain first-hand experience of the challenges and processes of the other, leading to increased empathy and understanding.

7. Customer-centric workshops. Organize workshops focused on customer journey mapping, personas, or pain points. Analyzing the customer experience cross-functionally helps in identifying

areas of improvement and aligns all teams towards the ultimate goal: customer satisfaction. Plus, there are things that folks from other teams might recognize that wouldn't even be noticeable to others. For instance, your marketing team might notice the exact way that something is worded, whereas your support team may see something as being unfriendly-to-the-customer when others wouldn't.

8. Access to product roadmaps. Give support and marketing teams access to product roadmaps. This way, they're prepared for what's coming, can preemptively address customer queries, and provide feedback on potential challenges they foresee. They can also plan out the amount of time that they will need when creating resources like documentation, videos, or FAQ pages.

9. Celebrate wins together. When a product enhancement, based on customer feedback, results in positive reviews or decreased complaints, celebrate it together. Similarly, if your team implements some new technology or strategy that improves *their* metrics, take the time to celebrate it. Recognizing collaborative achievements boosts morale and fosters camaraderie.

10. Feedback repository. Maintain a centralized repository where all customer feedback, complaints, and suggestions are stored. Make sure it's accessible to all teams, and everyone feels comfortable asking or discussing what you receive. Over time, this repository becomes a gold mine of insights, helping in data-driven decision-making.

11. Customer shadowing. Allow product teams to occasionally shadow support teams during customer interactions. This firsthand exposure to customer issues, complaints, and feedback can be an eye-opener and can shape product strategy effectively. Often it can be one thing to hear a support person complain about frequency of issues, but for a person responsible for

building something seeing the immediate pain it causes in the day-to-day can be much more impactful.

Getting support teams to work closely with other teams in the company is like getting all the members of a new band playing together. It's not just about making things run smoothly; it's about making sure everyone's on the same page, playing to the same tune. When teams chat and share more, they get a clearer picture of what customers like and what tweaks they need to make.

Remember, this isn't just a one-off thing. Markets change, customers' tastes evolve, and we've got to keep up with the beat. To get this right: keep at it, have everyone on board, and make sure you're always thinking about what's best for the customer.

# CHAPTER 7:

# The Finances of CX

Businesses are constantly seeking avenues to differentiate themselves and establish unique value propositions. Among these avenues, CX has emerged as a cornerstone for sustainable growth and brand loyalty (reference: Forrester Research, CX Index). Yet, as with any strategic initiative, the question invariably arises: what is the return on our investment? How do our efforts in enhancing customer experience translate to tangible financial benefits for the organization?

Understanding the financial dimensions of a CX strategy is not just about budgeting or measuring returns. It's about tying the ethereal aspects of customer emotions, perceptions, and experiences to concrete numbers that decision-makers, stakeholders, and even front-line teams can rally behind. This chapter delves deep into the intricate balance between the investments made in CX and the direct and indirect financial outcomes they generate. As we navigate through the financial intricacies of building and sustaining a CX team, we'll discover how to match these with the overarching business metrics that define a company's success.

The intention is to equip you, the reader, with the knowledge and tools to craft a CX strategy that is not only emotionally resonant and impactful but also financially sound and sustainable. Whether you are starting from scratch or looking to refine an existing strategy, understanding the financial dynamics is paramount. Let's embark on this journey to discover the fiscal side of memorable customer experiences.

## The Profit and Loss Statement

Okay, let's chat about why those in charge of Customer Experience (CX) should care about the often daunting world of Profit and Loss (P&L) statements. At first glance, CX—the center of customer happiness and brand love—might seem worlds apart from the dry numbers of finance. But, imagine you're spearheading a new project to improve customer support. It's not just about making customers smile; it's also about ensuring the numbers make sense. Can we afford it? Will it bring in more cash in the long run? That's where the P&L comes in. It tells you where the money's coming from, where it's going, and how much is left at the end of the day.

Having a grip on the P&L means that you are able to contextually understand where CX fits within the rest of the business, as well as being able to contribute more meaningfully to broader conversations about the future goals of the business. It enables you to see the bigger picture and make decisions that are good for customers and the bottom line, all while up-leveling your leadership by understanding the business as a whole. Let's dive in and break it all down, shall we?

## Understanding the Basics of P&L Statements

A Profit and Loss statement, often referred to as the income statement, offers a summarized view of a company's financial performance over a specified time frame. It's a crucial tool that showcases revenues, costs, and expenses, helping stakeholders understand how much profit or loss was generated. Here's a cheat sheet for a few key terms you might hear folks talk about:

- Revenues (or Sales): The top line of the P&L, representing the total income from goods sold or services provided during a particular period.
- Cost of Goods Sold (COGS): Direct costs associated with producing the goods or services sold by a company.
- Gross Profit: Obtained by subtracting COGS from Revenues.
- Operating Expenses: Includes Research and Development (R&D), Selling, General & Administrative (SG&A) expenses.

- Net Income (or Profit): Calculated by subtracting all expenses, including taxes and other non-operating costs, from the gross profit.

## Important Concepts for CX Leaders to Grasp

- Variable vs. Fixed Costs. While variable costs fluctuate based on production or sales volume (like raw materials or sales commissions), fixed costs remain unchanged regardless of the volume of production or sales (like rent or salaries). We go into this in detail in the following sections.
- Break-Even Point. The point where total revenues equal total costs, indicating that the business is neither making a profit nor a loss. It's vital for CX leaders to understand this, as enhancing CX might involve additional costs, which would, in turn, influence the break-even point.
- Operating Margin. Represents how much profit a company makes from its core business operations. A deeper insight into the operating margin can offer CX leaders a perspective on how much room there is to invest in CX initiatives without jeopardizing profitability.

## How CX Fits into the P&L

There are a few overarching ways that CX usually fits into a business' P&L:

- Revenues. Enhanced CX strategies can drive higher customer retention, leading to increased repeat purchases and, consequently, elevated revenues. For example, if a revamped customer support strategy results in a 10% increase in customer retention and each customer accounts for an average of $500 in sales, that's a significant boost in revenues.
- Cost of Goods Sold (COGS). Superior CX can streamline processes, potentially reducing COGS. An efficient feedback

mechanism, for instance, can lead to product improvements that reduce returns and associated costs.

- Operating Expenses. Investment in CX might initially raise operating expenses due to expenditures on tools, training, or campaigns. However, the long-term payoffs, such as reduced customer churn and increased word-of-mouth referrals, often outweigh these costs.

- Net Income. By driving customer loyalty and streamlining operations, effective CX initiatives can indirectly boost the net income. A study might reveal, for instance, that customers who have had a positive onboarding experience are 20% less likely to churn, translating to significant savings and increased profits in the long run.

Now that you have a high-level understanding of what you might see on a P&L, let's step into exploring the different smaller components that will be helpful for you to know.

## Understanding Your Costs

In order to strategically allocate resources and measure return on investment, understanding the nuances of CX team costs is essential. These costs can be categorized into direct costs, indirect costs, and variable costs—all terms that will be familiar to anyone who has ever worked with an accountant or done bookkeeping on their own. Let's dive deeper into each, elucidating them with examples and methods of calculation.

### Direct Costs

Direct costs are expenses that can be directly attributed to CX activities and are typically the most straightforward to calculate.

### Salaries

The most prominent direct cost, salaries encompass the wages of every member on your CX team, from managers and strategists to front-line representatives.

**Example**: If you have a team of five CX professionals with an average salary of $60,000 per annum, your annual direct cost from salaries is $300,000.

### Tools

These are the platforms and software used by the CX team, such as Customer Relationship Management (CRM) systems, feedback collection tools, or AI chatbots.

**Example**: A CRM subscription costing $1,000 per month would total $12,000 annually.

### Training

This encompasses any training programs or courses that CX teams might require to enhance their skills or understand the latest industry trends.

**Example**: If you invest in a yearly training program for your team costing $500 per member, for a team of five, this would amount to $2,500.

## Indirect Costs

Indirect costs, on the other hand, are not exclusively dedicated to CX activities but are spread across multiple departments or projects.

### Shared Resources

These could include shared digital platforms, co-working spaces, or even shared administrative support.

For example: If you have an office space that houses multiple teams, including CX, and costs $10,000 a month, and the CX team occupies 25%

of this space, the indirect cost allocation to the CX team would be $2,500 monthly or $30,000 annually.

### Overhead

These are the general operational costs, encompassing utilities, management salaries, or even company-wide subscriptions that benefit all departments.

Method of Calculation: Allocate these costs based on the proportion of the company's resources the CX team utilizes. For instance, if the CX team consists of 10% of the company's entire workforce, it would be reasonable to allocate 10% of the overhead costs to the CX team.

## Variable Costs

Variable costs are dependent on the specific initiatives or campaigns the CX team undertakes and can fluctuate based on volume or frequency.

### Campaigns

These are specific initiatives aimed at enhancing customer experience. It could be a product launch, software update announcements, or customer feedback drives.

**Example**: If you run a quarterly CX improvement campaign that costs $5,000 each time, your annual variable cost from these campaigns would be $20,000.

### Promotions

Special offers, discounts, or loyalty program initiatives aimed at improving customer retention and experience.

**Example**: Offering a 10% discount to long-time customers on a new service might cost your firm $10 per customer. If 1,000 customers avail of it, the cost is $10,000.

### Surveys

Research initiatives to gather customer feedback or measure satisfaction levels.

**Example**: Using a third-party service to conduct a comprehensive customer satisfaction survey might cost $7,000 annually.

When constructing a CX budget or evaluating the financial performance of your CX team, a deep understanding of these costs is paramount. By breaking down and regularly reviewing each category, businesses can not only allocate resources more efficiently but also find opportunities to optimize expenses and boost the effectiveness of their CX initiatives.

## CX's Impact on Sales and Growth

Any conversation about the cost structure of CX is incomplete without delving into its revenue implications. An efficient CX strategy isn't just about managing costs; it's about amplifying revenues. It serves as a catalyst for business growth in a multitude of ways, from fostering customer loyalty to extending customer lifetime value (CLV). Let's explore these facets in greater depth.

### Retention

Customer retention is akin to the heart's rhythm for any business—it ensures sustainability, long-term engagement, and profitability. Every single interaction between a brand and its customers acts as a checkpoint. A negative experience might divert the customer to a competitor, but a positive one has the potential to cement loyalty, making them more inclined to not just return but also advocate for the brand.

#### Factors Influencing Retention through CX

- Consistency: Customers expect a consistent experience. Whether it's the third or the thirtieth interaction, the quality of experience should be uniform. This predictability builds trust.

- Personalization: Recognizing returning customers and tailoring experiences based on their preferences can enhance loyalty. For instance, e-commerce platforms suggesting products based on past purchases can lead to increased sales.
    - Feedback Loops: Regularly collecting and acting upon feedback shows customers that their opinions are valued. This not only rectifies issues but often results in improved customer loyalty.
- Post-Purchase Engagement: Retention doesn't end with a sale. Post-purchase communication, support, and services can greatly influence a customer's decision to return.
- Brand Promise: Does the product deliver on the value that is promised?

Consider the hypothetical scenario of a business that achieved a 10% increase in repeat customers due to improved CX initiatives:

**Backdrop**: A small DTC peanut-roasting business typically sees 1,000 repeat customers annually. These customers, over the years, have come to trust the brand, largely due to the consistent value they receive. However, as the market grows competitive, there's a need for the brand to go the extra mile.

**CX Initiatives**: The brand decides to step into the modern era and introduces a loyalty program, enhances post-purchase communication, and offers personalized discounts to repeat buyers. As a result, the customer base becomes more engaged and feels valued.

**Outcome**: These CX strategies lead to a 10% increase in repeat customers. Now, if each of these customers spends an average of $200, the impact of the CX enhancements can be quantified.

An additional 10% of the original 1,000 repeat customers means 100 more repeat customers.

- With each spending $200, the revenue generated from these additional customers alone is $20,000.

**Method of Calculation:**

The formula encapsulates this increase: (Percentage Increase in Repeat Customers) × (Average Spend per Repeat Customer) × (Original Number of Repeat Customers)

In this case: (10/100) × $200 × 1,000 = $20,000

## Increasing LTV

The journey of customer loyalty extends far beyond the initial interaction or the first purchase. At its core, an effective CX strategy understands this continuity and aims to keep the customer engaged, ensuring they return time and time again. By doing so, businesses not only secure a sale but also lay the foundation for long-lasting relationships, turning a momentary transaction into a continuum of brand experiences and sales.

### Factors Influencing Repeat Purchases through Enhanced CX:

- Seamless User Experience: Whether it's the user-friendliness of a website, the ease of finding products, or the simplicity of the checkout process, a hassle-free user experience can influence customers to return.

- Reward Programs: Offering reward points, loyalty discounts, or exclusive member offers can provide customers with a tangible incentive to come back.

- Quality Assurance: Ensuring that the product or service consistently meets or exceeds expectations is a surefire way to gain repeat business.

- Proactive Customer Support: Addressing concerns even before they arise, or promptly resolving them when they do, can significantly enhance a customer's trust and likelihood to repurchase.

Consider a business where a satisfied customer typically makes two purchases a year, each amounting to $150.

**Backdrop:** This customer has been consistent in their purchasing pattern, driven by the existing quality of service and product. However, as the competition intensifies and options multiply, there's a greater onus on brands to keep their customers engaged.

**CX Initiatives**: The business introduces a multi-pronged approach. They revamp their loyalty program, offering exclusive deals to frequent buyers. They also invest in post-purchase communication, sharing care guides, or complementary product suggestions. Furthermore, the company bolsters its customer support, addressing issues proactively.

**Outcome:** As a result of these amplified CX initiatives, the satisfied customer's purchasing behavior shifts. Instead of buying twice a year, they now make purchases four times annually. This change doubles their annual expenditure with the brand, enhancing their Customer Lifetime Value (CLV).

- The increase in purchases: 4 (post-CX improvement) − 2 (pre-CX improvement) = 2 additional purchases.
- With each purchase valued at $150, the increase in annual expenditure is $300, taking their total annual spending from $300 to $600.

Method of Calculation:

The formula to gauge this enhanced spending is: (Number of Purchases per Year after Improved CX − Number of Purchases per Year Before Improved CX) × Average Purchase Value

In this instance: (4 − 2) × $150 = $300 (increase in expenditure)

## Customer Referrals and Word-of-Mouth

At the confluence of loyalty and external outreach lies the power of customer advocacy. When customers are delighted, they don't just keep it to themselves. They share, recommend, and often become unsolicited brand ambassadors. This phenomenon, more colloquially termed as word-of-mouth (or a "flywheel"), can create a cascading effect, drawing in new customers and reinforcing the brand's reputation. Such organic testimonials often outweigh the impact of paid advertisements, as trust and personal experience form the bedrock of these recommendations.

## Factors Influencing Advocacy through Stellar CX:

- Genuine Engagement: Customers can discern between transactional interactions and genuine engagement. When they feel genuinely valued, they are more likely to advocate for the brand.
- Encouraging Reviews and Testimonials: By creating easy avenues for customers to leave reviews and share their experiences, businesses can organically boost their outreach.
- Exclusive Referral Programs: Offering incentives for referrals can further galvanize satisfied customers to introduce friends and family to the brand.
- Staying Top-of-Mind: Regular, non-intrusive communication through newsletters, updates, or exclusive previews can remind customers of their positive experiences, prompting them to share and recommend more actively.
- Repeat business: Specifically for B2B SaaS, if a prior customer moves to another new company, and continues to be a loyal advocate for your business.

Consider this as an example: a business revamps its CX strategy and subsequently observes a 15% increase in customer referrals.

**Backdrop:** The business consistently acquired 500 new customers monthly. Although these figures were decent, the brand realized that leveraging their existing customer base could exponentially increase this number.

**CX Initiatives:** The brand starts by amplifying its post-purchase engagement, sending thank you notes and asking for feedback. They also roll out a referral program where both the referrer and the referee receive discounts. Furthermore, they initiate a monthly newsletter detailing new products, exclusive offers, and featuring customer testimonials.

**Outcome:** These initiatives resonate with their customers, leading to a 15% rise in referrals. If the brand typically brings in 500 new customers each month, this uptick translates to an additional 75 customers. Given that each of these customers spends an average of $100, this translates to an additional revenue of $7,500 monthly, purely from referrals.

**Method of Calculation:**

To quantify this increase: (Percentage Increase in Customer Referrals) × (Average Monthly New Customers) × (Average Spent per New Customer)

In this scenario: (15/100) × 500 × $100 = $7,500

The revenue implications of a well-executed CX strategy are profound. It transforms the brand–customer dynamic from a mere transactional relationship to a deeply entrenched bond of loyalty and advocacy. To truly appreciate the financial value of CX, it's imperative to recognize the intertwined relationship between customer experiences, sales, and business growth. Through regular monitoring and realignment, businesses can leverage CX as a formidable tool for revenue enhancement and long-term sustainability.

# The Intangible Value of CX

Not everything of value can be directly measured in dollars and cents. While revenue and profitability are pivotal, certain intangible assets create the bedrock upon which sustainable businesses thrive. Customer Experience (CX) transcends beyond just immediate sales or referrals; it radiates outwards, affecting aspects of business that might not be immediately quantifiable but are undeniably valuable.

## Brand Reputation and Perception in the Market

A brand's reputation can be made or broken in the span of a few online reviews or social media posts. Enhanced CX ensures that the narrative surrounding a brand is overwhelmingly positive.

Consider Apple. Its brand isn't just built on innovative products but also on an unparalleled user experience, from product design to customer service. This has not only driven sales but has also cemented Apple's reputation as a premium, customer-centric brand.

The Ripple Effect: A sterling brand reputation leads to increased trust, which can open doors to collaborations, attract top-tier talent, and make marketing campaigns more effective by building upon an already positive public perception.

## Employee Satisfaction and Retention

Happy customers invariably make the job of front-line staff, be it in sales, support, or services, far more pleasant. When employees see that their company is committed to delivering exceptional CX, it can boost morale, increase job satisfaction, and subsequently lead to higher retention rates.

Zappos, an online shoe retailer, places a significant emphasis on both customer and employee happiness. Their commitment to CX not only resulted in customer loyalty but also created an enviable company culture, making it a desirable place to work.

The Ripple Effect: Reduced employee turnover translates to decreased hiring and training costs. Plus, long-tenured employees, familiar with the company's ethos and customers, often provide superior service, reinforcing the cycle of excellent CX.

## Risks and Costs of Negative Customer Experiences

Negative experiences don't just risk the loss of a single customer. In the age of social media, one dissatisfied customer can share their displeasure with thousands, leading to cascading impacts on brand perception.

United Airlines faced a PR nightmare in 2017 when a video of a passenger being forcibly removed from an overbooked flight went viral. The incident was not just a customer service failure but had tangible consequences, including a drop in stock value and boycott calls.

The Ripple Effect: Rebuilding a tarnished reputation takes time, money, and immense effort. There's also the hidden cost of lost potential customers, those who choose a competitor based on negative reviews or bad press. Moreover, remedial actions, such as refunds, compensations, or extensive PR campaigns to manage such situations, can be significantly costly.

The intangible aspects of CX, though not always directly reflected on the balance sheet, hold the potential to significantly influence a company's fortunes. They form the undercurrents that drive business momentum, shaping not just how customers perceive a brand but also how employees, competitors, and even investors view its value and potential. Investing in CX is, thus, an investment in crafting a holistic, resilient, and admired brand identity.

# Key Business Metrics Influenced by CX

Customer experience (CX) is intricately woven into the fabric of business performance. To understand the weight and scope of CX's influence, it's crucial to zoom into specific business metrics. These metrics serve as tangible barometers of a company's CX efficacy and provide actionable insights for continuous improvement.

## Customer Retention Rate (CRR)

The percentage of customers a company retains over a specified period. For example, if a subscription-based software company started the year with 100 customers and lost 5 by the end, but gained 20 new ones, the retention rate would focus only on the original customers, leading to a 95% CRR.

Exceptional CX can be a pivotal factor in retaining customers, ensuring they continue choosing your service or product over competitors.

## Net Promoter Score (NPS)

A metric to gauge customer loyalty by asking customers how likely they are to recommend the company/product to others. For instance, companies like Apple consistently achieve high NPS scores, underlining their customers' loyalty and satisfaction levels.

High NPS indicates that customers are not just satisfied, but are also promoters of the brand, often a direct outcome of superior CX.

## Customer Satisfaction Score (CSAT)

Measures customer satisfaction with a company's product or service. Consider, after a support call, many companies send a short survey asking, "Were you satisfied with the service you received?" Responses typically fall on a scale, with higher scores indicating higher satisfaction.

CSAT directly reflects the quality of customer interactions, making it a critical gauge of CX performance.

## Customer Churn Rate

The percentage of customers that stop using a company's product or service during a particular period. For instance, in the competitive world of streaming services, platforms like Netflix need to constantly innovate and deliver quality content to maintain low churn rates.

A higher churn rate can indicate dissatisfaction, making it essential to probe and address CX-related issues.

## Average Ticket Resolution Time

The average time taken to resolve customer issues or complaints. For instance, companies like Amazon pride themselves on quick resolution times, ensuring customer issues are addressed promptly.

Faster resolution often translates to better customer satisfaction, highlighting the efficiency and effectiveness of the support team.

## First Contact Resolution Rate

The percentage of customer issues resolved during the first interaction. Higher rates indicate that customers don't have to repeatedly reach out, leading to enhanced satisfaction.

## Customer Lifetime Value (CLV)

Predicted net profit attributed to the entire relationship with a customer. For instance, Starbucks customers often remain loyal for years, making purchases frequently, which boosts their CLV.

Exceptional CX ensures customers remain loyal and increase their spending over time, amplifying the CLV.

## Customer Effort Score (CES)

Measures the ease with which customers can get their issues resolved. For example, simplified return processes in companies like Zappos lead to high CES scores, indicating minimal effort on the customer's part.

A low CES signifies that customers can achieve their goals with ease, directly boosting their overall experience.

The mosaic of business metrics paints a vivid picture of how deeply CX influences various facets of a company. Whether it's building loyalty, fostering satisfaction, or streamlining support processes, an effective CX strategy doesn't just touch upon these metrics—it elevates them. By monitoring and iterating based on these metrics, businesses can continually refine their CX, ensuring they not only meet but consistently exceed customer expectations.

# Creating a CX Financial Dashboard

Constructing a robust CX financial dashboard is a blend of clarity, relevance, and strategic alignment. Such a dashboard acts as a centralized hub, illuminating how customer experience aligns with and influences financial outcomes. Here's a step-by-step guide to crafting a CX financial dashboard tailored for your business needs.

## Selecting the Right Metrics

Metrics should be chosen based on their alignment with your organization's objectives, challenges, and industry-specific nuances.

For example, a SaaS (Software as a Service) company might prioritize metrics like Customer Churn Rate and CLV due to their subscription-based business model. On the other hand, a retail e-commerce store might emphasize CSAT scores and Average Ticket Resolution Time, given the high volume of daily transactions and customer interactions.

### Action Steps

1. Initiate a brainstorming session involving primary stakeholders.
2. Highlight metrics with a direct financial implication.
3. Ensure a mix of both leading (predictive) and lagging (historical) indicators.

## Integrating CX Metrics with Existing Business Performance Metrics

When juxtaposed against broader business performance metrics, CX metrics offer richer insights, revealing correlations, trends, and potential areas for improvement.

For example, if an e-commerce platform observes a surge in Customer Churn Rate, aligning this data with metrics like website downtime or delivery delays can unveil deeper causal insights.

Action Steps

1. Pinpoint key business performance metrics that intersect with CX.
2. Develop integrated views where CX and business metrics coexist for enhanced insights.
3. Continually assess correlations to identify patterns or anomalies.

## Using Visualization Tools

Data, when raw, can be daunting. With the right visualization tools, this data can be transformed into engaging, easily digestible visual narratives.

For example, tools like Tableau, Power BI, or Google Data Studio can convert raw CX and financial data into interactive dashboards. Instead of mere numbers, trends can be represented using line graphs, pie charts can display proportions, and heat maps can indicate focus areas.

Action Steps

1. Opt for a visualization tool that meshes well with your data sources and provides necessary customization.
2. Design keeping the target audience in mind, ensuring clarity for all stakeholders.
3. Emphasize clear design, utilizing color coding, legends, and annotations for clarity.

A well-constructed CX financial dashboard bridges data with actionable decisions. By adeptly selecting and integrating metrics, and presenting them compellingly, organizations can ensure that their customer experience narrative remains central, shaping strategic initiatives and fortifying financial performance.

That said, you do not by any means need a perfect CX dashboard—in fact, getting started with something small is better than nothing.

# Calculating the ROI of Your CX Initiatives

To underscore the importance of customer experience (CX) in a language that every stakeholder understands, one must bring numbers and financial outcomes to the table. ROI, or Return on Investment, serves as a critical metric that quantifies the value generated from CX initiatives. But how exactly do you measure the ROI of your CX endeavors? Let's explore.

## The Formula for Calculating ROI in CX

At its core, calculating the ROI for CX initiatives follows the conventional ROI formula, which is:

```
ROI= (((Net Profit from CX Initiatives) - (Cost of CX Initiatives)) / (Cost of CX Initiatives)) × 100
```

Where:

- Net Profit from CX Initiatives is the additional revenue generated due to CX efforts minus the costs associated with those efforts.
- Cost of CX Initiatives includes expenditures related to tools, training, personnel, and other related expenses.

Here are a few examples of putting this equation into play:

Revamping a Website for User Experience (UX):

- Investment: A company invests $50,000 to redesign its website, making it more user-friendly and intuitive.
- Outcome: As a result, online sales increase by 20%, resulting in an additional $200,000 in revenue over the year.

- ROI Calculation: Using the above formula, the ROI is $\frac{\$200{,}000 - \$50{,}000}{\$50{,}000} \times 100\% = 300\%$.

Introduction of a 24/7 Customer Support Chatbot:

- Investment: Implementation and maintenance costs amount to $20,000.
- Outcome: Reduction in support tickets, increased customer satisfaction, and additional sales due to instant query resolution generate an additional $80,000 in revenue.
- ROI Calculation: The ROI is $\frac{\$80{,}000 - \$20{,}000}{\$20{,}000} \times 100\% = 300\%$.

Employee Training Program for Enhanced Customer Interactions:

- Investment: Training sessions, materials, and related expenses come to $30,000.
- Outcome: Higher CSAT scores lead to increased customer retention, yielding an added $90,000 in revenue.
- ROI Calculation: The ROI is $\frac{\$90{,}000 - \$30{,}000}{\$30{,}000} \times 100\% = 200\%$.

## Factors That Can Influence ROI

- Market Changes: Economic downturns, shifts in consumer behavior, or global events (e.g., a pandemic) can impact the returns on your CX initiatives, regardless of their quality.
- Competitive Landscape: The entry of a strong competitor or the rollout of similar CX initiatives by rivals can dilute your ROI.
- Internal Changes: Organizational shifts, such as changes in leadership, strategy, or even technological disruptions, can either boost or hinder the ROI of CX projects.

- Evolving Customer Expectations: As industries innovate and set new standards, customer expectations can change rapidly, affecting the longevity and impact of previous CX efforts.

While ROI serves as a compelling metric to gauge the value of CX efforts, it's crucial to view it within the broader business context. A holistic approach, factoring in both tangible and intangible benefits, ensures that CX remains a strategic pillar in organizational growth and sustainability.

# Budgeting for CX: Aligning with Business Goals

Budgeting for customer experience (CX) is not merely about allocating funds. It's a strategic endeavor that intertwines with your organization's broader objectives, ensuring that every dollar invested in CX echoes with the aspirations of the business. Let's delve into the nuances of crafting a CX budget that harmoniously aligns with your business goals.

## Projecting Future CX Costs Based on Strategic Goals

Anticipating future costs is foundational in crafting a robust CX budget. This involves a close examination of your business's strategic objectives and understanding the role CX plays in reaching those milestones.

For example, if your company's goal for the coming year is to penetrate a new market demographic, your CX budget might need allocations for market research, cultural training for your support team, and possibly, localization of your digital assets.

Action Steps:

1. Collaborate with department heads to comprehend the broader business goals.
2. Identify the CX initiatives that align with these goals.
3. Estimate the resources—both financial and logistical—required for each initiative.

## Justifying CX Investments to Key Stakeholders

Every expenditure in a business, especially sizable ones like CX initiatives, often requires validation. Articulating the value proposition of CX investments is essential to secure stakeholder buy-in.

For example, let's consider a proposal to invest in a state-of-the-art CRM system. Instead of merely presenting the cost, highlight how the CRM can enhance customer data analysis, streamline communications, and potentially increase sales conversions by X%, translating to a projected Y% growth in revenue.

Action Steps:

1. Quantify potential benefits wherever possible.
2. Highlight long-term value in addition to immediate gains.
3. Relate investments back to overarching business goals and the strategic roadmap.

## Prioritizing CX Initiatives Based on Projected Financial Outcomes

Given finite resources, it's crucial to ensure that CX investments yield the most bang for the buck. Leveraging data can illuminate which initiatives hold the most promise in terms of financial outcomes.

For example, if data suggests that a significant percentage of cart abandonments on your e-commerce platform occur due to lengthy checkout processes, prioritizing a streamlined checkout experience can be more financially rewarding than, say, a website redesign that is more aesthetic than functional.

Action Steps:

1. Gather historical data on past CX initiatives and their ROI.
2. Use predictive analytics to estimate the potential financial outcomes of proposed initiatives.

3. Rank initiatives based on their projected ROI, ensuring that those with the highest potential impact are prioritized in the budget.

Crafting a CX budget is a delicate balance between financial prudence and strategic ambition. By aligning closely with business objectives, justifying investments articulately, and letting data guide prioritization, businesses can ensure that their CX budget not only elevates customer experience but also propels the organization closer to its overarching goals.

# Demonstrating the Financial Value of CX to Leadership

The undeniable connection between CX excellence and business growth is well-understood within the CX domain. Yet, making this connection palpable to leadership often calls for a distinct, structured communication approach. This section explores ways to convey the profound financial value of CX to key decision-makers.

## Communicating the Tangible and Intangible Benefits of CX

Rewards springing from an effective CX strategy can be both tangible and intangible. On the tangible side, revenue is often a direct beneficiary of CX improvements. For instance, a company that revamped its website for better user experience might witness a 20% hike in conversion rates. This improvement could mean an added $500,000 in monthly revenue. Simultaneously, refining CX processes can lead to cost efficiencies. By introducing self-help modules and streamlining customer support, a firm might reduce its support tickets by 30%, saving $15,000 monthly.

On the intangible front, CX elevates the brand and organizational culture. A superior CX strategy can bolster brand reputation, laying the groundwork for lasting customer trust and loyalty. Moreover, when employees recognize their role in a customer-centric organization, it often enhances workplace morale and satisfaction.

## Overcoming Objections and Hurdles in CX Budget Approval

Securing approval for CX initiatives requires tact and a deep understanding of potential objections. An effective way to gain trust is by showcasing a clear return on investment (ROI). When proposing, for example, the adoption of a new customer feedback tool, illustrate its potential benefits. Demonstrate how a hypothetical 10% rise in customer satisfaction might lead to a 5% increase in repeat patronage.

Another powerful strategy is competitive analysis. By highlighting how competitors are gaining an edge with their CX strategies, you can inspire change within your organization. If there's hesitancy towards major changes, it can be useful to suggest starting with a pilot project. This scaled-down version, if successful, can then be leveraged to make a case for larger-scale implementations.

## Building Cross-Departmental Support for CX Investments

Promoting a sense of collective ownership over CX is pivotal. To achieve this, inter-departmental workshops can be organized. Such sessions can illuminate how CX initiatives can enhance roles across the board.

When introducing a new CX tool or process, emphasize its universal benefits. A new CRM system, for instance, might not only streamline the sales process but also offer valuable insights for the marketing team and expedite ticket resolution for support.

It's equally essential to establish a shared CX ethos across the organization. Every team should recognize that delivering an exceptional CX is not just the prerogative of a single team; it's a collective mission. Recognizing and celebrating inter-departmental collaborations that lead to CX victories can foster this sentiment.

Conveying the value of CX in terms that resonate with leadership can be a nuanced task. By shedding light on both the immediate and long-term gains and by championing a culture of collaboration, CX professionals stand a better chance of seeing their strategies endorsed and funded by leadership.

## Continuous Monitoring and Iteration

In the dynamic landscape of customer experience (CX), merely implementing initiatives is not the culmination of the journey. Ensuring that these strategies are perpetually aligned with the desired financial outcomes requires vigilance and adaptability. This section underscores the pivotal role of ongoing monitoring and iterative adjustments in maximizing the financial benefits of CX.

## Regular Financial Reviews of CX Initiatives

At the core of effective CX management lies the tenet of consistent financial reviews. Imagine a scenario where a company has rolled out a new omnichannel support system. While it promises enhanced user satisfaction, its financial implications over time must be assessed. After six months, upon review, the company discovers that although customer satisfaction has soared by 10%, the operational costs have unexpectedly surged by 20%. Without regular reviews, such critical insights would remain elusive, potentially leading to financial drains.

By periodically analyzing the financial metrics associated with CX projects, companies can ensure that their investments are yielding the desired return and are in harmony with broader organizational goals.

### Adapting and Pivoting Based on Financial Performance

The fluid nature of the business environment mandates agility. Say, for instance, a retail company invests heavily in a Virtual Reality (VR) shopping experience, anticipating it to be the next big trend. However, after a year, financial reviews reveal that despite its novelty, the VR module isn't generating anticipated sales. Such insights should act as catalysts for change. The company might then decide to pivot, reallocating resources to more fruitful endeavors like enhancing their mobile shopping experience.

The key is to remain attuned to the financial pulse of CX initiatives and be prepared to make informed alterations when required.

### Creating a Feedback Loop between CX and Finance Teams

One of the most potent tools in ensuring the financial effectiveness of CX strategies is fostering robust communication between CX and finance teams. Consider a situation where the CX team wants to introduce a new loyalty program. Before its launch, the finance team, having access to purchasing data, points out that a significant portion of repeat buyers comes from a demographic not covered in the initial program design. With this feedback, the CX team can refine the program, ensuring a more inclusive and potentially more profitable rollout.

This symbiotic relationship ensures that CX initiatives are not just driven by experiential goals but are firmly rooted in financial prudence.

A robust CX strategy, while inherently customer-centric, must also remain financially astute. Through regular financial assessments, the agility to adapt, and by weaving a tight-knit feedback mechanism between the CX and finance arms, companies can ensure that their customer experience endeavors are both groundbreaking and economically sound.

## Where to Next?

Our exploration has underscored the profound influence of CX not only in shaping perceptions, brand loyalty, and customer satisfaction but also in driving tangible financial results. From calculating the direct and indirect costs associated with CX teams to demonstrating the exponential potential of positive customer advocacy, it becomes clear that effective CX strategies are not mere feel-good endeavors but crucial financial assets. Brands that harness the potential of financially informed CX strategies are better positioned to maximize their return on investment, ensuring that every dollar spent creates value both for the business and its customers.

## Encouraging a Culture of Financial Responsibility within the CX Team

As the custodians of customer experience, the CX team's responsibilities transcend delivering exceptional interactions. Imbibing a culture of financial responsibility within the CX team ensures that their strategies are always grounded in economic realities. This amalgamation of customer-centric thinking and financial responsibility ensures that initiatives are not only innovative but also sustainable and in line with broader organizational goals.

## Preparing for the Future

The world of business is in a constant state of flux, with technologies, customer preferences, and market dynamics perennially shifting. In this ever-changing milieu, it's essential that the financial goals and strategies of the CX team exhibit malleability. By perpetually monitoring, iterating, and aligning with the evolving business landscape, CX teams can ensure their initiatives remain relevant, impactful, and financially beneficial.

In the grand tapestry of business, CX stands out as a vivid and vital thread. But, for its colors to truly shine, for its patterns to truly resonate, it must be woven with threads of financial insight and prudence. As we navigate the future, let's champion CX strategies that are not just emotionally resonant but also financially astute, ensuring a brighter future for businesses and their customers alike.

# CHAPTER 8:

# Scaling Up

As your organization grows and evolves, so should your CX strategy. It's my hope that this chapter encompasses the vast journey of building CX from its foundation: emphasizing the phase where startups transition into established entities, and sometimes even empires. Scaling isn't just about growing bigger; it's about growing smarter, more efficient, and more attuned to the ever-changing needs of your customer base.

As you might expect, scaling your CX operations isn't without its hurdles. The process presents a blend of challenges—be it the need to stay consistent with your core values while adapting to new demands, or ensuring that the quality of service remains intact even as the volume of interactions surges. But alongside these challenges come immense rewards: a more loyal customer base, streamlined operations, and a team that's more engaged and empowered.

As we delve into this chapter, we'll explore the various facets of scaling CX operations, offering insights into not just the "how" but also the "when" and the "why." Whether you started this book as a one-person operation and are looking towards the future, or picked this up specifically for this learning, I hope this chapter helps.

## How to Know When It's Time for a Change

One of the most pivotal aspects of scaling up any operation, particularly with customer experience, is timing. When do you push forward with aggressive expansion? When do you hold back, refining your current processes and strategies? To strike the right balance, you need to be deeply attuned to the signs and indicators that suggest change is on the horizon.

Every business has its unique set of dynamics, but there are universally recognized signals that your CX operations may need to grow:

1. Increasing volume. One of the most straightforward indicators is a noticeable uptick in customer interactions. Whether it's more support tickets, emails, or calls, if your current team struggles to manage the increased volume, it's time to think about scaling.

2. Declining service levels. If previously met service level agreements (SLAs) are now regularly missed, or response and resolution times are lengthening, these are clear signs your team might be overwhelmed and it's time to think about ways to scale.

3. Negative customer feedback. If customers begin to complain about slower response times, unresolved issues, or lack of availability, it suggests that your current CX infrastructure is insufficient.

4. Staff burnout. We talked about ways to avoid burnout in the chapter around building your dream team, but sometimes even those things can't protect your ICs. An overburdened team can lead to increased employee turnover, more sick days, and general burnout. If your staff seems continually overwhelmed, it's an indicator that you need more hands or better tools.

5. Changes in product/service offering. Launching a new product or expanding into a new market segment often comes with a surge in customer interactions. If there's a significant change in your offerings, it's wise to anticipate the need for scaled CX operations. This is also the case for business expansion, such as pushing into a new market or sales channel.

6. Inefficiencies in current processes. If the current tools, saved replies, macros, or processes seem to hinder the team rather than help, or if there's a lot of time spent on tasks that could be automated, it's time to reassess and scale your operations.

7. Backlogs. If there's a growing backlog of customer inquiries, complaints, or issues that remain unresolved, it's a warning sign that your team can't keep up with the demand, and you should investigate ways to help: either through staffing or tooling.

8. Loss of key accounts or customers. If you're losing valuable customers and feedback suggests it's due to service quality or response times, then it's a clarion call to reevaluate your operations.

## What Happens If You're Late?

Waiting too long to address these signs can lead to dire consequences. Customer dissatisfaction might spike, leading to a decline in loyalty and, potentially, revenue. Your team might suffer, too; they could become overworked, leading to burnout, decreased morale, and high turnover rates. On the flip side, scaling too hastily presents its own set of challenges. You might find yourself with an oversized team, leading to increased operational costs and potential lay-offs in your future. Without proper planning and training, the quality of service could decline, even with more hands on deck. Additionally, hastily implemented systems or processes might not integrate well, leading to inefficiencies down the line.

Recognizing when it's time to scale is both an art and a science. It requires keen observation, a deep understanding of your business' rhythms, and a willingness to act decisively. Balancing the urgency of scaling with the foresight of strategic planning will position your CX operations for long-term success.

# Training and Development

Let's get real: growing your operations isn't just about getting a bigger team or fancy new software. It's about making sure everyone on the team feels knowledgeable, and that they're ready for whatever the next customer curveball might be. Training and development are huge levels up in this arena.

So you know that feeling when you find out about a new update or feature only after a customer asks? It's a bit like being asked about last night's score of the "big game" and not even knowing if it was basketball, baseball or something more obscure (cricket, anyone?). Continuous learning is your team's ticket to always staying in the loop. As your business picks up steam, customers will expect more, and your old playbook might not cut it. Regular training sessions make sure everyone's on their A-game, not just doing their job but doing it confidently. And hey, who doesn't like feeling like they're on top of their game?

## Mixing Up the Training Methods

If you look back, there's a good chance you'll recall those relaxed training sessions—maybe two colleagues chatting about procedures over a cup of coffee or a donut. The beauty of this approach is its personal touch. There's something about the casualness and immediacy of face-to-face discussions that make the learning stick. These individualized sessions help in building trust, understanding the unique perspectives of each team member, and allowing for real-time feedback. But, unfortunately, they don't typically scale forever and as your team gets larger, these get trickier and trickier to maintain and facilitate. What are some other ways to share knowledge?

### Group Workshops

When 1:1 coffee chats are no longer hitting the mark, it's time to move on to a larger group. These aren't just about passing on knowledge but can also be a fantastic way to bond. Everyone's in the same boat, trying to understand a new concept or a change in protocol. They can share their experiences, laugh about common customer stories, and even work out kinks in the system together. Plus, there's something to be said about the energy of a collective. Ideas bounce around, problems get multiple perspectives, and solutions become more comprehensive.

## Virtual Learning and Beyond

Training's no exception to the digital shift that the world saw in 2020. Especially when considering those who work unconventional hours or juggle multiple responsibilities, digital learning tools become invaluable. Online courses offer flexibility—employees can proceed at their own pace, rewind sections they find tricky, or even dive deeper into areas of interest. Webinars bring in experts from various fields, offering fresh insights without the constraints of geography. And if you're keen on blending the best of real-world and digital experiences, consider virtual reality setups. They can simulate complex customer interactions, giving your team a safe space to practice and refine their skills.

## Specialized Sessions

As the saying goes, "different strokes for different folks." As your customer experience operations evolve and mature, there'll be moments when a generic training session just won't cut it. Maybe it's a deep dive into brand-new CRM software, or perhaps it's a strategy brainstorm for managing high-value clients. These sessions, tailored to specific challenges or tools, ensure that your team isn't just prepared; they're experts, ready to handle niche situations with aplomb.

Training isn't a one-size-fits-all game. As your company morphs, embracing different phases of growth and change, your training methodologies should keep pace. It's not just about ensuring everyone knows their job; it's about fostering a culture of continuous learning. A well-trained, adaptable team isn't just efficient—it's a force to be reckoned with, ready to face the challenges of tomorrow head-on.

# Rewarding and Recognizing a Job Well Done

Scaling a Customer Experience (CX) strategy involves much more than just numbers and KPIs; it's also about the people driving the process. As we navigate the complexities of expansion, it's vital to prioritize and value the contributions of our team. In this section, we'll delve into the importance of fostering a cohesive team spirit, striking the right balance with feedback, and understanding the role of timely recognition. After all, as we grow, ensuring that our team feels seen and appreciated is what truly sets the foundation for sustainable success.

Beyond feeling *seen*, the members of your team have to feel unified. One of the most significant advantages of team unity is ensuring consistency in service delivery. As your company expands, there will naturally be an increase in the volume of customer interactions. If the team is cohesive and aligned, regardless of who handles a customer query, the quality and style of service remains consistent. This uniformity is essential for building and maintaining a robust brand reputation. Customers come to know and rely on the consistent experience they get every time they engage with your company.

Efficient problem-solving is another crucial benefit of a unified team. A team that shares common processes and goals is better equipped to address issues. When everyone operates from the same playbook, there's a marked decrease in confusion, leading to faster resolutions and a smoother overall customer experience. This efficiency extends to communication as well. With everyone understanding the company's direction and objectives, internal communications become more productive, and the messages relayed to customers become clearer and more coherent.

The collective growth and shared learning experience of a team cannot be underestimated. The adage "Together we rise" rings particularly true for scaling operations. Teams that share experiences, both the highs and the lows, gain insights and knowledge that might be overlooked on an individual basis. As these shared experiences accumulate, the team's collective wisdom grows, making it more adept at navigating the challenges of scaling.

Another noteworthy aspect is adaptability. Scaling often demands the introduction of new tools, processes, and sometimes even a shift in strategy. A team that shares a vision and purpose tends to be more adaptable and receptive to these changes. This unity makes transitions smoother, reducing the friction that often accompanies change. Moreover, a positive, unified work environment plays a critical role in boosting morale and reducing turnover. When team members feel they belong and that their contributions matter, it not only elevates their performance but also makes them more likely to stay, an essential factor when considering the costs and time associated with training new staff.

Lastly, the shared sense of ownership and accountability in a unified team is a powerful force. Every team member feels a deep sense of responsibility towards the company's mission and its customers. This collective approach ensures that everyone remains deeply invested in offering the best CX possible. In the grand scheme of things, as businesses evolve and scale their CX strategies, having a cohesive team acts as a foundation, ensuring that amidst all the changes, the customer's needs and experiences remain at the forefront.

So now we know it's important, but how do we do it?

## Encouraging Collaboration

Encouraging collaboration is key. Collaborative teams can share knowledge, address issues more effectively, and present a united front to the customer. Here are some key strategies to foster collaboration:

- Shared goals or objectives: Begin by setting team-wide objectives that require collaborative efforts to achieve. When everyone works towards a common goal, collaboration happens organically.
- Cross-training: Allow team members to understand different roles by switching tasks periodically. This helps them appreciate the challenges and insights of their colleagues, and encourages a culture where everyone helps out.

- Regular team meetings: Set up routine check-ins where the team can discuss challenges, share updates, and celebrate wins. This regular communication can foster understanding and unity.

- Good tools: Utilize tools like Slack, Trello, or Microsoft Teams, which promote real-time communication, document sharing, and task management. These tools can help in streamlining communication and ensuring everyone is on the same page. Encourage an open-door policy where team members can approach leaders and peers with questions, concerns, or suggestions without fear of backlash.

- Feedback loops: Create an environment where team members are encouraged to provide feedback on processes, policies, and interactions. This can be through suggestion boxes, regular retrospectives, or team workshops. If they feel like their suggestions are listened to, considered, and applied they will be more invested in the long-term success of your team and company.

- Team-building activities: Organize activities that aren't directly related to work, such as team lunches, outings, or games. These help in building interpersonal relationships, leading to better professional collaboration.

- Recognize and reward collaboration: Highlight and reward individuals or teams that showcase exceptional collaborative efforts. This sets a precedent and motivates others to collaborate.

- Group problem-solving: Encourage teams to brainstorm and problem-solve together. Not only does this foster collaboration, but it often leads to more innovative solutions.

- Knowledge sharing: Schedule regular sessions where team members can share knowledge on various topics, whether it's a new tool, strategy, or a recent challenging scenario they tackled.

Fostering collaboration within the CX team not only improves team dynamics but directly impacts the quality of service provided to customers. When teams collaborate effectively, they can pool their knowledge, resources, and expertise to create the best possible customer experiences. If you're looking for tips to get better integration between your support team and *other* teams within your business (also important), see the end of Chapter 6.

## Value Your People

At the heart of every thriving organization is a workforce that feels appreciated and valued. Rewards play a pivotal role in communicating that appreciation, especially in the often-challenging times that accompany scaling operations. Among the tangible rewards, bonuses certainly stand out. A financial bonus directly linked to the team's or individual's performance not only boosts morale but also injects a sense of accomplishment into the employee. Gifts, whether they're branded company merchandise or something personalized, also have a special touch. They act as a constant reminder of the company's gratitude and appreciation.

But beyond the physical and monetary, intangible rewards often strike a deeper chord. For instance, offering a surprise day off can serve as a rejuvenating break, allowing employees to come back with a refreshed mindset. Likewise, flexible working hours can be a game-changer for many, especially those juggling multiple responsibilities. This kind of flexibility communicates trust, showing employees that the company respects their time and trusts them to manage it efficiently.

Lastly, never underestimate the magic of simple words. Sometimes, a genuine "Thank you!" or "Great job!" note accompanied by the specifics around what you liked, can mean the world. This type of gesture doesn't just acknowledge effort and achievement but also builds a bond between the team and the leadership. The underlying message? The company sees and values every small and big contribution. When employees recognize this, they're not just working for a paycheck; they're investing their passion and dedication, driving them to consistently put their best foot forward.

## Constructive and Positive Feedback

Feedback's a two-way street. On one side, there are constructive insights that help team members grow and refine their skills. This type of feedback is not about pointing fingers but instead offering thoughts into how the recipient can be even better. On the other side, there's positive reinforcement. Highlighting what someone did right, and encouraging them to keep up the excellent work. Striking the right balance ensures employees feel supported and recognized, while also understanding areas of potential improvement.

## Recognize Achievements

Now, onto one of the most enjoyable parts: celebrating successes! It could be as grand as an awards ceremony or as simple as a shout-out in a team meeting. Perhaps even feature standout employees in company newsletters or on your intranet. The medium doesn't matter; it's the gesture that counts. By making recognition a regular affair, you're sending a clear message: hard work doesn't go unnoticed.

As your CX strategies scale, keep an eye on the human element. Machines and systems play their part, but it's the people, their dedication, and their teamwork that truly fuel growth. Remember to celebrate the big wins and the small victories; after all, every step forward is a stride towards success.

# Always Be Growing

As your company grows, your CX operations will inevitably face waves of challenges that demand adaptive strategies. One of the truths of scaling is that processes will, and should, evolve. Ignoring this evolution can be as catastrophic as a ship's captain ignoring an oncoming storm. The key lies not in resisting this evolution but in navigating it with precision and foresight.

## Embrace the Inevitable

No matter how perfect your initial CX strategy might seem, it won't remain static. As the company grows, factors such as customer expectations, team size, technology, and market dynamics will change. This shift means your once-perfect strategy might start showing cracks. The objective isn't to craft an unchangeable plan but to anticipate these shifts and have mechanisms in place to adapt to them. By being proactive in expecting change, businesses can maintain a high-quality customer experience throughout their scaling journey.

## Best Practices for Reviewing Your Processes

So, if evolution is inevitable, how does one ensure they're evolving in the right direction? The answer lies in regular process reviews. Here are some best practices:

- Schedule Them: Whether it's quarterly, bi-annually, or annually, have a set time-frame for reviewing processes.
- Involve Various Teams: A 360-degree view can only be achieved if representatives from various teams participate, offering different perspectives.
- Focus on Data: Ground your reviews in data. Look at metrics, KPIs, and any other tangible numbers to guide your discussions.
- Have Clear Objectives: Know what you're aiming to achieve from these reviews. Is it to increase efficiency, boost customer satisfaction, or reduce overheads? Going in without a specific eye will lead you nowhere.

## Use Feedback to Refine

Feedback is gold. In the context of CX, there are two main veins to mine: employees and customers.

Employees are on the front line. They understand the ins and outs of processes, and they can pinpoint bottlenecks, redundancies, or areas of improvement. Regularly solicit feedback from them. This not only helps refine strategies but also makes employees feel valued and heard.

On the other hand, customers offer an outside perspective. They can highlight areas where your CX strategy might be lacking from a user's viewpoint. Tools like surveys, feedback forms, or even direct conversations can be instrumental.

But gathering feedback is just one part of the equation. It's essential to then incorporate this feedback into your strategies. If you don't actually put the feedback to work and make changes to your strategy based on it, there is no point in wasting your energy collecting it.

Scaling your CX operations is not a one-time task. It's a continuous journey of adaptation, refinement, and evolution. As the landscape changes, so should your strategy. By recognizing the inevitability of process evolution, conducting regular reviews, and valuing feedback, businesses can ensure that their CX remains top-notch, no matter how big they grow.

So, as you navigate the waters of business growth, remember to keep your compass attuned to the winds of change.

# Changing Management Structures

Every thriving company experiences those winds of change. As your customer support team expands to accommodate increasing demands, your management structure will inevitably need to adapt. No two companies will look alike: a startup's management style varies from that of a well-established organization. Let's delve deep into how management structures change as customer support operations scale and how to navigate this complex yet rewarding journey.

## Management Structures Across Growth Stages

**Startup Phase—Flat Structure:** In the initial stages, many startups adopt a flat structure. Here the barriers between executives and employees are minimal. Team members often wear multiple hats, and decision-making is more collaborative. Such a structure allows for agility, rapid decision-making, and a close-knit environment.

**Midsize Phase—Functional Structure:** As a company grows beyond its startup phase, roles begin to diversify. Departments form around functions, like sales, marketing, and, of course, customer support. Within the support team, you might see distinct groups like tech support, customer success, and account management. Managers often oversee these specific functions.

**Large Phase—Divisional or Matrix Structure:** When a company becomes large, having only functional divisions might become inefficient. Here, a divisional or matrix structure can come into play. In the context of customer support, teams might be organized around product lines, customer segments, or regions. These teams will have their managers and support structures while still collaborating across divisions when necessary.

## Knowing When to Switch Gears

Recognizing when to shift your management structure is akin to the delicate balancing act of a tightrope walker. It requires both the precision of science and the intuition of art. Many of the signals that hint at a need for change in your org are often echoed in other areas, such as knowing when you need to staff up, or change tools. Familiar faces in this domain, like the looming shadow of increased complexity, the whispered concerns in team feedback, or the discernible murmurs from your customer feedback, are telling indicators that it's time for a managerial tune-up.

Yet, understanding that a transition is in order isn't the hard part—it's the change itself that can be tricky. Much like steering a large ship, altering the course of a management structure can encounter resistance, unpredictable waves, and the possibility of venturing off course. It's pivotal to anticipate potential challenges and be equipped with the strategies to overcome them. Here are some hurdles that might emerge on this transformative journey.

- Resistance to Change. People are often wary of change, especially if they've grown accustomed to a particular way of working. It's essential to communicate the reasons for the shift, involve employees in the transition process, and provide adequate training.
- Over-Complexity. While diversifying roles is crucial, creating too many layers can lead to bureaucracy. Aim for a balance: ensure clarity without stifling efficiency.
- Losing Company Culture. As you scale, there's a risk that the company's foundational culture might get diluted. Keep reiterating core values, mission, and vision. Embed these principles in training programs, so newcomers are well-guided.

The journey from a startup to a well-established organization is exhilarating. As your customer support team grows, the way you manage will need to evolve. By understanding the best-fit structures for each stage, recognizing when a shift is due, and navigating the inherent challenges, you set the stage for not just growth but also sustained excellence in customer support.

Remember, it's not about outgrowing your roots, but about providing a more extensive canopy of exceptional support.

**CHAPTER 9:**

# Creating a Customer-First Company Culture

We've all been around the block with the classic saying, "The customer is always right." And let's be honest, while it's catchy, it's not entirely true. Customers, like all of us, can sometimes get things wrong, and that's okay. But here's the twist: even if they aren't always right, they should always feel central to what we're doing. This chapter is about that shift in perspective.

Building a genuine customer-first culture isn't about sticking to outdated mantras or just adding some flashy customer testimonials in the office. It's about an authentic alignment—ensuring everyone, from those fresh-faced interns to the seasoned executives, is thinking about our customers' experiences in every move they make.

Imagine a business where the primary compass isn't just profit or efficiency but the experiences and feedback from those who use our services or buy our products. A place where, even when the relationship with the customer becomes fractured, we're still zoomed in on understanding their perspective and improving their journey.

Excited? You should be! As we delve deeper into this chapter, we'll explore strategies and insights to help shift your company's mindset. We're aiming for a dynamic where the customer isn't just an external entity but an integral part of the narrative you're building. Ready to get everyone on board this train? Choo-choo!

## Getting Started

Starting your journey towards a customer-centric company culture can often seem daunting, especially with the multitude of strategies and advice available. But whether you're a seasoned pro in customer-centricity or just dipping your toes into its vast waters, it's reassuring to know there's always a straightforward entry point. Think of it like diving into a pool: while some might opt for the high dive, there's nothing wrong with entering from the shallow end and gradually working your way deeper.

The goal isn't about how grand your initial leap is, but ensuring that every step you take is deliberate, progressive, and centers the customer's experience. In this guide, we'll walk you through some easy steps to kick-start or enhance your organization's commitment to placing customers at the heart of your operations. So, regardless of where you stand in your customer-centric journey, there's a path forward that's both manageable and effective.

1. Lead by example. The initiative for a customer-centric culture should start at the top. Leaders and managers should demonstrate a genuine interest in customer satisfaction, actively seeking feedback and making customer-centric decisions. This should not just be about the appearance of caring, either, but genuine involvement and understanding of customer personas and their life-cycle.

2. Hire for empathy. We mentioned this in the "building your dream team" chapter, but during the hiring process, prioritize candidates who demonstrate empathy and a genuine interest in understanding and helping others. These innate qualities can be powerful drivers of a customer-centric mindset.

3. Regular training. Invest in regular customer service training and development opportunities for your team. This helps them to feel more invested in the company and be stronger advocates for the things that are important (or unimportant) to the customer, and also continue to excel in their career.

4. Open feedback channels. Establish easy-to-use channels for customers to provide feedback. Whether it's through surveys,

feedback forms, or direct interactions, make sure customers feel heard and valued. And, beyond just making sure that they feel heard, try to make changes based on customer feedback, and let them know when you do.

5. Reward and recognize. Celebrate employees who go above and beyond for customers. Whether it's through monthly awards, shout-outs in team meetings, or other incentives, recognizing outstanding customer service can motivate others to follow suit. If you're looking for more ideas, check out the earlier chapter on team building.

6. Encourage inter-departmental collaboration. Break down silos within the company. Foster a sense of collaboration between departments so that everyone, from product development to marketing, understands and prioritizes the customer's perspective. If you're looking for more, view our chapter (page number here).

7. Implement regular reviews. Periodically assess your company's customer-centricity. Look at feedback, address pain points, and continuously refine your approach based on real customer experiences.

8. Incorporate customer stories. Share customer testimonials, stories, and feedback in internal meetings or company newsletters. These real-world examples can drive home the importance of the customer's perspective.

9. Foster a feedback culture internally. Encourage employees to speak up about potential areas of improvement. When staff feel comfortable sharing their insights and observations, it can lead to valuable adjustments in how the company approaches customer service. Everyone views your customers and their experience differently, so make sure you are opening yourself up to all perspectives.

10. Empower your customer-facing teams. This point will now be explained at length.

I see customer-facing teams all over LinkedIn: tales of customers caught in the endless loop of "hold" music, going round in circles with chatbots, or feeling the frustration of inflexible policies—I've made some posts about them myself! When you're internal, it's easy to see these processes from a bird's-eye view, focusing on efficiency and the bottom line. But for the customer on the other side, such experiences can make or break their relationship with your brand.

One of the best ways to ease this pain is to empower your teams to do the work that they are most uniquely equipped to do.

But, we know. Empowerment is a pretty big buzzword in the business world, but when we delve into the essence of it, it's quite simple: Trusting your teams with the autonomy to make decisions. This includes your CX team. When you give them the authority to, say, grant refunds outside of a strictly defined policy, you're not just making their jobs easier; you're also showing your customers that their satisfaction is a priority (and that you trust the people helping them!).

Consider this scenario: a customer realizes your product isn't quite the right fit for them. Sure, they might cancel, but that doesn't mean they won't speak highly of your service or recommend it to someone for whom it's better suited. However, if that customer encounters barriers when trying to cancel or is denied a justified refund, their perception of your brand takes a hit. Their story about your brand could shift from "It wasn't right for me, but their team was fantastic!" to "I had such a hard time trying to get a refund." Which narrative would you prefer echoing in the market?

Word of mouth and referrals remain among the most trusted and effective ways people discover new products and services. Even in our digital age, a friend's recommendation can carry more weight than a dozen online reviews. Making the cancellation or refund process fuss-free might seem like a small gesture, but its ripple effects can be immense. A smooth experience can turn even a departing customer into a brand advocate, while a negative one can do just the opposite.

A principle worth highlighting: Don't make it difficult for customers to reach out or to walk away. No one likes feeling trapped or ignored. Make sure that your customer service channels are easily accessible, responsive, and above all, empathetic. A human touch, understanding, and flexibility can transform even challenging situations into opportunities for building trust.

Empowering your customer-facing teams is more than just a management strategy; it's a growth strategy. It's about seeing the bigger picture, understanding that every customer interaction shapes your brand's narrative. By prioritizing customer satisfaction and trust over short-term gains, you're not only enhancing your brand's reputation but also planting seeds for future growth through referrals and positive word of mouth. So, go ahead, entrust your teams with more autonomy and watch as customer trust and brand loyalty flourish.

## How to Get Other Teams Involved in CX

We've all heard it said: "Customer experience (CX) is everyone's responsibility." But how often do we see this principle put into actual practice? While it's tempting to pigeonhole CX as the sole domain of a singular team—say, the Customer Service department—the most forward-thinking companies understand that delivering a standout experience requires all hands on deck.

### Show the Big Picture

It's essential to recognize that from product development to marketing, sales to IT, every team plays a pivotal role in the customer journey. For instance, a well-designed product by the R&D team can drastically reduce customer complaints, while timely and relevant marketing campaigns can enhance a customer's brand perception.

Action Tip: Organize cross-functional workshops showcasing real customer stories, both good and bad. Highlighting specific instances where different departments made an impact can drive home the collective role everyone plays.

## Establish Clear Communication Channels

In many organizations, there's a goldmine of customer insights hidden away in various departments. For example, the sales team may have invaluable feedback on why a customer chose not to make a purchase, while the IT team might have data on app glitches causing user frustration.

Action Tip: Consider implementing a centralized feedback repository or platform where departments can share their customer insights. Regular cross-departmental meetings can also facilitate information exchange, ensuring no valuable insight goes unnoticed.

## Celebrate Wins as a Collective

When the marketing team rolls out a successful campaign or the product team launches a much-requested feature, it's not just their victory; it's a win for the customer and, by extension, the entire company.

Action Tip: Establish a company-wide recognition system, celebrating teams that have made significant strides in improving CX. This could range from "Customer Hero" awards to dedicated shout-outs in company newsletters.

## Encourage a Culture of Empathy

Beyond metrics and KPIs, fostering genuine empathy towards customers can be a game-changer. When teams can put themselves in the customers' shoes, they naturally gravitate towards creating solutions that cater to real needs.

Action Tip: Encourage teams to regularly interact with customers. This could be through attending customer service calls, joining focus group discussions, or even going on field visits. The more direct interactions they have, the more empathy they'll cultivate.

## Offer Collaborative Training Sessions

Instead of isolated training sessions for each department, consider organizing joint sessions focused on holistic customer experience. A mixed group of, say, developers, marketers, and customer service reps brainstorming together can lead to out-of-the-box solutions.

Action Tip: Host collaborative training sessions where mixed teams work on real-world customer scenarios. For example, a session could involve addressing a specific customer pain point, with each department brainstorming solutions from their perspective. We have a great example of one of these in the next section.

Great CX isn't a sprint; it's a relay race where the baton is passed between departments, each playing their part in creating a seamless experience. By fostering inter-departmental collaboration and rooting every action in customer-centricity, companies can ensure that every team member, irrespective of their role, feels invested in delivering exceptional customer experiences.

# Pathing Insights from CX to Other Teams

Creating a pathway for insights to flow from CX to other departments is pivotal for a business aiming to be truly customer-centric. The feedback and insights from customers can provide valuable data that, when shared and acted upon, can drive improvement across the board. Here are some of the best ways to ensure this flow of information.

## Integrated CRM Systems

Modern businesses thrive on data, and CRM systems are the backbone for storing crucial customer data. By adopting an all-encompassing CRM system, departments can access a gold mine of customer information, from feedback to purchasing behavior. For instance, if a customer reports a product flaw, the product development team can instantly view this feedback and start rectifying it. Similarly, sales can tailor pitches based on customer interactions, leading to better conversions.

## Regular Cross-Departmental Meetings

Simply collecting feedback isn't enough; it must be discussed and acted upon. Regular meetings bridge the gap between departments, ensuring everyone is aligned. For instance, if marketing is aware of common customer pain points, they can shape campaigns around addressing those issues. These meetings become a hub for collaborative problem-solving, ensuring every department is customer-focused.

Here are some ideas for meetings that you might introduce:

- Monthly Customer Insight Roundtables: The CX team shares recent feedback, both positive and negative, with representatives from all departments. This allows everyone to hear directly about customer praises, pain points, and suggestions.

- Product-Feedback Sync-Ups: Regular sessions between the product team and customer support can help address common product-related issues and potential enhancements. This direct line ensures that the product team is always in the loop about customer feedback.

- Marketing and Support Alignment Meetings: Marketing teams can gain a deeper understanding of customer personas by listening to real-world customer queries and concerns from the support team. Similarly, support can get a heads-up on upcoming campaigns or product launches.

- Sales-Customer Support Handoff Discussions: These meetings ensure smooth transitions for new clients. The sales team can communicate specific promises or expectations set during the sales process, and the support team can prepare accordingly.

- Quarterly Strategy Brainstorms: Representatives from all departments gather to brainstorm strategies based on recent customer feedback and evolving market conditions. This collective approach can lead to innovative solutions that cater to customer needs.

- Operational Review Workshops: The operations team meets with both the sales and support teams to understand any logistical challenges customers might face, be it shipping concerns, billing issues, or anything in between.

- Training and Onboarding Syncs: HR collaborates with CX and other customer-facing departments to ensure that new hires are thoroughly trained in the company's customer-first philosophy and practices.

- Data and Analytics Deep Dives: Data analysts, together with the CX and sales teams, explore patterns in customer behavior, segment feedback, and devise metrics that can better gauge customer satisfaction.

- Tech Stack Review Meetings: IT, marketing, sales, and customer support come together to review and discuss the current tech tools and platforms in use. They can explore if any tool needs an upgrade or if there's a need for new software to better serve customers.

- Annual Customer-Centricity Retreats: An off-site meeting or workshop where teams from every department gather to celebrate successes, learn from failures, and chart out the roadmap for the coming year with the customer at its heart.

## Feedback Loop Systems

Think of this as an organized conveyor belt for customer insights. Instead of feedback getting lost in the abyss of shared inboxes, it's systematically routed to the right department. So, if a customer suggests a new feature, it goes straight to the product team's pipeline, ensuring quicker action and letting customers know their voice matters.

This will not just happen naturally. Here are ten key steps to take to get a feedback loop setup.

1. Identify Key Touchpoints. Determine where and when you'll solicit feedback. This could be post-purchase, after customer service interactions, or at the end of a user session on your app or website.

2. Choose Feedback Tools. Decide on tools or platforms to collect feedback. This could be as simple as email surveys, feedback forms on your website, or more sophisticated tools like NPS (Net Promoter Score) surveys or customer feedback management software.

3. Simplify the Feedback Process. Make it easy for customers to provide feedback. Limit the number of questions, use clear and concise language, and ensure that the process is quick.

4. Categorize Feedback. Once feedback starts coming in, classify it into different categories like product feedback, service feedback, website experience, and so on. This will help in routing the feedback to the relevant department or team.

5. Analyze and Interpret. After categorization, analyze the feedback to identify patterns or recurring issues. This will help in prioritizing actions.

6. Route Feedback. Ensure feedback reaches the right teams or departments. For instance, product-related feedback should go to the product team, while issues about service can be addressed by the customer service department.

7. Act on Feedback. This is the crux of the loop. Take actionable steps based on the feedback received. It could mean making

product changes, tweaking your website, or training your customer service team on specific issues.

8. Close the Loop with the Customer. Once an action is taken based on feedback, communicate back to the customer. Let them know their feedback was valued and acted upon. This could be done through personalized emails, newsletters, or direct phone calls.
9. Measure the Impact. Over time, measure the impact of the changes you've made based on feedback. Has customer satisfaction improved? Are there fewer complaints about a previously problematic feature?
10. Iterate and Improve. Use metrics and subsequent rounds of feedback to continuously refine your products, services, and processes. Adjust your feedback loop based on what you learn.

## Internal Communication Channels

Platforms like Slack or Teams aren't just for sharing memes or setting up lunch outings. They can be powerful tools where real-time customer insights are shared. For instance, a dedicated Slack channel for customer feedback ensures that any urgent issues are immediately flagged and resolved, improving response times. These should be shared between teams at the company that have a stake, and can make meaningful improvements in the event that something goes wrong. For instance, Marketing, Sales, CX, and Engineering.

## Incorporate CX Data into Business Analytics

Customer insights are a piece of the larger business puzzle. By integrating them into wider business metrics, companies can identify trends, gaps, and opportunities. For instance, a spike in customer complaints might correlate with a recent product change, signaling the need for swift rectification. You can also match up key CX insights with company metrics like lifetime value (LTV) or customer acquisition cost (CAC), to make what you do even more contextualized for other teams.

## Joint Workshops and Training

It's one thing to share feedback; it's another to collaboratively address it. Workshops offer a hands-on approach where teams tackle real-world customer scenarios. This not only fosters inter-departmental collaboration but also generates innovative solutions grounded in customer-centric thinking. Here's an example of a day-long workshop that you might conduct (or break into several segments over a few days) to create more connection between your product and support team.

---

**Joint Workshop:** Product Team and Customer Support Team . "Understanding Customer Pain Points to Drive Product Enhancements"

**Objective**

To bridge the gap between the Product Team (responsible for designing and updating the product) and the Customer Support Team (often the first line of defense in handling customer issues and feedback) to promote a more customer-centric product development approach.

**Agenda**

Introduction (15 minutes)

- Brief on the importance of cross-team collaboration in achieving customer-centricity.
- Objective and expected outcomes of the workshop.

Pain Point Presentation (45 minutes)

The Customer Support Team presents common customer complaints, issues, and feedback collected over the past quarter. This should include direct quotes, possible frequency of each issue, and any patterns they've noticed.

Product Team Insights (45 minutes)

The Product Team discusses the current roadmap, existing features in development, and their perspective on the feedback presented. They explain certain product decisions made in the past, giving the Customer Support Team a deeper understanding of the product's direction.

Breakout Sessions (1 hour)

Participants break into smaller groups, mixing members from both teams. Each group is given a specific customer pain point to discuss. They should come up with potential solutions or improvements that address the issue.

Group Presentations (1 hour)

Each breakout group presents their pain point and proposed solutions. Discussions should be encouraged to understand the feasibility, potential impact, and priority of each suggestion.

Feedback Integration Discussion (30 minutes)

Discuss how the feedback from the workshop can be integrated into the product roadmap.

Determine what changes can be made in the short term and what might be longer-term goals.

Action Plan and Next Steps (30 minutes)

Jointly develop an action plan to address the main takeaways from the workshop. Assign responsibilities and timelines.

Schedule a follow-up meeting to review progress and ensure accountability.

Wrap-up and Feedback on Workshop (15 minutes)

A brief wrap-up, thanking everyone for their participation.

Distribute a short feedback form on the workshop to understand what went well and what can be improved for future sessions.

> **Outcome**
> By the end of this joint workshop, both teams will have a deeper understanding of the customer's perspective and the challenges faced by each team. The Product Team gets direct insights into real-world user challenges, and the Customer Support Team gains clarity on the product's direction and rationale behind certain design choices. This mutual understanding fosters better internal communication and drives more customer-focused product development.

## Feedback Repository

Imagine having a library of customer insights at your fingertips. A centralized database acts as this reservoir, allowing teams to pull insights for various initiatives. Whether the marketing team is crafting a new campaign or R&D is brainstorming product features, they have direct access to what customers are saying.

You could use a CRM, Ticketing System, feedback collection platform, social listening platform, or even a chat tool like Slack to aggregate this information. Ultimately, it should all be pulled into a centralized place, using code, manual entry, or automation.

## Appoint CX Ambassadors

These are your internal CX champions. By having dedicated individuals in each department, you ensure there's always a conduit for customer insights. These ambassadors act as a bridge, ensuring their teams are always aligned with the customer's perspective.

This can be great if the person has originally or historically worked in support!

# Voice of the Customer

One of the most effective ways to truly understand your customers and cultivate cross-company value of CX is through the Voice of the

Customer (VoC) strategies. But what are they, and how can you harness their power? Don't worry. We've got you.

What Is the Voice of the Customer (VoC)

VoC is a research and feedback-gathering method that captures customer needs, desires, preferences, and aversions directly from them. By prioritizing the customer's voice, businesses can make informed decisions that align products, services, and experiences with genuine customer needs, enhancing satisfaction and loyalty.

VoC isn't just about collecting feedback after a purchase or service experience. It's a holistic approach to gathering insights on every aspect of the customer's interaction with a brand. This includes understanding their needs (both met and unmet), their desires (what they aspire to achieve with a product or service), their preferences (how they would like their interactions to unfold), and their aversions (elements they dislike or find off-putting).

One of the hallmarks of VoC is that it sources feedback directly from the customer. Instead of making assumptions or relying solely on market trends, VoC seeks to hear the customer's perspective in their own words. This can be through various mediums, from one-on-one interviews, focus groups, and direct observations to digital methods like online surveys and social media listening.

While every business will have internal metrics and KPIs, a true VoC strategy places the customer's viewpoint at the forefront. It's a shift from inward-facing metrics (like sales targets) to outward-facing metrics (like customer satisfaction scores or Net Promoter Score). The philosophy here is simple: If you cater to the customer's needs and exceed their expectations, business success will naturally follow.

By continually gathering and analyzing VoC data, businesses can make strategic decisions rooted in real-world insights. Whether it's tweaking a product feature, overhauling a service protocol, or introducing a new offering, VoC ensures that such decisions resonate with the customers' genuine needs and desires. In other words, you're not shooting in the dark; you're making choices backed by concrete customer data.

## Benefits of a VoC Strategy

Voice of the Customer is about fostering a two-way dialogue with your customers. It's about listening intently, acting on feedback, and continually refining the brand experience to make it more in tune with what customers truly seek. In an age where competition is fierce, and customers are more discerning than ever, a VoC strategy might just be the differentiating factor that sets a business apart. Here are a few of its key benefits.

### Better Product Development

When a business truly grasps its customer needs and pain points, it's in a prime position to innovate and iterate. This could mean introducing entirely new products that fill a gap in the market or tweaking current offerings to better serve users. The essence of product development is solving problems for the customer, and what better way to identify those problems than by listening directly to them?

Moreover, when customers feel that a product has been crafted with their specific needs in mind, they're more likely to resonate with it, leading to higher adoption rates and more favorable feedback. In short, anchoring product development around customer insights ensures that business offerings are always relevant, timely, and tailored to meet actual market demands.

### Enhanced Customer Experience

Offering a great product or service often isn't enough. How a customer feels when they interact with a brand can be just as crucial. Armed with insights into what truly matters to the customer, businesses can refine every touchpoint, from the first point of contact to post-purchase support.

This could involve simplifying a checkout process, offering more personalized recommendations, or even something as straightforward as reducing wait times in a call queue. By consistently striving to reduce friction and elevate positive interactions, businesses not only meet customer expectations but often exceed them. The result? Memorable experiences that foster loyalty and create customers who are enthusiastic about returning.

## Increased Revenue

It's a simple equation: happy customers lead to better business outcomes. When customers feel valued and satisfied, they're not only more likely to stick around but also to deepen their relationship with the brand. This could translate into buying more products, upgrading their current service package, or even branching out into other offerings from the same brand. Furthermore, satisfied customers often become brand advocates, sharing their positive experiences with friends, family, and their broader networks.

This word-of-mouth marketing is invaluable, driving new customer acquisition without the significant costs associated with traditional advertising. In essence, by focusing on customer happiness and meeting their needs, businesses set themselves up for sustained revenue growth, both through retaining existing customers and attracting new ones.

## Crafting Your VoC Strategy

Crafting a comprehensive and actionable VoC strategy is the linchpin to success in making use of customer insights. This section delves into the steps to create a robust VoC framework, ensuring that you can not only listen to your customers but also adapt and evolve based on their feedback.

1. Set Clear Objectives

Every successful strategy begins with well-defined objectives. Before diving into the world of Voice of the Customer (VoC), it's crucial to pinpoint exactly what you aim to achieve. Perhaps there's a feature of your software that's generating mixed reviews and you want a clearer understanding. Or maybe you've noticed a slight decline in your post-sales support ratings.

For example, a streaming service might wish to understand why a specific show isn't being watched to its end by most viewers. By having a clear goal, such as enhancing user experience or refining post-sales support, you're better poised to design your VoC approach with precision and purpose.

2. Choose Your Tools

With the digital age in full swing, there are more tools than ever to gather customer feedback. From traditional methods like interviews and feedback forms to more modern approaches like social listening tools, each offers its unique perspective.

An online retailer, for instance, might utilize post-purchase surveys to gauge satisfaction, while a restaurant chain might lean heavily on social media reviews to gather diner sentiments. Your tool choice should align with where your customers are most active and where you believe you'll procure the most candid insights.

3. Segment Your Audience

It's a well-acknowledged fact in marketing and CX: No two customers are completely alike. By segmenting your audience—say, based on how frequently they use your product, their purchasing behavior, or even demographic factors like age or region—you can curate more tailored questions.

Consider a SaaS company; they might segment users who've just started a trial differently from long-term subscribers, hoping to understand the early-stage user experience versus sustained utility.

4. Ask the Right Questions

Formulating your questions is an art. They need to be clear to avoid confusion, concise enough to retain attention, and open-ended when you're fishing for detailed feedback.

For instance, a hotel chain might ask, "What's one thing we could have done to make your stay exceptional?" rather than a simple "Did you enjoy your stay?" By encouraging more descriptive feedback, you're better armed with actionable insights.

Collect Feedback

With your tools in hand and questions ready, it's action time. Whether you're launching a survey after a product purchase, initiating one-on-one interviews, or monitoring feedback via chosen platforms, this phase is about gathering raw data.

For example, an e-commerce platform might introduce a pop-up survey post-checkout to gauge the shopping experience, looking for insights on navigation ease, product selection, and checkout efficiency.

6. Analyze and Interpret

Once feedback streams in, the real work begins. Raw data, in isolation, offers limited value. Businesses need to sift through the feedback, identifying recurring themes, pain points, or unique suggestions.

A tech company might notice a recurring theme around users struggling with a new interface, signaling the need for an interface tweak or more robust user education.

7. Implement Changes

The power of VoC shines through when businesses action the feedback. It's not just about collecting insights; it's about effecting change.

If a coffee shop chain consistently receives feedback about a particular drink being too sweet, a recipe revision might be in order. By making necessary adjustments, whether to a product, service, or protocol, businesses underline their commitment to customer-centricity.

8. Review and Refine

Voice of the Customer isn't a "set and forget" strategy. As the market evolves, customer preferences change, and businesses grow, so it's imperative to revisit your VoC strategy.

An annual subscription service, for instance, might review its feedback mechanisms each year before renewal campaigns, ensuring they're capturing the most relevant insights. By staying adaptable, you ensure your VoC remains a potent tool in your business arsenal.

## Getting Started with VoC

Diving into the Voice of the Customer (VoC) world can feel like a lot at first. But think of it as trying out a new hobby; it's always best to start small and pick things up as you go along. For starters, kick off with something manageable like a quick survey after a purchase or maybe a chatty focus group. Think about that little boutique down the street. Before switching up their whole product line, they could test the waters with feedback forms for a couple of items. It's like testing a recipe before hosting a big dinner party.

Now, for the VoC magic to really work, it's not just about the fancy tools or the neatly designed surveys. It's about getting everyone, from Dave in product design to Sarah in sales, on board and excited. Imagine if Dave could get a lowdown from Sarah about what customers are saying and then tinker around with his designs? That's how businesses create stuff that people really want.

When it comes to feedback, timing is key. It's a bit like asking someone their opinion about a movie right after the credits roll versus a month later. If an online tech store pings a customer right after they've bought a new gadget, the response is likely to be raw and real. Pop in an instant email survey or a quick chatbot message, and you'll capture those initial reactions, be it sheer joy or a bit of frustration.

The heart of a solid VoC strategy, though? Being real. Customers can spot a half-hearted effort from a mile away. If they feel like their feedback is going into some corporate black hole, they won't bother. But if they see that cafe down the road tweaking its menu based on suggestions, or a software app rolling out features that users have been clamoring for, they'll know their voice matters.

Let's be honest: Not all feedback will be sunshine and rainbows. Some of it might sting, like finding out people don't love that new feature as much as you thought they would. But that's okay. It's like getting honest advice from a friend. Instead of shying away from it, embracing these critiques can be the roadmap to making things even better. After all, every piece of feedback, good or bad, is a step towards creating something awesome.

## Key Challenges and Overcoming Them

There's no denying the magic of Voice of the Customer (VoC) in shaping a company's direction. The ability to tap directly into the desires and grievances of your audience is a superpower. However, with great power comes—you guessed it—a couple of hitches.

### Drowning in Feedback

My worst nightmare is being at a party where everyone's talking to me. At once. Overwhelming, right? That's what feedback can feel like initially. With the myriad of channels available—from social media to emails, surveys, and more—the flood of information can be staggering.

The Fix: Embrace technology to your advantage. Utilize advanced analytics and AI-powered tools that can sift through the noise, helping you categorize and prioritize feedback. Instead of trying to respond to every single comment, focus on discerning patterns and overarching themes.

### Biased or Unclear Feedback

You've sent out a survey, and the results are… confusing. Some feedback is contradictory, and other pieces seem overly positive or negative. It's like getting mixed reviews on a new recipe—some find it too spicy, others too bland.

The Fix: Diversify your feedback channels. Don't rely solely on one medium. A mix of surveys, one-on-one interviews, focus groups, and even third-party reviews can give a more rounded perspective. And always encourage respondents to be specific—the more detailed the feedback, the more actionable it becomes.

## Integrating Feedback into Tangible Strategies

Okay, so you've got the feedback. Now what? The challenge lies in translating these insights into actionable steps for different departments, from R&D to marketing.

The Fix: Create a cross-functional team responsible for distilling the feedback and deciding on actionable steps. For example, if customers are consistently asking for a feature in your app, the tech team needs to be in the loop. Monthly or quarterly meetings can ensure everyone's on the same page, making feedback-driven changes.

## Maintaining a Genuine Commitment

It's easy for companies to say, "We value customer feedback." But if customers feel their suggestions fall into a black hole, never to be addressed or acknowledged, they might wonder if you really do.

The Fix: Keep the communication channels open. Update your customers on the changes you're making based on their feedback. A simple newsletter or update on your website can go a long way in showing your audience that you genuinely value their input.

Weaving a narrative centered around the customer is not just a strategic choice—it's a defining ethos. As we journeyed through the intricacies of building a customer-centric company, it's evident that this transformation isn't merely about implementing a set of processes or practices. At its core, it's about cultivating a mindset, a culture, and a commitment that places the customer at the epicenter of every decision, every action, and every interaction.

The steps and strategies explored within these pages are guideposts, vital in their own right. Yet the essence of true customer-centricity transcends beyond methodologies. It lies in our ability to empathize, to listen intently, and to adapt with both agility and authenticity. It's about ensuring that every team member, from the C-suite to the front lines, resonates with a shared vision—that of enriching and elevating the lives of those we serve.

As this chapter closes, it's essential to remember that the journey towards customer-centricity is continuous, dynamic, and ever-evolving. Voice of the Customer strategies, when executed well, can be a goldmine of insights, driving businesses closer to their customers and fostering lasting relationships. While the path might have its bumps, the destination—a business that resonates deeply with its customers—is worth every effort. Remember, in the cacophony of today's business world, sometimes the most crucial voice is that of your customer. Listen closely.

# CHAPTER 10:

# Bringing in Help

Every once in a while, even the most seasoned CX teams hit a wall. Maybe it's a tricky challenge, a new market, or just the need for a fresh set of eyes. That's when ringing up some outside help can make all the difference. In this chapter, we'll chat about the ins and outs of bringing in external pros to team up with your in-house crew.

Think of it as calling a buddy to help you move a couch—it's not that you can't do it alone, but having an extra hand (especially if they've moved a ton of couches before) just makes everything smoother. We'll dig into when it makes sense to give your team that extra boost, and how to make sure everyone's playing to the same beat once you do. By the end, you'll see that merging the strengths of your internal champs with outside aces isn't just smart—it's a game-changer for creating standout customer experiences. Let's dive in!

## What Is Outsourcing?

Think of outsourcing like this: You're throwing a big party and you decide to hire a caterer instead of cooking all the food yourself. Why? Because you want to focus on being a great host and enjoy your own party. Plus, the caterer probably has way better cooking skills and all the right equipment. Maybe you've got two kids like me, and very little help in the kitchen to boot. In the business world, outsourcing is pretty much the same concept.

Let's say you run a tech startup. Your expertise is in developing products, not necessarily in answering customer service calls 24/7. So, you hire an external company specialized in customer support to handle that for you. This way, you get to focus on what you're really good at—like creating the next big app—while a team of pros handles the customer queries.

It's a win-win. You're maximizing efficiency and getting specialized help where you need it. Just remember, though, you're still the host of the party. So, choose your "caterers" wisely and make sure they're up to your standards!

# What Are Its benefits?

Every touchpoint, every interaction, and every resolution matters. With soaring customer expectations and the constant race to provide top-tier service, companies often face a crucial question: Should we handle customer support in-house or consider outsourcing?

An adept customer support outsourcing firm is equipped to handle the nuances of customer interactions, ensuring a delightful experience every step of the way. They've already helped tons of companies with issues similar to you and know where the pitfalls are. Here are some of the key benefits to consider.

## Expertise on Tap

Think of brands like Apple, known for their impeccable products. Yet even they rely on external partners for certain services. Outsourcing means tapping into seasoned professionals who live and breathe customer support. They're the "Apple Geniuses" of support, ready to tackle any issue with finesse.

## Cost Efficiency

Remember when bootstrapped startups like Slack were looking to make the most of every penny? Outsourcing offers a solution. Instead of heavy investments in hiring and training, businesses can leverage the infrastructure of established support firms, getting top-notch service without breaking the bank. Here's an example of the cost of a team of 15 across different geographies.

## Scalability

Recall the "Baby Yoda" craze? I still haven't watched "The Mandalorian" because of all of that. Products can suddenly trend, leading to a surge in queries. With outsourcing, it's easier to scale operations seamlessly during these high-demand periods, ensuring no fan is left unanswered.

## Diverse Skill Set

Consider companies like Samsung, which deal with a vast range of products. Outsourcing partners often boast teams with specialists in various fields. So, whether a customer has a query about a refrigerator or a smartphone, there's an expert ready to assist.

## 24/7 Support

Netflix, a global sensation, has viewers binge-watching at all hours. If they relied solely on a local in-house team, many international queries would face delays. But with outsourced teams across the globe, they can provide real-time assistance, anytime.

For instance, if a brand like Doc Martens launches a new shoe line globally, an in-house team might struggle to juggle the influx of international queries. But, with an outsourced team, a customer in Tokyo gets the same timely, informed response as one in Paris, making their shopping experience seamless and positive.

## Fresh Perspectives

Ever noticed how with some movie sequels with fresh directors, things are different, for better or worse? Similarly, an external support team can offer insights and feedback strategies that an in-house team might be too close to see.

However, it's essential to remember that while outsourcing has its array of benefits, the decision isn't one-size-fits-all. It's about finding a partner who not only has the skills but also vibes with your brand's essence.

They're your brand ambassadors, after all. Make the right choice, and your customer experience could very well be the talk of the town.

## What Are Its Downsides?

Outsourcing has undeniably become the magic bullet, especially when it comes to customer support. But just like that coffee shop on the corner with the alluring aroma but inconsistent brews, there can be a mismatch between expectations and delivery. As we pull back the curtain, let's delve into the challenges faced by many companies and stir in some real-world examples to get the full picture.

### Loss of Personal Touch

Take the charm of local mom-and-pop stores. The store owner knows your name, your go-to orders, and how your day's been. This personalized touch can be the first casualty when support is outsourced, depending on which company you are working with. For brands built on deep customer relationships, like Ben & Jerry's with its community-centric ethos, it is extra important to evaluate and find a BPO that can help co-create a nuanced understanding of their customer base.

### Communication Barriers

Ever played the "Telephone Game?" Information can get distorted as it's passed along. Similarly, when support is outsourced, particularly overseas, linguistic and cultural barriers can sometimes lead to misunderstandings. Think of a customer trying to explain a technical glitch to a support agent who interprets the issue differently due to language nuances. This is something that can be solved for in the interview process, but can be a downside if you don't think to assess for it.

### Limited Control Over Quality

Recall the backlash faced by fashion brands when their outsourced manufacturing practices came under scrutiny? In the same vein, maintaining consistent support quality can be challenging. Businesses can't always oversee outsourced teams as closely as in-house ones, leading to potential discrepancies in service levels. However, the more you put into the relationship as you are building it at the beginning (see some of the sections below on how to do this well), the less likely this is to be a concern.

### Security Concerns

Consider the confidentiality agreements at firms like JP Morgan or Goldman Sachs. Sharing customer data with third parties always carries a risk. Outsourced teams, although contractually bound, might not always adhere to the strict data protection standards required by some businesses, posing a potential threat to customer data.

### Inflexibility in Customization

Imagine ordering a bespoke suit, but you're only allowed to choose from preset designs. Similarly, outsourcing firms often have set processes, making it challenging for brands with unique requirements to get that "perfect fit." For a company like LEGO, which thrives on creativity and customization, such rigidity can hamper their customer service experience.

It's crucial to note that these challenges don't spell the end of outsourcing. They highlight the need for a meticulous selection process and forging partnerships with firms that align with your brand values and vision. After all, while outsourcing can offer a world of convenience, it's the nuances of execution that truly determine success or setback.

## How Will I Know If I Need Outsourcing?

As your business navigates the winding paths of growth, you're often faced with a pressing question: How do I maintain the same quality of service without stretching my resources too thin? It's like trying to serve the perfect latte during the morning rush—there's a point where even the most skilled barista needs an extra pair of hands. In customer experience, that metaphorical "extra pair of hands" often comes in the form of outsourcing.

But how do you discern the right time to embrace this solution? In this section, we'll uncover the tell-tale signs that indicate your business might be ready to venture into the world of outsourcing.

## Customer Support Is Taking You Away from Other (More Impactful) Responsibilities

If you find yourself spending more resources than you expected on managing and growing a customer support team, it could be a sign that outsourcing would be a more efficient way to grow.

Consider the following scenarios:

- Your support team gets little-to-no time to work on projects outside of the queue.

- Your team leads spend a majority of their time managing queue coverage.

- Your manager or director is bogged down in the day-to-day and unable to focus on forecasting.

- None of these individuals are making the most of their valuable time, or doing the things most impactful for a support strategy. You could outsource any of these responsibilities and free up space to improve your customer experience with more meaningful, fulfilling activities.

Josh Magsam, former Director of Support at Discogs, sees this point as the biggest benefit of outsourcing: "To do support well requires knowledge, people, tools, and resources. Outsourcing it can really help businesses tackle more fundamental tasks like product development and sales. By outsourcing, you are buying time, particularly on the management side."

## You Are Running Out of Space in the Office, and/or It Is Increasingly Hard to Source New Hires Where You Are Located

Maybe you've built a strong in-house team that does an amazing job talking to customers and leveraging insights, but it is becoming increasingly hard to fill those roles.

The budget you have does not allow you to hire the caliber of people you would like. Your recruiting team is overburdened and doesn't have time to do the type of outreach needed to hire the right people.

Or maybe there physically just isn't enough office space to house any new hires. When you get to this point, outsourcing probably makes sense. You can still keep a small, extra-knowledgeable team in-house to support experiments and manage the BPO.

Dane Barry, Head of Customer Support at Rachio (formerly Quality Assurance Manager at FCR), thinks that recruiting, hiring, and maintaining talent is the most crucial value that outsourcing companies bring.

"The primary benefit of outsourcing is recruiting and staffing. Anybody who has worked in HR knows that hiring and staffing take a huge amount of time and effort. By working with an outsourcing company, you remove that entire burden from your plate."

## Slower Response Times

Let's be real: In today's digital era, no one likes waiting. Especially not when you've got a question about a product or service you're using. Remember when your startup was just kicking off and your team would respond to queries within an hour? Those days set the expectation for your customers that you're always there, always listening.

But as businesses grow, things can get a bit more... chaotic. More products, more users, and suddenly, that one-hour response time starts to creep up. Before you know it, customers are waiting a whole day, or even longer. And that's when the alarm bells should start ringing.

Take, for instance, a user who's trying to navigate a new feature in your app. If they hit a roadblock and you get back to them swiftly, they're back on track in no time. But let them stew in confusion for a day? They might just decide to jump ship and try out your competitor.

In essence, when your response time starts to lag, it's not just about making customers wait. It's a sign that your customer support might be gasping for air, trying to keep up. It might be time to think about beefing up the team or considering—yep, you guessed it—outsourcing. After all, keeping that casual, friendly, and efficient chat with your customers is worth its weight in gold.

## You Don't Have the Expertise to Pick the Most Valuable Tools, Workflows, or Metrics

When people think about outsourcing, they often think of a large, sad, unskilled group of people sitting in cubicles answering angry customer phone calls. The truth is that a high-quality outsourcing company can handle angry customers with the best of them, but is often positioned to do far more.

A great BPO will also help you pick the right tools and workflows to scale your team efficiently and accomplish the customer experience goals you have in mind.

Beyond that, they can help you benchmark where you are in your industry and set goals for key customer service metrics like average time to first response, CSAT, and handle time.

A good BPO will have a point of view on systems and processes that can help your team scale efficiently; and a great BPO will help you implement them.

## You Want to Support Customers in New Languages and Time Zones

An obvious moment for outsourcing is when you realize you have customers who speak different languages or use your product while your team is offline. For example, our partner HeyGo, who needed 24/7 support but didn't have the bandwidth to staff it.

If you are a U.S.-based company, covering 24 hours in a day can be hard, especially if you care about your team members' quality of life. After all, working the graveyard shift can be difficult!

Many companies find that they would like to prioritize hiring someone who is naturally awake and working when customers are reaching out. A BPO makes it easy to find the right hires for customer service in other parts of the world.

## Surging Ticket Volumes

If the volume of customer inquiries is consistently increasing and your current team struggles to handle the load, it might be time to think about outsourcing. For instance, if you've just launched a new product and the demand spikes, an outsourced team can help manage the influx of questions.

Similarly, if you anticipate rapid growth or fluctuating support demands, having an outsourced team can offer the flexibility to scale up or down as needed. Think of a mobile app that goes viral; outsourcing can help handle the unpredictable surge in users.

## You Want to Offer a New Channel But Don't Want to Take on the Risk and Expenses Associated with It

Let's say you've been offering email and chat support, but realize you need to offer phone support, too. You'll need to figure out the best phone system to use, how to set up an IVR system, get headsets for your team, and make sure the people you hired to do email and chat support are up to the challenge.

Or, you could hire an outsourcing company that has the processes and people to bring it to life on your behalf.

Mary, from a large eCommerce business, put it this way:

Outsourcing makes sense when you need capabilities that your company doesn't have in-house, or need to scale up and down quickly.

We first decided to outsource because we needed phone support, but didn't want to set up the infrastructure for it in-house. We had an internal team focused on email support and needed a partner that already had the equipment and experience ready to go so we could quickly scale that channel.

## What are some questions I can ask during the evaluation process?

Bright promises, impressive testimonials, and charismatic sales pitches may have already been showered upon you. After a few initial interactions, you might find yourself thinking, "These all seem perfect for my needs!" But that's the catch, isn't it? In a sea of promising options, how do you pinpoint the real gems?

Sales calls can paint a rosy picture, and while it's easy to get swept away, your business deserves a partner that doesn't just talk the talk but walks the walk. So, how do you ensure the glossy promises made on that initial call turn into tangible results for your company? You ask the right questions. Let's dive into some essential queries that will help you discern the truly exceptional BPOs from the good talkers.

### Get Your Ducks in a Row Internally First

Before you even begin talking to BPOs, you should list all the qualities that are most important to you in a partner. Be sure to include key stakeholders from your marketing team, IT/Security department, and operations department.

- What are our values? What values am I looking for in an outsourcing partner?

- How do I want to work with the outsourcing partner? Will I be meeting with them weekly? Monthly?
- What tools and systems will we use to keep everyone in the loop?
- How much will I lean on the partner to ensure quality versus doing that in-house?
- How much will I rely on the partner for training new agents versus doing that in-house?
- What technical expertise do agents working for our company need to have? How will I have an outsourcing partner guarantee this?
- How will scheduling work?
- If DEI (Diversity, Equity, and Inclusion) is important at our company, how will that be reflected in an outsourcing partner?
- What level of privacy/security/confidentiality is essential to us? How can we guarantee that in a partner?
- How does our ticket volume fluctuate throughout the year? What are the peaks and valleys? How can a partner scale up and down to meet our volume needs?
- What languages and time zones do we need covered?
- What other types of work do we do besides support tickets? How important is it that an outsourcing company is flexible in what it can deliver on as we grow?
- Where do we think we'll be as a company in one year? Three years? How can I be sure the outsourcing company we pick can scale to meet our needs as we grow?

Once you've decided on all the qualities you are looking for in a BPO, you can assign each a level of importance. Use that when speaking with potential BPOs, so you can grade them on each quality and multiply it by the assigned weight.

If you consistently do this for each company you talk to, you will have quantitative data to help guide your decision. Then, ask them the following questions as you go.

## References

Talking to references is the best way to verify that anything is actually as good as it says it is. It's no different for a high-quality BPO. If you're looking for more validation on your decision, ask for two or three references to speak to.

When you're speaking with the references, try to gain insight into any pros or cons of working with your potential new BPO. Beyond that, if you know other companies working with that outsourcer that are not on the reference list, definitely check with them as well.

If you hear different things from their existing customers than what you heard on the sales call, it's a sign that you may need to do more due diligence to ensure that the company performs as well as they say they do.

## Employee Attrition

Don't be afraid to ask for detailed information about attrition. A BPO that is focused on quality will have voluntary attrition rates between two and four percent a month. If it's anything more than that, you should consider asking more questions about why.

High attrition could mean employees are underpaid or the company culture isn't great. Either one of those things will ultimately impact your customers. High attrition overall also means there will likely be turnover on your team.

When you constantly have team members revolving through your team, the quality of service your customers receive degrades and causes additional friction in training up new team members.

Mary, from before, counts attrition as one of the most important data points to look at in the sales process:

If you see really low attrition rates, it means people are engaged, which is a good indicator of things behind the scenes. If you see a high attrition rate, that's not good.

## Recruiting Strategies

Digging into an outsourcing company's recruiting strategy can teach you a lot about what it will be like to work with them. Consider asking about the following.

- What is the profile of typical hires at their company?
- How many years of experience do employees at different levels typically have?
- How do they evaluate candidates' language skills?
- How long does it take to bring on new team members?
- How will the outsourcing company match candidates for your specific company?
- Can you look at writing samples and background information for candidates that will be placed on your team?
- Can you see the assessments they use for front-line agents and managers?

A BPO's ability to quickly hire great talent is one of the main reasons to hire one in the first place, so pay close attention to their ability to do it well and whether it aligns with how your business approaches hiring.

## Meet the Team

If you get close to signing a contract, you should ask to meet the management layer that you will be working with. These are the folks you'll be meeting with on a weekly or monthly basis for reporting, performance, and training purposes.

Make sure you like and trust them. Do they seem like accountable managers that you would actually enjoy working with? If not, pass on the company. A mismatch with management will cause a lot of headaches for you down the road, and can make for an unenjoyable work environment for anyone on the team.

A BPO is working to level up your whole team—it's important to have values and personalities that complement each other.

Don't stop there, though. If the management layer seems good, ask to meet with some front-line employees. They likely won't be the exact ones assigned to your team, but it will give you a good sense of what to expect for the ones who will be.

These are the folks that will talk to your customers day in and day out, so you should have the experience of talking to them, too. Use your conversations to gauge how you would feel about this person speaking with your customers.

> Mary watches out for a couple of things during these calls:
>
> There's a lot of generic customer service jargon that people can say back to you, like "Yes, we ensure quality and CSAT are important." It's easy to say things like that, but just knowing how to run a contact center is not enough. You need to be more detailed about what you are looking for.
>
> Specific data points and use cases are important to dig into. For example, in a recent RFP (Request for Proposal), we were really specific about needing non-English support in these exact languages, or complex finance support. You need to get in a room with the team and ask follow-up questions.

## Outsourcing Company Size

Another thing to consider is the size of your program compared to the size of the BPO. A ten-person team is likely not going to get a lot of attention at a 20,000 person company.

If you're running a team of 20 or fewer agents, you would be best-served by a smaller BPO (150 to 1,000 employees). There are BPOs that can get your team started with additional help as small as a single agent, or a pool of shared team members.

If you're running a team of 21 to 100 agents, you could work with a large BPO, but you'll still get more attention from a company with 500 to 2,500 employees (assuming they can meet your operational needs).

If you'll be scaling to hundreds of agents in a short period of time, that is when you would want to limit your search to a large BPO with 2,500 to 20,000+ global employees.

## Matching Candidates to Brands

Does the outsourcing company make an effort to match their employees to customers based on product knowledge and interest? For instance, if you are an ecommerce business, will they strive to place employees within your program that already have ecommerce experience?

Companies that do the research on your product and their employees to ensure a good match will go a long way in terms of quality of service and employee retention.

# How Do I Know If They Are Ethically Sound?

Partnering with a Business Process Outsourcing (BPO) firm is no longer just about cost savings and operational efficiency. With increasing awareness around global issues, corporate responsibility has moved to the forefront, and businesses are expected to uphold a high ethical standard. This expectation extends to their partners, including BPOs.

When considering an outsourcing partner, it's crucial to ascertain not just their service quality and expertise, but also their commitment to ethical practices. After all, the actions of your BPO can reflect on your brand, potentially impacting its reputation. Thus, ensuring that the BPO you're evaluating adheres to ethical standards is not only morally right but also smart business. In this section, we'll delve into how you can assess whether a BPO operates ethically and aligns with your company's values.

Darnell Witt, EVP and Head of Solutions at PartnerHero, former Senior Director of Support and Community at Vimeo, explains why some BPOs may not always act ethically:

> The rumors you heard are true, BUT they aren't true across the board. If you do a Google search for the world's worst employers, call centers and outsourcing companies will be among what you find, and they are there for a reason.
>
> The business model of many outsourcing companies is to increase profitability by churning and burning through low-level employees and always widening the gap between what they charge customers and what they pay their employees.
>
> They have an incentive to pay as low as the market allows. That being said, there are plenty of outsourcing companies that have chosen a different approach. These are companies that want to build long-term relationships with their customers and employees.

But how will you know the difference when evaluating different companies? Below are the key indicators you can use to determine if a company is treating employees well and in it for the long run or using a "churn and burn" approach.

The good news for you is that being able to differentiate between the two will also help you determine if the vendor you are talking to can provide quality service or not.

## Indicator Number 1: Employee Retention Rates

This is the second time we've mentioned this, and for good reason! The employees of a BPO are the number one indicator of business health. You should ask each vendor that you speak to about employee retention.

Vendors should be able to provide you with a report that shows monthly and annual numbers for both voluntary and involuntary attrition.

Again, attrition should not be above 4% monthly. You should also ask for average tenure across their different teams. If the numbers look high, that is a bad sign. Of all the indicators you can use to determine if a company is good or bad, this is the most important one.

## Indicator Number 2: Current Employees

When you're conducting your reference interviews with managers and current employees, dive a bit into the ethics of the business.

Ask them how long they've worked at the company, what their experience has been like, and to describe their day-to-day activities. This will give you a sense of whether the company has hiring and operating standards similar to your own.

## Indicator Number 3: Pricing

Pricing and how employees are treated do not always track linearly. That being said, if the companies you're looking at all seem pretty similar, but one or two have dramatically lower pricing, that should be a red flag.

You should ask questions to better understand how they are able to provide a quality service at that price and, specifically, if it's at the expense of providing a living wage to front-line workers.

Companies that are offering prices on the lower end or below are likely paying employees less, and you may see more burnout and attrition.

## Indicator Number 4: Pay Rates and Benefits

Don't be shy to ask the outsourcing companies you're looking at how much they pay, what benefits they offer, and whether your agents will be employees or contractors.

Be wary of companies that over-rely on contractors and don't offer a solid benefits package.

## Indicator Number 5: References

We spoke about references earlier—if there is one thing you do to vet an outsourcing company, it's to speak to their references. And, the topic of employee welfare should be on your list of questions.

What has their experience of employee turnover been? How adept are the program managers and team leads?

What are the best ways to outsource with success?

In finding an outsourcing company, it's easy to overlook the preparation that needs to happen internally to set the relationship up for success. The first weeks and months are critical for the future of your new team.

Putting in some extra work in the beginning will pay huge dividends as time goes on. But what does this mean?

## Set Clear Mutual Expectations

From the get-go, both parties should have a clear understanding of what is expected. Whether it's response times, quality metrics, or any other KPI, set clear targets. For instance, if you want your customers to receive a response within 12 hours, make sure the BPO knows this and has the resources to achieve it.

## Comprehensive Training

Your BPO team should be an extension of your brand. Invest time in training them not just about the processes, but also about your company's values, culture, and the essence of what makes your brand unique. Consider the example of a health and wellness brand that prides itself on empathy and understanding. Training sessions should emphasize these values so that they come across in every customer interaction.

> Here's what Mary has to say:
>
> Try thinking about it from their perspective. Do they have the resources they need? Were they adequately trained? Do they have access to the permissions necessary to take action on the backend?
>
> It can be difficult when you are 10+ years into building a company and the tools have been built up over time for an internal team. These tools and systems may not be made for an outsourced agent.
>
> It depends where you are in the lifecycle of the company, but most companies probably need to go back and figure out how to make their systems simpler and more streamlined to optimize for an outsourcing company.

First, make a list of all the types of tickets and workflows you are asking your outsourcing partner to take on. Evaluate your training materials for these processes.

- Are they up to date? Are they clear? Are they engaging?
- Is there a test component to make sure agents have understood the material?
- Does the training include how to handle edge cases and how to escalate issues that come up?

If the answer to any of these questions is "No," you have two options: update your training to make sure the answer to all the questions is "Yes," or work with your new partner to get dedicated training resources that you can work with to ensure your trainings are ready for prime-time.

The worst option is to share inadequate training with your new team, which will lead to disappointment and more work in the long run.

To make sure agents are ready, Dane from Rachio likes to do mock phone calls and tickets.

> The best way to test if an agent is ready is through mock support interactions. You can also set up quizzes as part of training, so you can quiz and make sure they understand material they were trained on.
>
> A lot of your success is dependent on how much you put into it. Make sure you are always engaged, and that there's plenty of face-to-face (or Zoom) interaction.
>
> It's so important that you treat your new partner like a partner. Make sure you are incorporating them into your internal structure. The last thing you want is to create a silo.

## Establish Regular Check-Ins

In the beginning, frequent check-ins can iron out any hiccups. Whether it's a weekly meeting or a bi-weekly report, ensure there are avenues for open dialogue. A tech startup, for example, experienced a surge in specific product-related queries after launching a new feature. Regular check-ins allowed them to quickly relay this to the BPO, ensuring agents were prepared with answers.

## Use Technology to Your Advantage

Leverage modern tools and platforms that allow for seamless communication, monitoring, and reporting. This can be especially important if your BPO operates from a different time zone. A fashion e-commerce business might utilize chat tools for real-time communication and cloud-based platforms to share relevant product updates or feedback instantly.

## Solicit Feedback

The BPO agents are on the front lines, interacting with your customers daily. Encourage them to share insights, as they can offer a fresh perspective on potential pain points or areas of improvement. For instance, agents might notice that many customers are confused about a specific section of your return policy, prompting a possible revision or clearer communication on your website.

## Foster a Partnership Mentality

View the BPO as a partner, not just a vendor. When they feel invested in your success, they're more likely to go the extra mile. Celebrate achievements together and work collaboratively on challenges. A digital payment platform, upon hitting a customer satisfaction milestone, sent out appreciation packages to their BPO team, fostering goodwill and camaraderie.

Starting a partnership with a BPO is like any new relationship. The initial stages require effort, understanding, and open communication. But with the right foundation, this partnership can lead to enhanced customer satisfaction, streamlined operations, and a brighter future for your business. So, as you embark on this journey, keep these steps in mind to pave the way for success.

# Maintaining Ongoing Success

Although the decision to outsource can propel your business to new heights, the key to realizing its full potential lies in nurturing a healthy and fruitful relationship with your outsourcing partner. So, how do you ensure that the collaboration remains beneficial and harmonious? Here's a guide to help.

## Open and Transparent Communication

Start with a solid foundation of open dialogue. The clearer you are about your expectations, goals, and constraints, the easier it is for your outsourcing partner to meet (and perhaps even exceed) them. Use tools like video conferencing, collaborative platforms, and regular meetings to keep the lines of communication open. For instance, a weekly catch-up might be the perfect opportunity to address any concerns and highlight achievements.

## Set Clear Expectations from the Start

Before diving into any project, it's crucial to outline your objectives and expectations. Are there specific benchmarks or KPIs you want to hit? Maybe there's a particular workflow you prefer. By setting these parameters early on, both parties can work cohesively towards a shared goal. A software company, for example, might provide its outsourcing partner with detailed specifications and desired outcomes for a software development project.

## Foster Cultural Understanding

Cultural differences can sometimes lead to misunderstandings. Take the time to learn about your partner's culture and business etiquette. This gesture not only helps in navigating potential pitfalls but also demonstrates respect. A simple step, like understanding local holidays or knowing the correct way to address colleagues, can go a long way in fostering goodwill.

## Provide Timely Feedback

Feedback is the lifeblood of improvement. Whether it's positive reinforcement or constructive criticism, providing timely feedback ensures that your outsourcing partner can adapt and improve. Did the customer service team handle a spike in queries exceptionally well during a product launch? Let them know! Similarly, if there are areas of concern, addressing them sooner rather than later can prevent bigger issues down the line.

## Invest in Training

Even the best outsourcing firms can benefit from a deeper understanding of your product, service, or company culture. Regular training sessions can align your partner more closely with your brand ethos. For example, if you're an eco-conscious brand, running a workshop on sustainability practices can ensure that your values are upheld across all interactions.

## Build Mutual Trust

Like any relationship, trust is paramount. This means honoring commitments, respecting expertise, and valuing the input of your outsourcing partner. Regular check-ins, transparency in decision-making, and acknowledging successes are all ways to foster this trust.

## Celebrate Milestones Together

Every project will have its ups and downs, but it's essential to celebrate the wins. Did you hit a significant sales target or achieve a project milestone ahead of schedule? Celebrate these successes with your partner. Recognizing shared achievements fosters camaraderie and motivation for future endeavors.

Outsourcing can be a game-changer for businesses looking to optimize operations and scale efficiently. However, the true magic unfolds when there's a harmonious, healthy relationship at its core. By nurturing this partnership with respect, open communication, and mutual understanding, both parties can flourish in their shared journey towards success. But what if you *don't* want to outsource? Are there other options for you? You betcha.

# Are There Alternatives to Outsourcing?

When it comes to providing top-notch customer support, there's no one-size-fits-all approach. While outsourcing is a popular and effective strategy for many businesses, it's not the only option on the table. Let's dive into the alternatives and consider their benefits, potential challenges, and best use-cases.

## In-House Customer Support Team

Keeping operations in-house often emerges as the preferred choice for businesses seeking a hands-on approach. By choosing this model, companies retain full control over training programs, ensuring that quality standards are met and that response times remain swift. Additionally, proximity plays a role: having your team close, possibly within the same building or city, fosters a deeper sense of company culture and unity. When a customer issue arises, in-house teams can confer, collaborate, and solve problems in real-time.

**Example**: Consider the dynamics at a luxury boutique brand that prides itself on delivering personalized, top-tier service. To ensure every customer interaction is in harmony with the brand's values and high standards, they might opt for an in-house team, embedding the brand's essence into each communication.

## Utilizing Chatbots and AI

Chatbots and AI-driven support systems are gaining traction. These automated assistants can manage routine queries tirelessly, 24/7, without the need for breaks or shifts. Businesses can leverage them to offer prompt responses for basic issues, which is not only cost-efficient but also easily scalable. As traffic grows, chatbots can handle the surge without compromising on response time.

**Example**: Imagine a bustling e-commerce platform where users frequently seek information on order deliveries, product specifications, or return procedures. Instead of overwhelming human agents, the platform deploys chatbots to field these routine questions, ensuring that users get instant answers.

## Self-Service Portals

Empowering customers to help themselves is a strategy that many modern businesses are adopting. By curating a rich and detailed self-service portal—complete with FAQs, how-to guides, and video tutorials—companies allow users to find answers independently. This not only reduces the pressure on formal support but also caters to customers who prefer self-sufficiency.

**Example**: A cutting-edge software-as-a-service (SaaS) company could build a comprehensive online resource center. Here, customers might find step-by-step guides, video walkthroughs, and troubleshooting techniques, offering a self-directed support journey.

## Community Support

There's power in community—a truth that many brands harness for support. By establishing a dedicated forum or online community, companies cultivate spaces where customers can engage, share experiences, and offer solutions to one another. These platforms not only relieve some strain from official support channels but also build a sense of camaraderie among users.

**Example**: A popular video game developer, observing the enthusiastic player base, might create forums where gamers can exchange strategies, discuss challenges, and even share Easter eggs or hidden features they've discovered.

## On-Demand Expertise

Sometimes, the best approach is to call in the experts—but only when required. Some businesses, rather than maintaining a full-fledged team year-round, collaborate with specialists on an ad-hoc basis. This ensures that customers receive top-tier, knowledgeable support while the company avoids the overhead of a permanent, full-time team.

**Example**: A digital platform catering to budding photographers might periodically collaborate with renowned professionals in the field. These experts could conduct Q&A sessions, offer guidance on technique, or even review user-submitted photographs, elevating the platform's value proposition.

## Peer-to-Peer Support Networks

A step beyond community forums is the structured peer-to-peer support network. Here, companies identify and train a segment of their user base to guide and assist their peers. It's not just about resolving issues—it's about creating a system where passionate users guide newcomers, fostering a dynamic sense of community and mentorship.

**Example**: Picture a fitness application with a global user base. To foster engagement and ensure newcomers receive guidance, the app might initiate a program where seasoned users, perhaps those who've achieved significant milestones, mentor beginners, sharing routines, diet tips, and motivation.

The decision on how to provide customer support should align with a company's values, customer expectations, and available resources. While outsourcing offers scalability and cost benefits, the alternatives can provide unique advantages in terms of quality, brand loyalty, and customer engagement. By assessing the specific needs of your business and understanding the pros and cons of each approach, you can craft a customer support strategy that ensures success, satisfaction, and sustainability.

# CHAPTER 11:
# The End

This chapter sat unwritten for longer than I care to admit. Final chapters are always so conclusive, and I am terrible at goodbyes. Secretly, or perhaps not so secretly, I really don't want you to go. And, beyond that, how can I put a point on something that is as infinite as CX? How do I answer "where do we go from here?" without a crystal ball.

The world has come a long way since I started in support over 20 years ago. The technologies that we have at our fingertips are endless, and continue to expand. I can't answer where we go from here. I can, however, answer how to continue leveling yourself up:

- Be curious.
- Reference books, other people, and the internet often.
- Ask questions.

I wrote this book hopeful that it would sit on desks and in backpacks. I dream of it being handed down from leader to leader. I envisioned it being written in and questioned, beaten up like my son's *Stardew Valley* guidebook. I knew that it wouldn't always be right because times change and, well, printed books don't. But, I hope you change, too. I hope you learn and grow and that this book has a part in it. I wish you the very, very best of luck.

# INDEX

## A

Abandon Rate 55
accessibility 55, 78, 88, 89, 93, 102
Accessibility 89
account management 14, 18, 97, 258
adoption 79, 165, 189, 242, 275
Adoption 79
AI chatbots 223
ambassadors 82, 229, 273, 286
Ambassadors 273
analytics 9, 46, 48, 57, 137, 162, 188, 196, 209, 213, 240, 280
Analytics 25, 53, 68, 78, 88, 268, 270
Appcues 1, 7, 10, 22, 64
App Integration 54
applicants 62, 180, 181
Applicants 181
attrition 294, 295, 299, 300
Attrition 294
automation 9, 15, 158, 159, 160, 161, 162, 163, 164, 165, 166, 168, 273
Automation 67, 157, 159, 161, 162, 164, 166
Average Handling Time (AHT) 153

## B

BPO 286, 289, 290, 291, 293, 294, 295, 296, 297, 298, 299, 300, 301, 302, 303
brand 30, 134, 226, 231
Brand 30, 134, 226, 231
brand loyalty 31, 69, 82, 121, 219, 244, 264, 308
budget 137, 242
Budget 137, 242
budgeting 136, 137, 138, 239
Budgeting 136, 137, 138, 239

## C

call center 8
campaign 1, 103, 186
Campaign 1, 103, 186
categories 146
Categories 146
categorization 25, 70, 77, 89
Categorization 25, 70, 77, 89
CES 142, 234
channel 13, 14, 20, 21, 23, 32, 33, 39, 41, 44, 47, 53, 59, 61, 63, 66, 70, 79, 91, 92, 93, 104, 105, 106, 109, 111, 119, 214, 247, 270, 291, 292
Channel 63, 70, 104, 291
chat 36, 37, 39, 40, 41, 42, 44, 45, 46, 47, 105

Chat 36, 37, 39, 40, 41, 42, 44, 45, 46, 47, 105
chatbots 71, 78, 160, 167, 195, 306
Chatbots 71, 78, 160, 167, 195, 306
chat duration 45
Chat Duration 45
chat support 13, 38, 42, 44, 45, 119, 291
Chat Support 13, 38, 42, 44, 45, 119, 291
chat transcripts 44
Chat Transcripts 44
CLV 225, 228, 234, 235
cocial 56, 58, 60, 61, 62, 63, 65, 69, 70, 88, 105, 182
collaboration 25, 68, 108, 174, 197, 252
Collaboration 25, 68, 108, 174, 197, 252
Compliance 26, 68, 147
CRM 41, 54, 68, 78, 87, 142, 164, 223, 240, 242, 250, 266, 273
CSAT 34, 56, 69, 119
culture 14, 177, 187, 245, 259, 260, 265
Culture 14, 177, 187, 245, 259, 260, 265
customer catisfaction (CSAT) 34, 56, 69, 119
customer-centric culture 261
Customer-Centric Culture 14
customer data analysis 240
customer effort score 234
Customer Effort Score 234
customer experience 2, 4, 152, 219, 230, 250, 275
Customer Experience 2, 4, 152, 219, 230, 250, 275
customer feedback management 269
Customer First 174
Customer Lifetime Value 228, 234
customer relationship management 54, 142, 223
Customer Relationship Management 54, 142, 223
customer retention 233
Customer Retention 233
Customer Satisfaction (CSAT) 34, 56, 69, 119
customer support iii, iv, v, 26, 124, 136, 155, 161, 166, 174, 176, 227, 238, 267, 271, 272, 273, 288, 289, 306
Customer Support iii, iv, v, 26, 124, 136, 155, 161, 166, 174, 176, 227, 238, 267, 271, 272, 273, 288, 289, 306
CX strategy 6, 7, 8, 9, 11, 12, 14, 15, 92, 159, 219, 225, 227, 229, 230, 234, 241, 244, 246, 256, 257

## D

data analysis  240
data-driven decision-making  217
data privacy  68
demographic  7, 13, 21, 239, 244, 277
distributed teams  53
Distributed Teams  191
documentation  4, 12, 14, 26, 40, 44, 66, 101, 103, 115, 139, 146, 147, 215, 217
Documentation  4, 12, 14, 26, 40, 44, 66, 101, 103, 115, 139, 146, 147, 215, 217
domain  80, 97, 106, 241, 258, 264
Domain  80, 97, 106, 241, 258, 264

## E

emotional intelligence  173
employee training  238
Employee Training  238

## F

feedback loop  130, 132, 167, 244, 268
Feedback Loop  130, 132, 167, 244, 268
feedback management  269
first call resolution  55, 156
First Call Resolution  55, 156
first contact resolution (FCR)  34
First Contact Resolution (FCR)  34
follow-the-sun  102
Follow-the-Sun  102
forum  80
Forum  80
friction  115, 117, 164, 252, 276, 294

## G

growth  v, 90, 169, 198, 205, 225, 258
Growth  v, 90, 169, 198, 205, 225, 258

## H

help center  176
help desk software  105, 107, 108
Help desk software  107, 108
Help Desk Software  107, 108

## I

incident management  106
Incident Management  106
indirect costs  222, 244
Indirect Costs  223
integration  25, 53, 54, 67, 68, 78, 87, 88, 272
Integration  25, 53, 54, 67, 68, 78, 87, 88, 272
interactive voice response (IVR)  53, 55, 72

Interactive Voice Response (IVR)  53, 55, 72
interviewing  183, 185
Interviewing  183, 185

## K

KPIs (Key Performance Indicators)  44

## L

language  176
Language  176
levels  126
Levels  126
loyalty  4, 31, 36, 46, 69, 82, 92, 100, 121, 126, 127, 133, 134, 163, 191, 214, 219, 222, 224, 225, 226, 227, 228, 230, 231, 233, 234, 241, 244, 248, 264, 274, 276, 308
Loyalty  170

## M

machine learning  160, 167, 196
Machine Learning  160, 167, 196
market research  60, 239
Meta  56, 61, 62, 67, 70, 105
metrics  28, 70, 91, 108, 119, 142, 145, 198, 207, 211, 232, 235, 290
Metrics  28, 70, 91, 108, 119, 142, 145, 198, 207, 211, 232, 235, 290
multichannel  93, 108, 109, 111
Multichannel  93, 108, 109, 111

## N

Net Promoter Score (NPS)  35, 56, 156, 233

## O

omnichannel  108, 109
Omnichannel  108, 109
onboarding  2, 4, 6, 18, 136, 165, 173, 177, 186, 187, 188, 222
Onboarding  2, 4, 6, 18, 136, 165, 173, 177, 186, 187, 188, 222
on-call  193, 194
On-Call  193

## P

partnership  145, 303, 305
Partnership  145, 303, 305
post-purchase  3, 95, 226, 228, 229, 269, 275, 277
predictive analytics  240
Predictive Analytics  240

## Q

QA Manager  144, 145, 146

## R

referral  181, 229
Referral  181, 229
resolution  25, 29, 45, 46, 53, 68, 69, 70, 80, 84, 87, 90, 93, 96, 99, 106, 111, 116, 117, 118, 119, 120, 121, 123, 125, 128, 130, 131, 132, 133, 171, 184, 185, 200, 208, 209, 211, 213, 234, 238, 242, 247, 284
Resolution  25, 29, 45, 46, 53, 68, 69, 70, 80, 84, 87, 90, 93, 96, 99, 106, 111, 116, 117, 118, 119, 120, 121, 123, 125, 128, 130, 131, 132, 133, 171, 184, 185, 200, 208, 209, 211, 213, 234, 238, 242, 247, 284
roadmap  27, 209, 211, 240, 268, 272, 280

## S

SaaS  6, 7, 28, 72, 124, 137, 229, 235, 277, 307
scheduling  152, 190, 191, 192, 193, 293
Scheduling  152, 190, 191, 192, 193, 293
self-service  16, 18, 36, 70, 71, 72, 73, 74, 75, 76, 77, 79, 80, 81, 106, 160, 167, 307
sentiment  26, 41, 68, 187, 204, 242
Sentiment  26
Sentiment Analysis  26
Service Level Agreements (SLAs)  113, 115, 123, 150
SLA compliance  117
Social  56, 58, 60, 61, 62, 63, 65, 69, 70, 88, 105, 182
social listening tools  277
social media listening  274
structure  103, 104, 127, 128, 140, 141, 142, 152, 166, 191, 225, 257, 258, 302
Structure  18, 197, 200, 258
survey  13, 20, 34, 40, 41, 90, 225, 233, 278, 279, 280
Survey  40

## T

tag  63, 89, 212
tagging  68, 85
Tagging  77, 89
team collaboration  271
Team Collaboration  174
ticket management  106
ticket volume  35, 120
Ticket Volume  35, 120
tone  26, 30, 32, 33, 42, 52, 53, 65, 86, 112, 127, 133, 134, 135, 147, 197
touchpoint  6, 31, 51, 77, 161, 275, 284
Touchpoint  6, 31, 51, 77, 161, 275, 284
training  26, 76, 91, 128, 132, 136, 142, 223, 238,

248, 249, 250, 266, 268, 271, 301, 305
Training  26, 76, 91, 128, 132, 136, 142, 223, 238,
  248, 249, 250, 266, 268, 271, 301, 305
transcript  43, 48
Transcript  43, 48
Trust and Safety  168, 169, 170, 171

## U

User Experience (UX)  237

## V

voice recognition  53